D1088921

AUTODESK® REVIT®
ARCHITECTURE 2010
IN PRACTICE

Kogent Learning Solutions, Inc.

JONES AND BARTLETT PUBLISHERS

Sudbury, Massachusetts

BOSTON   TORONTO   LONDON   SINGAPORE

World Headquarters

Jones and Bartlett Publishers
40 Tall Pine Drive
Sudbury, MA 01776
978-443-5000
info@jbpub.com
www.jbpub.com

Jones and Bartlett Publishers
Canada
6339 Ormindale Way
Mississauga, Ontario L5V 1J2
Canada

Jones and Bartlett Publishers
International
Barb House, Barb Mews
London W6 7PA
United Kingdom

Jones and Bartlett's books and products are available through most bookstores and online booksellers. To contact Jones and Bartlett Publishers directly, call 800-832-0034, fax 978-443-8000, or visit our website www.jbpub.com.

Substantial discounts on bulk quantities of Jones and Bartlett's publications are available to corporations, professional associations, and other qualified organizations. For details and specific discount information, contact the special sales department at Jones and Bartlett via the above contact information or send an email to specialsales@jbpub.com.

Autodesk® Revit® Architecture software helps you explore early design concepts and forms, and more accurately maintain your vision through design, documentation, and construction. When you make a change, it's automatically updated across the project. The essential building information modeling (BIM) data provided by Autodesk Revit Architecture software supports sustainable design, clash detection, construction planning, and fabrication.

Production Credits

Publisher: David Pallai
Editorial Assistant: Molly Whitman
Production Assistant: Ashlee Hazeltine
Associate Marketing Manager: Lindsay Ruggiero
V.P., Manufacturing and Inventory Control:
  Therese Connell

Composition: diacriTech
Art Rendering: diacriTech
Cover and Title Page Design: Scott Moden
Cover Image: © r.nagy/ShutterStock, Inc.
Printing and Binding: Malloy, Inc.
Cover Printing: Malloy, Inc.

Library of Congress Cataloging-in-Publication Data
Autodesk Revit Architecture 2010 in practice/Kogent Learning Solutions, Inc. – 1st ed.
  p. cm.
  Includes index.
  ISBN-13: 978-0-7637-7630-5 (pbk.)
  ISBN-10: 0-7637-7630-0 (ibid.)
  1. Architectural drawing–Computer-aided design. 2. Architectural design–Data processing. I. Kogent Learning
    Solutions, Inc.
  NA2728.A87 2009
  720.28'40285536–dc22

                            2009034455

6048
Printed in the United States of America
13 12 11 10 09   10 9 8 7 6 5 4 3 2 1

TABLE OF CONTENTS

INTRODUCING AUTODESK® REVIT® ARCHITECTURE 2010

Chapter **1**

In This Chapter

◊ Understanding the Basic Concepts and Principles of Autodesk Revit Architecture 2010
◊ New and Improved Features of Autodesk Revit Architecture 2010
◊ Installing Autodesk Revit Architecture 2010
◊ Opening Autodesk Revit Architecture 2010
◊ Understanding the User Interface
◊ Using Autodesk Revit Architecture 2010 Help
◊ Exiting Autodesk Revit Architecture 2010

In day-to-day life, you may have seen many architectural construction works in progress, such as buildings, malls, and bridges. Architecture of a building often refers to the main structure along with the design of the total built environment both around and inside the main structure. The built environment includes all the details of the proposed structure—from the macro level of the integration of a building with its surrounding context, such as town planning and urban design, to the micro level of architectural and construction details, such as furniture and other household materials.

Autodesk® Revit® Architecture 2010 is a building information modeling (BIM) software package that has revolutionized the architectural designing industry. The software allows architects and engineers to conceptualize, design, and document a building model using a single integrated platform. BIM is a new computer-aided design (CAD) paradigm that allows three-dimensional (3D) and parametric object-based designs. The objects in Autodesk Revit Architecture 2010 are fully integrated to provide a proper coordination of information across all its representations; therefore, a change in an object at one place reflects a change in the objects at all the associative places.

This chapter starts with a brief discussion on the basic concepts and principles of Autodesk Revit Architecture 2010 and its various new and improved features. It then explains how to install and open Autodesk Revit Architecture 2010. In addition, it describes the new user interface of Autodesk Revit Architecture 2010 and discusses how to get assistance from its help feature. Finally, exiting Autodesk Revit Architecture 2010 is covered.

1.1 UNDERSTANDING THE BASIC CONCEPTS AND PRINCIPLES OF AUTODESK REVIT ARCHITECTURE 2010

Before starting your work with Autodesk Revit Architecture 2010, you should be familiar with the basic terms used to create a building model as well as their concepts and principles. In this section, we discuss the most commonly used terms of Autodesk Revit Architecture 2010, such as *project, level, families*, and *element categories.* Let's start our discussion with the Autodesk Revit Architecture project.

The Autodesk Revit Architecture Project

The Autodesk Revit Architecture project is very much similar to actual architectural projects. As in actual architectural projects, the different components, such as drawings, 3D views, specifications, schedules, and cost estimates, are inherently linked together; the Autodesk Revit Architecture project links the 3D building model to its parametric documentation. Such a project contains all the information related to the design of the building model. This information is stored in a database known as building information modeling. When you create a project in Autodesk Revit Architecture and save it, a file is created with the .rvt extension. The project file consists of all the information related to the building model, such as components used to design the model, 3D views, drawing sheets, schedules, cost estimates, renderings, and walkthroughs.

Because the Autodesk Revit Architecture model includes only a single project file, you can easily alter the design, and those changes will be reflected in all the associated areas of the project. In addition, it is easy to manage the project when there is only a single project file.

Levels in a Building Model

Autodesk Revit Architecture divides the building model into different levels. The levels are finite horizontal planes that act as a reference for other elements that are hosted on a level, such as the roof, floor, and ceiling. In simple words, a level is a horizontal surface that establishes floor-to-floor heights and other critical horizontal work planes. Graphically, the levels are represented with a line and a level symbol that can be placed at one or both ends of the level line. The levels that are defined in a building model can relate to different floor levels of the building project. Each element created in the project belongs to a specific level.

The Autodesk Revit Architecture Families

An Autodesk Revit Architecture family includes all the elements that you add to an Autodesk Revit Architecture project—from the structural members, such as walls, roofs, windows, and doors, to the documentation members, such as callouts, fixtures, tags, and detail components. In addition, the family groups the elements with common parameters as well as with a related graphical representation. The elements of the same family may have different values for some or all of their parameters, but they all have common characteristics. When you create a family and save it, a file is created with the .rfa extension.

Element Categories

Autodesk Revit Architecture is not limited to the building elements, but may also contain other associated elements, such as annotations, imported files, and links. These elements are classified into the following categories:

- Model
- Annotation
- Datum
- View

A category groups the elements that you use to create or document a building model. Apart from these four categories, Autodesk Revit Architecture includes categories such as imported, workset, filter, and Revit. The Revit category is included when a Autodesk Revit Architecture project is linked to another Autodesk Revit Architecture project.

Model Category

The model category includes the building elements that are used to create a building model. **Table 1.1** lists these building elements.

Element	Description
Wall	Defines the spatial arrangement of a building and acts as the host for the door and window elements
Floor	Defines the bottom horizontal surface of a room or a building
Roof	Defines the exterior surface that covers the top of a building

TABLE 1.1   Elements under the model category

Continued

Element	Description
Ceiling	Defines the upper interior surface of a room or a building
Door	Defines an opening in the wall for creating an entrance to a room or a building
Window	Defines an opening in the wall to admit light and air to a room or a building
Stair	Defines a series of steps to connect two levels of a building

TABLE 1.1 Elements under the model category

Annotation Category

The annotation category includes all annotation elements, symbols, and descriptive data that are added to a view to describe the building. **Table 1.2** lists the annotation elements.

Element	Description
Dimension	Specifies an annotation that displays the sizes and distances in a project
Text note	Specifies an annotation that contains text and may contain a leader line and arrow
Tag	Specifies an annotation that is used to identify elements in a project
Symbol	Specifies an annotation that represents elements in a graphical form
Keynote	Specifies an annotation that annotates drawing to identify building materials and to standardized information related to the building model

TABLE 1.2 Elements under the annotation category

Datum Category

The datum category includes the datum elements, such as levels, grids, and reference planes. The datum elements are the nonphysical items that help to design the model of a building by placing the elements at appropriate locations. **Table 1.3** lists the elements in the datum category.

Element	Description
Grid	Displays a series of lines in the drawing area to help you draw or place elements in a building design
Level	Specifies a finite horizontal plane that acts as a reference for the level-hosted elements, such as roof, floor, and ceiling
Reference Plane	Specifies a two-dimensional plane, used while designing families of model elements or placing the elements in a building design

TABLE 1.3   Elements under the datum category

View Category

The view category includes parametric elements that define how the information should be displayed. A parametric element can change its size, material, and graphic look, but still keeps itself as the same fundamental element. A view does not alter the model; it only acts as a filter through which you can view the model from different perspectives. **Table 1.4** lists the elements of the view category.

Element	Description
Floor plan	Specifies a drawing model to display the layout of walls and other building components
Ceiling plan	Specifies a drawing model to display the design of a ceiling
Elevation	Specifies an orthographic view of a vertical part of a building model
Section	Displays a building model as if the building model were cut vertically to show its interior details
3D view	Displays a three-dimensional representation of a building model
Callout view	Displays a detailed and enlarged drawing of a portion of a view
Walkthrough	Represents a simulated building model to display a view where a person walks through along a specified path to show all the facets of the building model

TABLE 1.4   Elements under the view category

In this section, you have learned about the elements within the different Autodesk Revit Architecture element categories. Let's now move on to discuss the new and improved features of Autodesk Revit Architecture 2010.

1.2 NEW AND IMPROVED FEATURES OF AUTODESK REVIT ARCHITECTURE 2010

Apart from updating some of the existing features, Autodesk Revit Architecture 2010 has introduced several new features that help to create projects easily and efficiently. Some of the new and enhanced features of Autodesk Revit Architecture 2010 are as follows:

- Enhanced user interface
- Conceptual design environment
- Interoperability
- Worksharing
- Visibility and graphics enhancements
- Details and annotations
- Macros development with Revit VSTA
- Documentation

Note: VSTA refers to Visual Studio Tools for Application.

Let's discuss all of these features, one by one.

Enhanced User Interface

The Autodesk Revit Architecture 2010 user interface has been redesigned to provide a completely different appearance as compared to the user interface available in earlier versions. The toolbar, menu bar, and design bar are replaced by a single ribbon in the new user interface. The ribbon organizes all the tools under different tabs and panels, thereby allowing you to access all the tools from a single place.

Autodesk Revit Architecture 2010 also provides learning tools, such as User Interface Overview, User Interface Tour, and Where Is My Command?, to help you understand the new features and functionalities incorporated in the new user interface. These learning tools will assist you in making the transition from Autodesk Revit Architecture 2009 to Autodesk Revit Architecture 2010. The User Interface Overview tool provides an interactive display to describe the different parts of the user interface as you move the mouse pointer over each part. You can also use the User Interface Tour tool to watch an animation of the user interface. The Where Is My Command? tool provides you with a list of all commands and their locations on the Autodesk Revit Architecture 2010 ribbon.

The new user interface also provides tooltips, an InfoCenter, and an improved spell checker. Tooltips display a description of the tool as you move the mouse pointer over a tool on the ribbon. InfoCenter provides a toolbar that contains a collection of tools that can be used to find information about Autodesk Revit Architecture 2010. Using the improved spell checker, you can easily specify a language for the main dictionary and create custom dictionaries.

Conceptual Design Environment

Autodesk Revit Architecture 2010 introduces a new feature called conceptual design environment, which you can use to explore the design concepts before you attempt to create a detailed building information modeling. In simple words, the conceptual design environment provides flexibility for architects, structural engineers, and interior designers by allowing them to express ideas and create parametric massing families early in the design process. The parametric massing families are the parameter-based designs created in the conceptual design environment. You can use these designs in the Autodesk Revit Architecture project environment to create a detailed architecture by creating the elements, such as walls, roofs, and floors.

The conceptual design environment is a type of family editor (a graphical editing mode used to create and modify families) that creates new massing families using advanced modeling tools and techniques. These newly created mass families can be integrated into the Autodesk Revit Architecture project environment and carried through to the final construction phase. The conceptual design environment provides you with a variety of features, such as flexible geometric form-making and manipulation tools; an improved drawing environment; tools to divide surfaces, apply patterns, and create flexible parametric components; and an integrated workflow.

Interoperability

Autodesk Revit Architecture 2010 has introduced as well as enhanced a variety of features geared toward ensuring interoperability among Autodesk products. The interoperability can be determined by using the Autodesk Exchange (ADSK) files as well as by sharing content online using Autodesk Seek. These features are described as follows:

- **Exporting Building Sites:** Allows you to export the digital design geometry, including the BIM data, of the buildings designed using Autodesk Revit Architecture to the application that accepts ADSK files, such as the files created in AutoCAD® Civil 3D®.
- **Project Base Points and Survey Points:** Allows you to export the coordinates of the survey point from the building site to the ASDK files.
- **Importing Building Components:** Allows you to import building components from the applications, which create ASDK files, to Revit Architecture.
- **Publishing Content to the Autodesk Seek Website:** Allows you to publish Autodesk Revit Architecture families, products, and design information to the Autodesk Seek website to share them online with other users.

- **Export to gbXML:** Allows you to export the building model to a Green Building XML schema (gbXML) file.

Worksharing

Worksharing is a feature that allows all team members to access a shared model simultaneously by using a central file. Autodesk Revit Architecture 2010 has been enhanced for worksharing with the following improvements:

- **Create New Local:** Opens a workshared project file (central file) as a local file. This creates a copy of the central file and renames the file as a local file. However, if a local file with the same name already exists, Revit Architecture prompts you to overwrite the existing file or to rename the new file.
- **Set Default Worksets to Open:** Allows you to set worksets for a workshared project that you want to open by default, when the project is opened next time.

> **Note:** The project that contains the shared model is called a *workshared* project; several team members can work on it at the same time. A *workset* refers to a collection of elements, such as walls, floors, ceilings, doors, and windows. When you enable worksharing, several default worksets are automatically created.

Visibility and Graphics Enhancements

The visibility and graphics capabilities of Autodesk Revit Architecture 2010 have been improved in the following areas:

- **Gradient Backgrounds for 3D Views:** Enable you to specify gradient backgrounds for 3D views as well as orthographic views and perspective views.
- **Halftone/Underlay Settings:** Enable you to control the weight and pattern of a line used for underlays as well as to control the brightness of the halftone elements.
- **Visibility Filters for Sections, Callouts, and Elevations:** Enable you to include elevations, sections, and callouts while using filters to control the visibility and graphic display of the elements.
- **Anti-aliasing:** Allows you to enable anti-aliasing for 3D views to smoothen the appearance of the curved lines.
- **Hardware Acceleration for Graphics:** Allows you to enable hardware acceleration to improve graphics display while performing certain functions,

such as refreshing the screen, switching to another window, or displaying annotations.
- **Highlight Color:** Allows you to highlight the elements with a color.
- **Hide by Filter:** Allows you to hide elements by using filters apart from hiding selected elements in a view or the elements in a category.

Details and Annotations

Autodesk Revit Architecture 2010 includes a feature named spot slope, which is a new type of spot dimension, for detailing and annotating elements in a building model. Using the spot slope, you can display a slope at a specific point on a face or an edge of a model element. Spot slopes can be placed in plan views, elevation views, and section views. Examples of objects using spot slope include roofs, beams, and piping.

Macros Development with Revit VSTA

The macros development feature of the older version is also enhanced with Revit VSTA to improve workflow and introduce new macro security features. In Autodesk Revit Architecture 2010, the Macro Manager has been redesigned to streamline the workflow. The streamlined workflow creates macros in the Autodesk Revit VSTA integrated development environment (IDE) and implements them at the document and application levels. In addition, the Macro Manager enhances the visibility and organization of the application programming interface (API) macro development. At the same time, the new security features prevent the workstation from running any unknown code. You can prevent the workstation from running such code by disabling macros at the application and document levels or by setting macros to prompt you to allow the code to run as they are detected.

Documentation

The documentation feature is also improved in Autodesk Revit Architecture 2010 with the introduction of architectural workflows. The architectural workflow allows you to map typical architectural tasks, such as creating elements of a model, to their corresponding software features and functionalities. It provides high-level information to Autodesk Revit Architecture. For instance, you can create different elements, such as a wall, roof, or staircase, as they would be created in the real world.

1.3 INSTALLING AUTODESK REVIT ARCHITECTURE 2010

You can install Autodesk Revit Architecture 2010 by using the Autodesk Revit Architecture 2010 installation wizard. The installation wizard provides a graphical user interface to guide you through the different installation phases.

> **Note:** You can install Autodesk Revit Architecture 2010 by using the installation DVD provided by your software vendor.

To ensure a smooth and complete installation of Autodesk Revit Architecture 2010, you need to ensure that your computer meets some fundamental software and hardware requirements. **Table 1.5** lists minimum as well as recommended software and hardware requirements to install the 32-bit Autodesk Revit Architecture 2010.

	Software	
	Minimum	**Recommended**
Operating system	Microsoft Windows Vista 32-bit (SP1) Ultimate, Business, or Home Premium Edition, or Microsoft Windows XP (SP1 or SP2) Professional or Home Edition	Windows XP Professional (SP2 or later)
Web browser	Microsoft Internet Explorer 6.0 (SP1 or later)	Microsoft Internet Explorer 6.0 (SP1 or later)
Software	DirectX 9 or later	DirectX 9 or later
	Hardware	
	Minimum	**Recommended**
Processor type	Intel Pentium 4 1.4 GHz or equivalent AMD processor	Intel Core 2 Duo 2.4 GHz or equivalent AMD processor
Hard disk space	5GB or higher	5GB or higher
RAM	3GB (1GB when rendering is not required)	4GB
Miscellaneous	1280 × 1024 monitor, display adapter capable of 24-bit color, a mouse-compliant pointing device, and a DVD-ROM drive	Video card supporting DirectX 9 (or later), and a two-button mouse with scroll wheel

TABLE 1.5   Minimum Software and Hardware Requirements for 32-Bit Autodesk Revit Architecture 2010

Table 1.6 lists minimum as well as recommended software and hardware requirements to install the 64-bit Autodesk Revit Architecture 2010.

	Software	
	Minimum	**Recommended**
Operating system	Microsoft Windows Vista 64-bit (SP1) Ultimate, Business, or Home Premium Edition, or Microsoft Windows XP (SP1 or SP2) Professional or Home Edition	Windows XP Professional (SP1) x64 edition
Web browser	Microsoft Internet Explorer 6.0 (SP1 or later)	Microsoft Internet Explorer 6.0 (SP1 or later)
Software	DirectX 9 or later	DirectX 9 or later
	Hardware	
	Minimum	**Recommended**
Processor type	Intel Pentium 4 1.4 GHz or equivalent AMD processor	Intel Core 2 Duo 2.40 GHz or equivalent AMD processor
Hard disk space	5GB or higher	5GB or higher
RAM	3GB	4GB
Miscellaneous	1280 × 1024 monitor, display adapter capable of 24-bit color, a mouse-compliant pointing device, and a DVD-ROM drive	Video card supporting Microsoft 9 (or later), and a two-button mouse with scroll wheel

TABLE 1.6   Minimum Software and Hardware Requirements for 64-Bit Autodesk Revit Architecture 2010

After equipping your system with the necessary software and hardware, perform the following steps to install Autodesk Revit Architecture 2010:

1. *Insert* the installation DVD of Autodesk Revit Architecture 2010 in the DVD drive. The DVD automatically starts running and displays the **Setup Initialization** wizard, as shown in **Figure 1.1**.

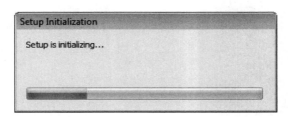

Setup Initialization

Setup is initializing...

FIGURE 1.1

After completing the initialization process, the **Autodesk Revit Architecture 2010** wizard appears, as shown in **Figure 1.2**.

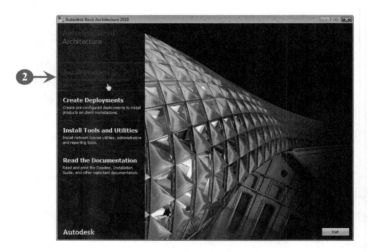

FIGURE 1.2

2. *Click* the **Install Products** button (Figure 1.2). The **Select the Products to Install** page of the **Autodesk Revit Architecture 2010** wizard appears, as shown in **Figure 1.3**.

FIGURE 1.3

3. *Select* the **Autodesk Revit Architecture 2010** check box, if not selected (Figure 1.3).
4. *Click* the **Next** button (Figure 1.3). The **Accept the License Agreement** page appears, as shown in **Figure 1.4**.

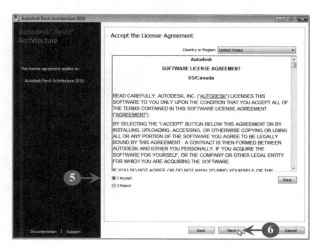

FIGURE 1.4

5. *Select* the **I Accept** radio button to accept the license agreement.
6. *Click* the **Next** button (Figure 1.4). The **Product and User Information** page appears, as shown in **Figure 1.5**.

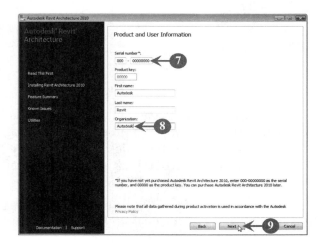

FIGURE 1.5

7. *Enter* the serial number and product key in the **Serial number** and **Product key** text boxes, respectively. In this case, we enter the serial number as **000-00000000** and product key as **00000** (Figure 1.5).

Note: If you have not yet purchased Autodesk Revit Architecture 2010 from Autodesk, enter the serial number mentioned at the bottom of the Product and User Information page.

---

8. *Enter* your first name, last name, and the name of the organization in the First name, Last name, and Organization text boxes, respectively, to provide the user information (Figure 1.5).
9. *Click* the **Next** button (Figure 1.5). The **Review–Configure–Install** page appears, as shown in **Figure 1.6**.

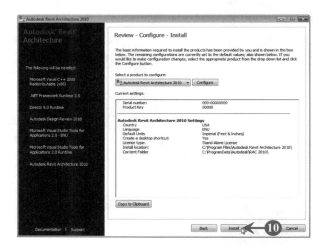

FIGURE 1.6

The **Review–Configure–Install** page allows you to configure a product, which you can select from the Select a product to configure drop-down list. After selecting a product, you need to click the **Configure** button to display the various configuration options. In this case, we do not configure the product and leave the configuration to default settings.

10. *Click* the **Install** button (Figure 1.6). The **Installing Components** page appears showing the installation of the components, as shown in **Figure 1.7**.

FIGURE 1.7

Once all the components are installed, the **Content Extraction** dialog box appears automatically to extract the files required to run Autodesk Revit Architecture 2010 smoothly. This process may take several minutes depending on the downloading speed of your system. As all the files are extracted, the **Installation Complete** page appears, as shown in **Figure 1.8**.

FIGURE 1.8

11. *Click* the **Finish** button (Figure 1.8). This closes the **Autodesk Revit Architecture 2010** wizard and completes the installation process.

Let's now learn how to open Autodesk Revit Architecture 2010.

1.4 OPENING AUTODESK REVIT ARCHITECTURE 2010

To work with Autodesk Revit Architecture 2010 to create and render building models, you need to open it. Perform the following steps to open Autodesk Revit Architecture 2010:

1. *Click* **Start > All Programs > Autodesk > Autodesk Revit Architecture 2010 > Autodesk Revit Architecture 2010,** as shown in **Figure 1.9**.

FIGURE 1.9

The **Autodesk Revit Architecture 2010** window opens and displays the **Product and License Information** dialog box, as shown in **Figure 1.10**.

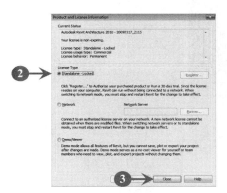

FIGURE 1.10

2. *Select* a license type. In this case, we select the **Standalone–Locked** radio button (Figure 1.10).

3. *Click* the **Close** button (Figure 1.10). The **New Features Workshop** page appears asking you to view the new features workshop, as shown in **Figure 1.11**.

FIGURE 1.11

4. *Select* a radio button to specify whether you want to view the workshop now or later or close this page permanently. In this case, we select the **No, don't show me this again** radio button (Figure 1.11).

5. *Click* the **OK** button (Figure 1.11). The **Autodesk Revit Architecture 2010** window opens and allows you to work with projects and families, as shown in **Figure 1.12**.

FIGURE 1.12

This completes our discussion on how to open Autodesk Revit Architecture 2010. We'll next investigate the Autodesk Revit Architecture 2010 user interface. Before doing so, *click* the **New link** under the Projects section to create a new Autodesk Revit Architecture project so that we can explore most parts of the user interface.

1.5 UNDERSTANDING THE USER INTERFACE

The user interface of Autodesk Revit Architecture has remained the same (menu based) since late 1990s. Therefore, a complete revamp of the design was felt to be needed for a long time. In response, Autodesk came up with a completely different user interface for Autodesk Revit Architecture 2010. In the new user interface, the menus and toolbars are replaced by a new tab-and-ribbon interface. In earlier versions of Autodesk Revit Architecture, the less commonly used commands were placed three or four levels down in the menu. This organization has been replaced with a single strip at the top of the user interface called the ribbon. All commands on the ribbon have been put under specified tabs and groups. Owing to its simple, yet unique single-strip design, the ribbon ensures that the bulk of the Autodesk Revit Architecture commands are at your fingertips at all times.

In this section, you'll learn about the user interface of Autodesk Revit Architecture 2010 in detail. Let's start the discussion with the title bar.

Title Bar

As in most other software, the title bar is always displayed at the top of the window. When you create a new project in Autodesk Revit Architecture 2010, by default the title bar displays the title Autodesk Revit Architecture 2010–[Project1–Floor Plan: Level 1], as shown in **Figure 1.13**.

FIGURE 1.13

When you save an Autodesk Revit Architecture project with a different name, the specified name appears on the title bar. For example, if you save your file with the file name **Personal,** then this name replaces the file name **Project1** and the title bar displays the file with the new name.

Application Button

The **Application** button is displayed at the upper-left corner of the Autodesk Revit Architecture 2010 window. **Figure 1.14** shows this button.

FIGURE 1.14

Clicking the **Application** button displays an application menu with various menu commands in the left pane and the recently used documents in the right pane, as shown in **Figure 1.15.**

FIGURE 1.15

You can see in Figure 1.15 that the application menu contains various menu commands in the left pane, such as New, Open, Save, Save As, Export, Publish, Print, Licensing, and Close. Apart from the recent documents, the right pane also contains a drop-down list containing various options to organize the recent documents, such as by ordered list, by access date, by size, and by type. In addition, the right pane displays the submenus related to the menu commands in the left pane. The submenus are available only for those menu commands that have a right arrow immediately next to them. They can be viewed by moving the mouse pointer over the menu commands in the left pane. For example, if you move the mouse pointer over the Open command, a submenu appears with various commands for Open in the right pane, as shown in **Figure 1.16**.

FIGURE 1.16

The use of the **Application** button is not only limited to opening, saving, and closing your project. It also allows you to export, print, and publish a file as well as to view and change the product and license information. The **Application** button can be considered as a major enhancement in the user interface in comparison to previous editions of Revit Architecture.

Quick Access Toolbar

The Quick Access toolbar is placed just next to the **Application** button on the title bar. You can access the most frequently used commands, such as New, Open, and Save, directly from this toolbar and save your time. **Figure 1.17** displays the Quick Access toolbar.

FIGURE 1.17

By default, the Quick Access toolbar contains the **Open, Save, Undo, Redo, Modify, Synchronize and Modify Settings,** and **3D View** buttons. However, you can also add or remove commands from the Quick Access toolbar, according to your requirements. An arrow icon to the right of the Quick Access toolbar is used to customize this toolbar.

Ribbon

The ribbon contains the group of tools used to create a project. It appears immediately as you create or open a file. The tools are organized as a set of tabs on the ribbon, where each tab groups the relevant tools. The ribbon contains the tools in the form of three types of buttons:

- **Button:** A simple button that allows you to access a tool.
- **Drop-down button:** A button with a drop-down arrow to display additional associated tools.
- **Split button:** A button that is divided into two areas by a line. The upper area allows you to access a frequently used tool and the lower area displays additional associated tools.

Figure 1.18 displays the ribbon of Autodesk Revit Architecture 2010.

FIGURE 1.18

As you can see in Figure 1.18, the ribbon is a collection of different tabs, which replaces the traditional way of using menus and toolbars. Some of the tabs available on the ribbon are Home, Insert, Annotate, Modify, Massing & Site, Collaborate, View, and Manage.

Tabs and Contextual Tabs

The tabs are placed just below the title bar on the ribbon. When you navigate through the ribbon, the tabs assist you to select the task that you would like to perform. You can see the various tabs on the ribbon, as shown in **Figure 1.19**.

FIGURE 1.19

Using the tabs, you can access the various tools of application easily and quickly. When you open or create a Revit Architecture project, by default the ribbon highlights the Home tab. You can move to the other tabs by clicking them. The tabs other than the Home tab present in Autodesk Revit Architecture 2010 are Insert, Annotate, Modify, Massing & Site, Collaborate, View, and Manage. Autodesk Revit Architecture 2010 also contains some tabs that are visible only on some certain predefined conditions or in the context of specific components; these tabs are referred as contextual tabs.

The contextual tabs are context-sensitive and appear at the extreme right side of all other tabs. They appear when you select some objects, such as a wall or a door. Contextual tabs provide tools to edit the functionalities of the selected object. **Figure 1.20** displays a contextual tab when a component is selected.

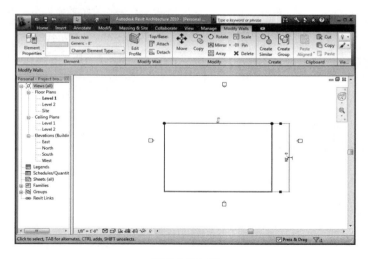

FIGURE 1.20

As you can see in Figure 1.20, when the wall component is selected, a new tab named Modify Walls is added to the ribbon. The Modify Walls tab provides the tools to deal with the wall component. Similarly, when you select a door or a window component, a contextual tab with tools used for doors or windows appears. When the object is not selected, the contextual tabs are hidden (they do not appear on the ribbon).

Panels and Expanded Panels

Panels refer to a collection of tools grouped under a tab. A tab may contain various panels containing different tools related to the same task. When you select a tab, the related tools are displayed on the ribbon. All of the tools available under a tab are organized in panels, as shown in **Figure 1.21**.

FIGURE 1.21

As you can see in Figure 1.21, the Home tab contains seven panels. These panels allow Revit Architecture architects to group the tools logically. For example, the Build panel contains the tools that are related to creating a building, and the Room & Area panel contains tools to create a room and calculate its area.

In addition, Autodesk Revit Architecture 2010 provides several expanded panels. The expanded panels are similar to panels but also include a drop-down arrow at their bottom. **Figure 1.22** displays an expanded panel.

FIGURE 1.22

Clicking the drop-down arrow expands the panel to display additional tools and controls, as shown in **Figure 1.23**.

FIGURE 1.23

The expanded panel automatically closes as you move the mouse pointer away from the panel. You can click the push-pin button at the lower-left corner of the expanded panel to keep the panel expanded.

Dialog Launcher

Autodesk Revit Architecture 2010 allows you to use the various options in the traditional way of dialog boxes, in case you are not comfortable or familiar with the new interface. For this purpose, a dialog launcher arrow is placed at the lower-right corner of the panels, as shown in **Figure 1.24**.

FIGURE 1.24

The dialog launcher arrow is used to open a dialog box containing commands in the traditional style. For example, clicking the dialog launcher in the Structure panel opens the Structural Settings dialog box, as shown in **Figure 1.25**.

FIGURE 1.25

These dialog box-based interfaces offer you more advanced options to work with Revit Architecture projects.

Tools

Tools refer to the different types of buttons that you need to create a project. These buttons are organized under different tabs on the ribbon. For example, the Home tab provides tools such as Wall, Door, Curtain System, Model Text, Area, and Room, as shown in **Figure 1.26**.

FIGURE 1.26

Similar to the Home tab, all other tabs on the ribbon also contains different sets of tools to work with a project.

Type Selector

The Type Selector is a drop-down list that is used to specify the type of the selected element. It appears under the Element panel for the currently selected tool. The content of the Type Selector changes depending on the current function or selected elements. While placing an element in the drawing area, you can use the Type Selector to specify the type of element that you want to add. **Figure 1.27** displays the Type Selector.

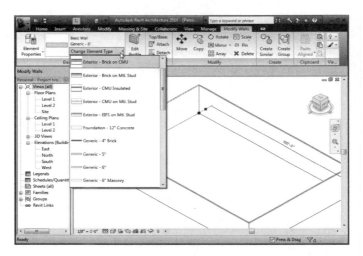

FIGURE 1.27

The Type Selector displays a list of family types from which you can choose an element to add it in the drawing area. The Type Selector appears under the contextual tab, as you can see in Figure 1.27.

InfoCenter

The InfoCenter is located on the title bar next to the project name. It allows you to search for information by using keywords, to access subscription services by using the Subscription Center panel, to access product updates and announcements by using the Communication Center panel, to access saved topics by using the Favorites panel, and to access topics in Help. **Figure 1.28** displays the InfoCenter.

FIGURE 1.28

You can collapse the InfoCenter by clicking the arrow on its left side.

Keytips and Tooltips

Keytips are another interesting feature provided by Autodesk Revit Architecture 2010. This feature lets you access commands displayed on the ribbon by using the keyboard. Thus you do not need to remember the different combinations for the keystrokes. If you want to know the keyboard shortcut of any command, just press the **ALT** key. As you press the **ALT** key, Autodesk Revit Architecture 2010 displays the associated shortcut keys on the ribbon, as shown in **Figure 1.29**.

FIGURE 1.29

As you can see in Figure 1.29, keytips are visible on the ribbon as keyboard shortcut indicators. You can use the key combinations displayed in the keytips to access a particular command.

Tooltips are pop-up boxes that provide information associated with the tools and the panels, as shown in **Figure 1.30**.

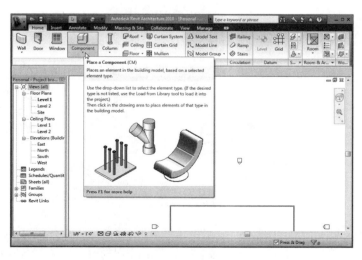

FIGURE 1.30

When you move the mouse pointer over a tool on the ribbon, by default a tooltip appears displaying brief information about that particular tool. If you leave the mouse pointer over the tool for another moment, additional information appears in the tooltip. In case you want to get detailed information about a particular tool, place the mouse pointer over it and press the **F1** key.

Options Bar

The options bar appears just below the ribbon. The fields of the options bar changes depending on the tool or component that you have currently selected. **Figure 1.31** shows the appearance of the options bar.

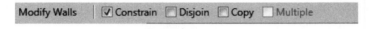

FIGURE 1.31

The fields displayed in Figure 1.31 are related to the wall component. When you select the wall component and click the **Move** button, the fields related with moving the wall appear on the options bar.

Project Browser

The Project Browser displays a logical hierarchy that organizes all views, plans, sections, elevations, schedules, sheets, families, groups, linked Revit models, and parts of the current project. **Figure 1.32** shows the Project Browser.

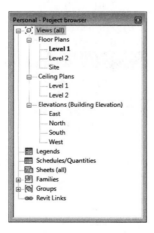

FIGURE 1.32

You can click the plus button beside the options to expand and see the lower-level items. Clicking on the minus button collapses and hides the items. You can easily and efficiently navigate and manage complex projects using the Project Browser.

Drawing Area

The drawing area is the white area displayed in the middle of the Autodesk Revit Architecture user interface. This area displays views as well as schedules and sheets of the current project. The drawing area is shown in **Figure 1.33**.

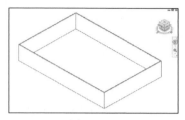

FIGURE 1.33

You can display one or more views in the drawing area. Each time you open a view in a project, the view appears at the top of all other views in the drawing area. It does not close the existing views. The existing views move underneath the current view. You can use the **Switch Windows** button under the Windows panel of the View tab to navigate through the various views that are currently open.

View Control Bar

The view control bar is placed between the drawing area and the status bar. **Figure 1.34** shows the appearance of the view control bar.

FIGURE 1.34

The view control bar contains a set of functions in the form of buttons, such as **Scale**, **Detail Level**, **Model Graphics Style**, **Shadows On/Off**, **Show/Hide Rendering Dialog**, **Crop Region On/Off**, **Show/Hide Crop Region**, **Temporary Hide/Isolate**, and **Reveal Hidden Elements.** These buttons alter the appearance of elements in the drawing area.

Status Bar

The status bar appears at the bottom of the Autodesk Revit Architecture 2010 window. While working with a tool, the left side of the status bar displays hints and tips on what to do. When you highlight a component, the status bar displays the family name and type of the highlighted component. In addition, when you first open a large file, the left side of the status bar displays the progress to indicate how much of the file has been downloaded. The status bar is shown in **Figure 1.35**.

Click to select, TAB for alternates, CTRL adds, SHIFT unselects.   ☑ Press & Drag   ▽:1

FIGURE 1.35

As you can see in Figure 1.35, some other controls also appear on the right side of the status bar. These controls may vary depending on the selected component. The most frequently used controls that appear on the right side are **Press & Drag**, **Editable Only**, **Active Only**, **Exclude Options**, and **Filter**.

After getting familiar with the user interface of the Autodesk Revit Architecture 2010, let's learn how to use its Help feature.

1.6 USING AUTODESK REVIT ARCHITECTURE 2010 HELP

Autodesk Revit Architecture 2010 includes a Help feature to provide assistance while you are working with it. You can access this feature in two ways—as online help or as context-sensitive help. Perform the following steps to use the online help of Autodesk Revit Architecture 2010:

1. *Click* the left part of the **Help** split button in the **InfoCenter** box, as shown in **Figure 1.36**.

FIGURE 1.36

The **Revit Architecture Help** window opens, as shown in **Figure 1.37**.

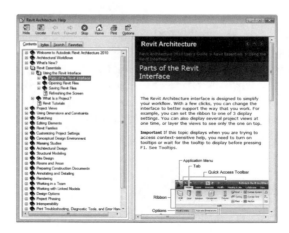

FIGURE 1.37

The **Revit Architecture Help** window consists of a toolbar and two panes, the navigation pane and the contents pane. The navigation pane has four help viewer tabs—Contents, Index, Search, and Favorites—which are used to move through different help topics. The contents pane displays information based on the topic selected in the left pane. The following tabs are present in the navigation pane:

- **Contents:** Lists all topics related to Autodesk Revit Architecture 2010 in the format of a table of contents.
- **Index:** Displays the help topics as keywords. The keywords are presented in an alphabetical order and provide you with the flexibility of conducting quick information searches in Autodesk Revit Architecture 2010.
- **Search:** Helps you find specific topics, which you type in the search box. The Search tab also includes an advanced search facility with which you can search for information using wildcard characters (* , ?) and Boolean operators (AND, OR, NEAR, NOT).
- **Favorites:** Helps you bookmark frequently accessed topics in the favorites list so that you can view information quickly.

2. *Select* the **Search** tab to search for a topic, as shown in **Figure 1.38**.

FIGURE 1.38

3. *Enter* the text in the **Type in the word(s) to search for** combo box that you want to search. In this case, we enter **user interface** (Figure 1.38).
4. *Click* the **List Topics** button (Figure 1.38). The topics related to the entered text appear in the **Select topic** list box, as shown in **Figure 1.39**.

FIGURE 1.39

5. *Select* an appropriate topic from the **Select topic** list box. In this case, we select **User Interface** (Figure 1.39).

6. *Click* the **Display** button (Figure 1.39). The information related to the **User Interface** topic appears in the contents pane, as shown in **Figure 1.40**.

FIGURE 1.40

After getting familiar with the Autodesk Revit Architecture 2010 Help feature, let's learn how to exit Autodesk Revit Architecture 2010.

1.7 EXITING AUTODESK REVIT ARCHITECTURE 2010

After working and saving your work in Autodesk Revit Architecture 2010, you need to close the application. Perform the following steps to exit Autodesk Revit Architecture 2010:

1. *Click* the **Application** button to open the application menu, as shown in **Figure 1.41**.

FIGURE 1.41

2. *Click* the **Exit Revit** button (Figure 1.41). This closes the **Autodesk Revit Architecture 2010** window.

Chapter 2

WORKING WITH PROJECTS AND ELEMENTS

In This Chapter

- ◇ Creating a New Project
- ◇ Sketching Elements
- ◇ Saving a Project
- ◇ Closing a Project
- ◇ Opening an Existing Project
- ◇ Selecting an Element
- ◇ Modifying an Element
- ◇ Moving an Element
- ◇ Rotating an Element
- ◇ Flipping an Element
- ◇ Mirroring an Element
- ◇ Resizing an Element
- ◇ Copying, Cutting, and Pasting an Element
- ◇ Trimming and Extending an Element
- ◇ Creating an Array of Elements
- ◇ Grouping Elements
- ◇ Aligning Elements
- ◇ Deleting an Element

Projects and elements are at the core of Autodesk Revit Architecture. Without creating a project and sketching elements, you cannot think about designing a building model. To create a final building model, you first need to create a project and then use different tools provided by Autodesk Revit Architecture, such as Wall, Door, Floor, and Window. While you are designing the project, you need to know how to work with the tools provided by Autodesk Revit Architecture. For example, when you create a building, you should know how to use the tools related to a building, such as Wall, Door, and Window.

In addition, you are required to know about the editing tools, such as Rotate and Scale, which help you to create a full-furnished building model.

In this chapter, you learn tasks for working with Autodesk Revit Architecture projects, such as creating, saving, closing, and opening a project. In addition, you learn to work with the operations on the elements in Autodesk Revit Architecture, such as those for sketching, modifying, moving, rotating, flipping, mirroring, and resizing an element. The chapter also explores the processes of copying, cutting, pasting, trimming, and extending an element; creating an array of elements; grouping elements; aligning elements; and deleting an element. We start our discussion by learning how to create a new project.

2.1 CREATING A NEW PROJECT

Creating a project is the first step toward designing the final building model. When you create a new project in Autodesk Revit Architecture, the project file uses the default settings defined in a project template. The default settings are specified in the **default.rte** file to help you start the designing process immediately, as all of the default tools appear under different tabs on the ribbon when the **default.rte** file is loaded into the project. Alternatively, you can create a custom template and then create a new project using that particular template.

To create a new project using the default settings, follow these steps:

1. *Open* the **Autodesk Revit Architecture 2010** window.
2. *Click* the **Application** button. The application menu appears, as shown in **Figure 2.1**.

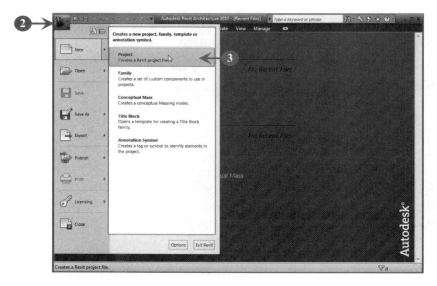

FIGURE 2.1

3. *Select* **New** > **Project** from the application menu (Figure 2.1). The **New Project** dialog box appears, as shown in **Figure 2.2**.

FIGURE 2.2

4. *Select* a radio button under the **Template file** group to specify whether you want to use a project template. In this case, we select the radio button beside the text box in which the project template file is specified (Figure 2.2).

5. *Select* the **Project** radio button under the **Create new** group (Figure 2.2).

Note: The Project template radio button allows you to create a custom project template.

---

6. *Click* the **OK** button (Figure 2.2). A new project, named **Project1**, is created, as shown in **Figure 2.3**.

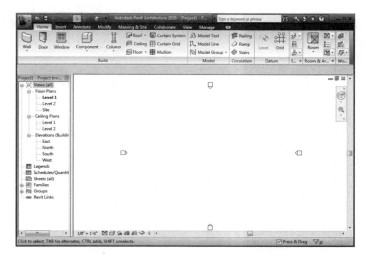

FIGURE 2.3

In Figure 2.3, you can see that the default project file name **Project1** appears on the title bar. Now you can create or sketch elements in the drawing area.

In the next section, we learn how to sketch elements in Autodesk Revit Architecture.

2.2 SKETCHING ELEMENTS

Sketching allows you to create an element of the building model. Sketching an element in Autodesk Revit Architecture can be done using two ways: by drawing lines or by picking existing elements from the ribbon, such as walls, doors, and windows. When *drawing* elements, you click and drag the mouse pointer in the drawing area according to the required element. When *picking* elements, you select an element from the ribbon and place it in the drawing area where you want to draw the respective element.

Adding elements that do not have predetermined shape and size, such as a roof, can be difficult. For adding such elements, you need to activate the sketch mode. In the sketch mode, the tools are displayed based on the type of element you are sketching. However, some elements, such as walls and doors, do not require the sketch mode.

Perform the following steps to sketch elements in Autodesk Revit Architecture:

1. *Create* a new project. (See Section 2.1, Creating a New Project.)
2. *Select* the **Home** tab, as shown in **Figure 2.4**.

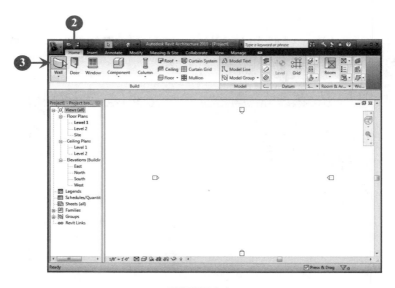

FIGURE 2.4

3. *Click* the button corresponding to the element that you want to sketch. In this case, we click the upper part of the **Wall** split button (Figure 2.4).

A contextual tab labeled **Place Wall** is added on the ribbon, which enables you to sketch a wall in the drawing area, as shown in **Figure 2.5**.

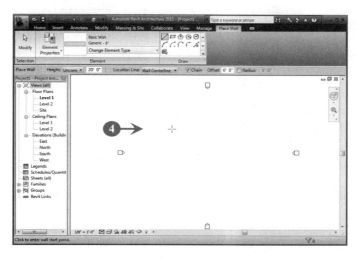

FIGURE 2.5

4. *Move* the mouse pointer to the location in the drawing area where you want to specify the starting point of the wall and then *click* the mouse button (Figure 2.5).

5. *Move* the mouse pointer in the drawing area to specify the length of the boundary of the wall and *click* the mouse button to specify the ending point of the wall, as shown in **Figure 2.6**.

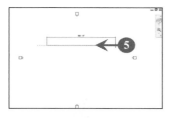

FIGURE 2.6

Note: The dimension of the wall increases as you move the mouse pointer away from the starting point.

6. *Press* the **ESC** key twice to exit the Wall tool.

7. To observe the wall in 3D view, *select* the **View** tab on the ribbon, as shown in **Figure 2.7**.

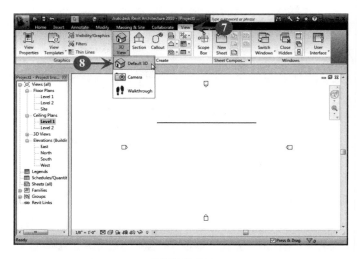

FIGURE 2.7

8. *Click* the lower part of the **3D View** split button and then *select* the **Default 3D** option from the drop-down list (Figure 2.7). The wall is displayed in 3D view, as shown in **Figure 2.8**.

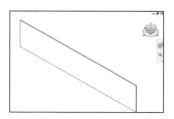

FIGURE 2.8

This completes our discussion about sketching a wall in Autodesk Revit Architecture. We next explore how to save a project.

2.3 SAVING A PROJECT

After creating a project and sketching the required elements, you need to save your project so that you can use it later when required. Perform the following steps to save the project:

1. Continuing from the previous section, *click* the **Application** button. The application menu appears, as shown in **Figure 2.9**.

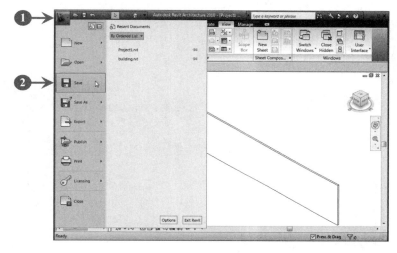

FIGURE 2.9

2. *Select* the **Save** option from the application menu (Figure 2.9). The **Save As** dialog box appears, as shown in **Figure 2.10**.

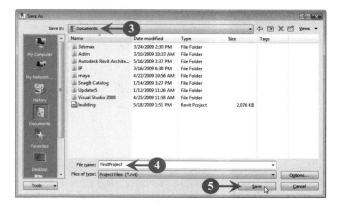

FIGURE 2.10

Note: The Save menu item opens the **Save As** dialog box, if the project is not saved earlier. Once you save a project and want to change the project name, you can open the **Save As** dialog box using the Save As menu item.

3. *Select* a location where you want to save the project from the **Save in** drop-down list. In this case, we *select* the **Documents** folder (Figure 2.10).

4. *Enter* the file name for the project in the **File name** text box. In this case, we *enter* the name **FirstProject** (Figure 2.10).

5. *Click* the **Save** button (Figure 2.10). The project is saved with the specified name, as shown in **Figure 2.11**.

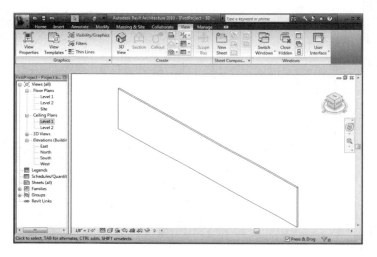

FIGURE 2.11

In Figure 2.11, you can see that the name of the project—that is, **FirstProject**—appears on the title bar.

In the next section, we learn how to close a project.

2.4 CLOSING A PROJECT

After creating and saving your project, you can close it. Closing a project does not mean that you need to close the **Autodesk Revit Architecture 2010** window. Autodesk Revit Architecture 2010 provides you with an option to close a project that is currently open without exiting this window. Perform the following steps to close the project:

1. Continuing from the previous section, *click* the **Application** button. The application menu appears, as shown in **Figure 2.12**.

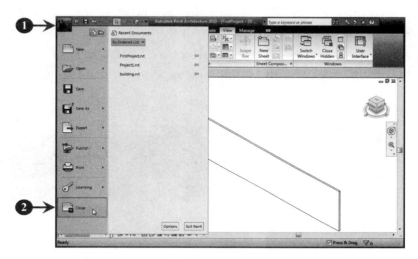

FIGURE 2.12

2. *Select* the **Close** option from the application menu (Figure 2.12). The project is closed without exiting the **Autodesk Revit Architecture 2010** window, as shown in **Figure 2.13**.

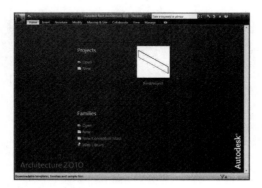

FIGURE 2.13

Now let's learn how to open a project that you have already created in Autodesk Revit Architecture.

2.5 OPENING AN EXISTING PROJECT

If you have to work on a project that you have created and saved on your computer earlier, you must open the project file first, before you start your work. Perform the following steps to open an existing project:

1. *Open* the **Autodesk Revit Architecture 2010** window.
2. *Click* the **Application** button. The application menu appears, as shown in **Figure 2.14**.

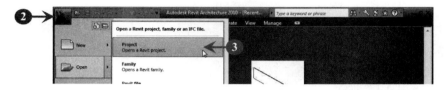

FIGURE 2.14

3. *Select* **Open > Project** from the application menu (Figure 2.14). The **Open** dialog box appears, as shown in **Figure 2.15**.

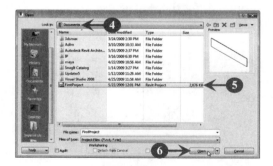

FIGURE 2.15

4. *Select* the location of the project file from the **Look in** drop-down list. In this case, we *select* the **Documents** folder (Figure 2.15).
5. *Select* the project file that you want to open—in this case, **FirstProject** (Figure 2.15).
6. *Click* the **Open** button (Figure 2.15). The project opens, as shown in **Figure 2.16**.

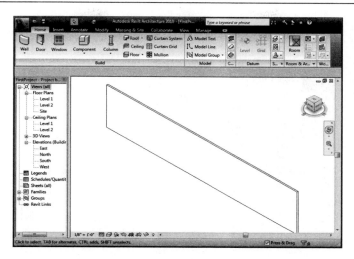

FIGURE 2.16

This completes our discussion about opening an existing project. Now let's learn how to select an element in Revit Architecture.

2.6 SELECTING AN ELEMENT

Selecting an element makes the element active in the viewport. When an element is selected, you can access and modify its parameters. Autodesk Revit Architecture 2010 includes the automatic highlighting feature to identify and select a specific element among a set of elements. When you move the mouse pointer over an element in the drawing area, the outline of the element is highlighted using a heavier line weight. When an element is highlighted, the description of the element appears on the status bar as well as within a tooltip below the mouse pointer. You can select an element by just clicking that particular element. Selecting an element in one view selects that particular element in all other views. For example, if you select a wall in the 3D view, the wall is also selected in the other views, such as the Plan, Elevation, and Legends views.

Perform the following steps to select an element in the drawing area of Autodesk Revit Architecture:

1. *Open* the **Autodesk Revit Architecture 2010** window.
2. *Create* an Autodesk Revit Architecture file and sketch the elements from which you want to select an element. In this case, we *create* the **Project1** file, which contains the wall, door, and window elements, as shown in **Figure 2.17**.

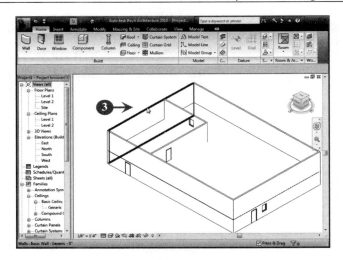

FIGURE 2.17

3. *Move* the mouse pointer over the element that you want to select. In this case, we *move* the mouse pointer over the wall element. The outline of the wall is highlighted (Figure 2.17).

4. *Click* the mouse button to select the wall. The wall is selected and the dimensions of the wall appear, as shown in **Figure 2.18**.

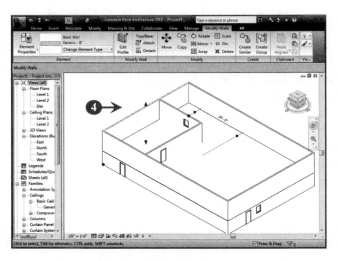

FIGURE 2.18

You can select multiple elements in the drawing area by pressing the **CTRL** key and then clicking each element that you want to select.

In this section, you have learned how to select an element. Let's move on to the next section, which explains how to modify an element.

2.7 MODIFYING AN ELEMENT

Modifying an element implies changing the structure and appearance of the element in the drawing area. When you select an element, the Modify <Element> tab appears on the ribbon to provide you with a set of tools to manipulate, modify, and manage the appearance of the selected element in the drawing area. For example, when you select a wall, the Modify Walls tab appears on the ribbon with a variety of tools specific to the wall element, which you can use to apply changes to the wall element.

You can modify an element by performing various tasks, such as changing its component types and line style, changing the cut profiles, measuring the elements, and joining and unjoining elements. Let's perform the following steps to change the component type of an element:

1. *Open* the **Autodesk Revit Architecture 2010** window.
2. *Open* the file in which you want to change the component type of an element. In this case, we *open* the **Project1** file.
3. *Select* the **Modify** tab on the ribbon, as shown in **Figure 2.19**.

FIGURE 2.19

4. *Click* the **Match Type** button under the **Clipboard** panel (Figure 2.19). The mouse pointer changes its appearance to the pointer with a paint brush and the **Match Type** tab is added on the ribbon, as shown in **Figure 2.20**.

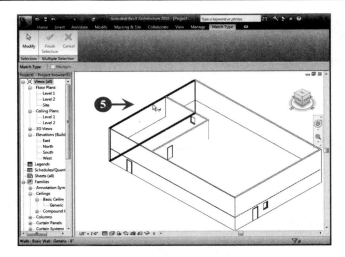

FIGURE 2.20

5. *Select* an element of the type to which you want to convert other elements. In this case, we *select* the wall of **Generic—8"** type (Figure 2.20). The paint brush appears as filled.

6. *Select* the element(s) that you want to modify (change the type, in our case) with the type of the selected element. In this case, we *select* the wall of **Generic—5"** type, as shown in **Figure 2.21**.

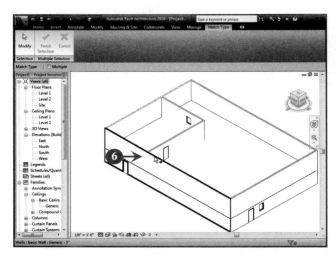

FIGURE 2.21

The wall having the Generic—5" type has been changed to the Generic—8" type, as shown in **Figure 2.22**.

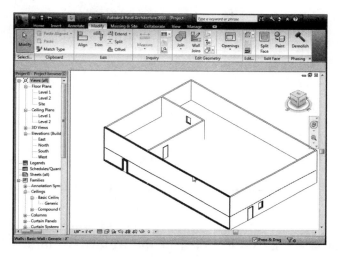

FIGURE 2.22

7. *Press* the **ESC** key twice to exit the Wall tool.

Now, when you move the mouse pointer over the wall of Generic—5" type, the type appears as Generic—8".

2.8 MOVING AN ELEMENT

Moving allows you to move a selected element to a new location in the drawing area. Autodesk Revit Architecture provides a variety of options to move an element in the drawing area, such as by changing the temporary dimensions, by dragging the element, by using the arrow keys, and by using the Move tool. The Move tool is a better choice than the other options, as it moves the elements by a specific distance and allows for more precise placement, which in turn increases the accuracy of the building model.

Perform the following steps to move an element in the drawing area:

1. *Open* the **Autodesk Revit Architecture 2010** window.
2. *Open* the file in which you want to move an element—in this case, **Project1**.
3. *Select* the element that you want to move. In this case, we *select* the window element, as shown in **Figure 2.23**.

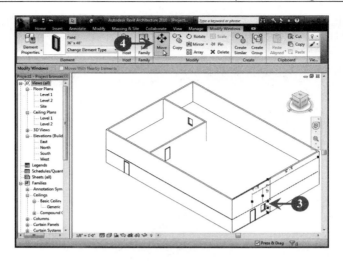

FIGURE 2.23

When you select the window element, the **Modify Windows** tab appears on the ribbon in the selected mode.

4. *Click* the **Move** button under the **Modify** panel (Figure 2.23). The mouse pointer changes its appearance to a cross double-headed arrow.
5. *Select* a check box on the options bar to specify a move option. In this case, we *select* the **Constrain** check box, as shown in **Figure 2.24**.

FIGURE 2.24

The options bar provides four check boxes:

- **Constrain:** Restricts the movement of elements along perpendicular or collinear vectors.
- **Disjoin:** Breaks the association between an element and its associated elements.
- **Copy:** Creates a copy of an element by retaining the original element. Selecting the Copy check box automatically selects the Disjoin check box.

- **Multiple:** Creates multiple copies of elements every time you click in the drawing area.

6. *Click* the selected element to specify a starting point for moving the element, as shown in **Figure 2.25**.

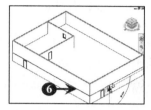

FIGURE 2.25

7. *Move* the mouse pointer to the location where you want to move the element (**Figure 2.26**).

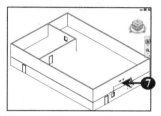

FIGURE 2.26

8. *Click* at the location where you want to place the element, as shown in **Figure 2.27**.

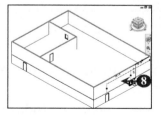

FIGURE 2.27

The window is moved to the new location, as shown in Figure 2.27.

2.9 ROTATING AN ELEMENT

Autodesk Revit Architecture provides the Rotate tool to rotate and change the orientation of an element. When you rotate an element along an axis, you do not have to rotate the mouse pointer, but rather move it either straight up and down or left and right. If you move the mouse pointer up or left, the element rotates in one direction. Alternatively, if you move the mouse pointer down or right, the element rotates in the opposite direction. The elements can be rotated along any axes.

Perform the following steps to rotate an element:

1. *Open* the **Autodesk Revit Architecture 2010** window.
2. *Open* the file in which you want to rotate an element—in this case, **Project1**.
3. *Select* the element(s) that you want to rotate. In this case, we *select* the wall element, as shown in **Figure 2.28**.

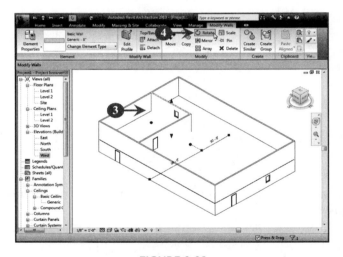

FIGURE 2.28

When you select the wall element, the **Modify Walls** tab appears on the ribbon in the selected mode.

4. *Click* the **Rotate** button under the **Modify** panel (Figure 2.28).
5. *Select* a check box on the options bar to specify the rotate option. In this case, we *select* the **Disjoin** check box, as shown in **Figure 2.29**.

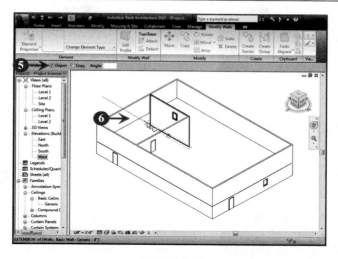

FIGURE 2.29

6. *Click* at a location in the drawing area to specify the first ray of rotation (Figure 2.29).

7. *Move* the mouse pointer left and right or up and down in the drawing area to the location where you want to specify the second ray of rotation. In this case, we *move* the mouse pointer to the left, as shown in **Figure 2.30**.

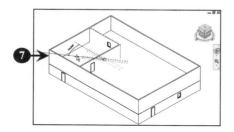

FIGURE 2.30

8. *Click* again at the location where you want to place the second ray. The wall is rotated, as shown in **Figure 2.31**.

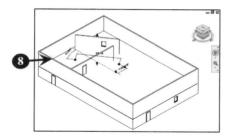

FIGURE 2.31

Similar to rotating a wall, you can also rotate multiple elements at a time by just selecting them and then using the Rotate tool on all of them at once.

Now, let's move to the next section to learn how to flip an element in Revit Architecture.

2.10 FLIPPING AN ELEMENT

Flipping an element changes the orientation of the element in the drawing area. After creating an element in Revit Architecture, you can flip it horizontally or vertically. Perform the following steps to flip an element:

1. *Open* the **Autodesk Revit Architecture 2010** window.
2. *Open* the file in which you want to flip an element. In this case, we *open* the **Parking Component** file, which contains numerous trees in the drawing area, as shown in **Figure 2.32**.

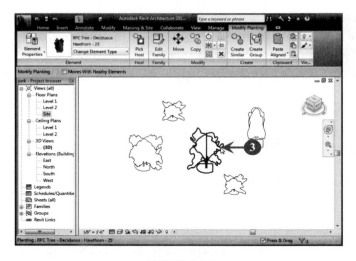

FIGURE 2.32

3. *Select* the element that you want to flip. In this case, we *select* the **Hawthorn** tree (Figure 2.32).
4. *Press* the **SPACEBAR** key on the keyboard to flip the element, as shown in **Figure 2.33**.

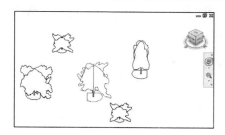

FIGURE 2.33

Each time you press the **SPACEBAR** key, the element flips.
Let's now learn how to mirror an element.

2.11 MIRRORING AN ELEMENT

Autodesk Revit Architecture allows you to create a mirror image of an element using the Mirror tool. Mirroring reverses the position of a selected element across an axis. You can either pick an existing reference of the mirror axis or draw a temporary axis interactively. Perform the following steps to mirror an element in Autodesk Revit Architecture:

1. *Open* the **Autodesk Revit Architecture 2010** window.
2. *Open* the file in which you want to mirror an element. In this case, we *open* the **Parking Component** file.
3. *Select* the element that you want to mirror. In this case, we *select* the **Siberian crab apple** tree, as shown in **Figure 2.34**.

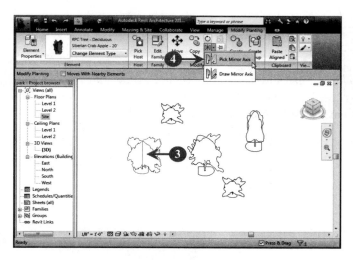

FIGURE 2.34

When you select the tree, the **Modify Planting** tab appears on the ribbon in the selected mode.

4. *Click* the **Mirror** split button and then *select* the **Pick Mirror Axis** option from the drop-down list (Figure 2.34).

Note: You can *select* the **Pick Mirror Axis** option to select the line that represents the mirror axis or *select* the **Draw Mirror Axis** option to draw a temporary mirror axis line.

5. *Clear* the **Copy** check box on the options bar to move only the selected item, irrespective of creating its copy, as shown in **Figure 2.35**.

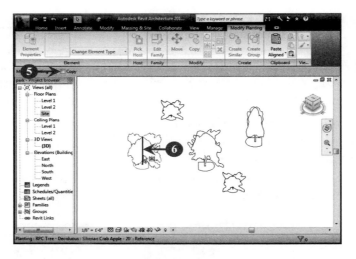

FIGURE 2.35

6. *Click* the mirror axis line about which you want to mirror the selected element (Figure 2.35). When you click the mirror axis line, the selected element appears, as shown in **Figure 2.36**.

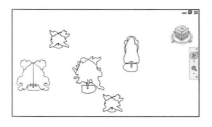

FIGURE 2.36

As you can see in Figure 2.36, the selected element is mirrored about the selected mirror axis.

2.12 RESIZING AN ELEMENT

When an element does not fit in the drawing area, you can change its size. You can either increase or decrease the size of an element in the drawing area, if required. Autodesk Revit Architecture provides the Scale tool to resize elements, such as lines, walls, images, DWG (Drawing) and DXF (Drawing Exchange Format) imports, reference planes, and position of dimensions. Resizing an element requires you to define an origin that is a fixed point from which the selected element and the elements related to it are equally resized.

Let's perform the following steps to resize an element in Autodesk Revit Architecture:

1. *Open* the **Autodesk Revit Architecture 2010** window.
2. *Open* the file in which you want to resize an element—in this case, the **Project1** file.
3. *Select* the element that you want to resize. In this case, we *select* the wall element, as shown in **Figure 2.37**.

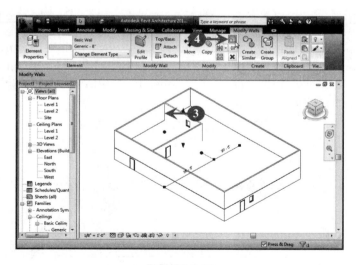

FIGURE 2.37

When you select the wall, the **Modify Walls** tab appears on the ribbon in the selected mode.

4. *Click* the **Scale** button under the **Modify** panel (Figure 2.37).

5. *Select* the **Graphical** radio button on the options bar to graphically scale the element, as shown in **Figure 2.38**.

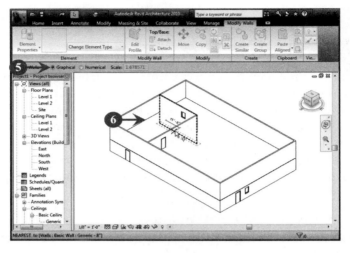

FIGURE 2.38

Note: Select the Numerical radio button to scale the element numerically and then enter the value in the Scale text box by which you want to scale the element.

6. *Click* at a location in the drawing area to set the origin (Figure 2.38).

7. *Move* the mouse pointer to the location where you want to define the first vector and then *click* the mouse button to set the length, as shown in **Figure 2.39**.

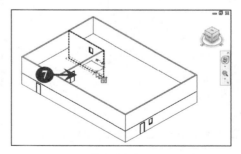

FIGURE 2.39

8. *Move* the mouse pointer again to the location where you want to define the second vector, as shown in **Figure 2.40**.

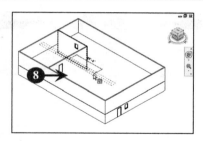

FIGURE 2.40

9. *Click* the mouse button to set the point for the second vector (Figure 2.41). As you can see in Figure 2.41, the wall is scaled to a new size and the window in the wall is shifted to a new location.

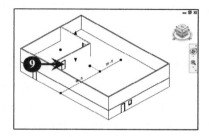

FIGURE 2.41

Let's now learn how to copy, cut, and paste an element in Autodesk Revit Architecture.

2.13 COPYING, CUTTING, AND PASTING AN ELEMENT

Copying allows you to create multiple copies of an element and place them in the drawing area. Autodesk Revit Architecture includes the Copy tool to create copies of an element. This tool does not place the copied element on the clipboard; rather, it is used when you want to place the selected element in the drawing area immediately. In contrast, the Copy to Clipboard tool is used to place an element on the clipboard.

Perform the following steps to copy an element:

1. *Open* the **Autodesk Revit Architecture 2010** window.
2. *Open* the file in which you want to create copies of an element—in this case, the **Project1** file.
3. *Select* the element(s) in the drawing area that you want to copy. In this case, we *select* the window element, as shown in **Figure 2.42**.

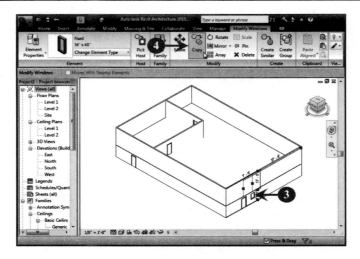

FIGURE 2.42

When you select the window element, the **Modify Windows** tab appears on the ribbon in the selected mode.

4. *Click* the **Copy** button under the **Modify** panel (Figure 2.42).
5. *Click* at a location in the drawing area to start moving and copying the element(s), as shown in **Figure 2.43**.

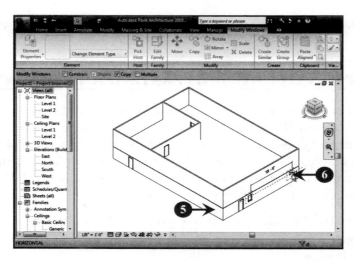

FIGURE 2.43

6. *Move* the mouse pointer away from the original element to the location where you want to place the copied element and then *click* the mouse button to

place the copied element (Figure 2.43). A copy of the selected element is created at the new location, as shown in **Figure 2.44**.

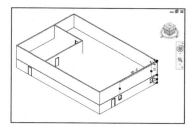

FIGURE 2.44

Alternatively, you can copy the elements to the clipboard and then paste them later from the clipboard in the drawing area or in another project. Perform the following steps to copy and paste an element to and from the clipboard, respectively:

1. *Open* the **Autodesk Revit Architecture 2010** window.
2. *Open* the file in which you want to create copies of an element—in this case, **Project1**.
3. *Select* the element(s) in the drawing area that you want to copy. In this case, we *select* the window element, as shown in **Figure 2.45**.

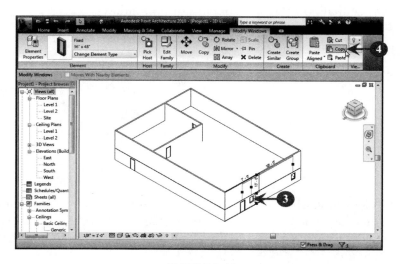

FIGURE 2.45

When you select the window element, the **Modify Windows** tab appears on the ribbon in the selected mode.

4. *Click* the **Copy** button under the **Clipboard** panel (Figure 2.45).

5. *Click* the **Paste** button under the **Clipboard** panel, as shown in **Figure 2.46**.

FIGURE 2.46

6. *Move* the mouse pointer to the location in the drawing area where you want to place the copied element, as shown in **Figure 2.47**.

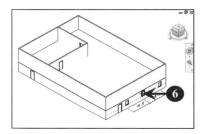

FIGURE 2.47

7. *Click* the mouse button to paste the copied element. In **Figure 2.48**, you can see that now the wall contains three windows.

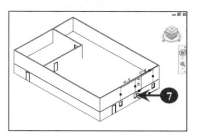

FIGURE 2.48

Unlike the Copy tool, which creates copies of the selected element without removing it from the original location, the Cut tool removes the selected elements and place them in the location where you want to paste the elements. Perform the following steps to cut and paste an element:

1. *Open* the **Autodesk Revit Architecture 2010** window.
2. *Open* the file from which you want to cut an element—in this case, **Project1**.
3. *Select* the element(s) in the drawing area that you want to cut. In this case, we *select* the window element, as shown in **Figure 2.49**.

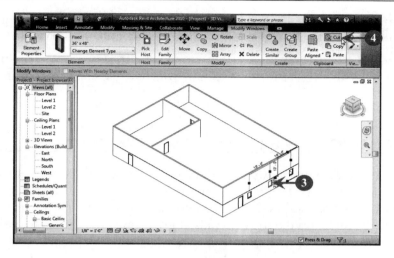

FIGURE 2.49

When you select the window element, the **Modify Windows** tab appears on the ribbon in the selected mode.

4. *Click* the **Cut** button under the **Clipboard** panel (Figure 2.49).
5. *Press* the **CTRL+V** keys on the keyboard.
6. *Move* the mouse pointer to the location in the drawing area where you want to place the cut element, as shown in **Figure 2.50**.

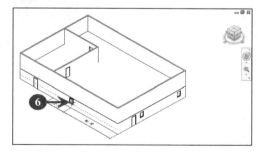

FIGURE 2.50

7. *Click* the mouse button to paste the element, as shown in **Figure 2.51**.

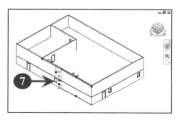

FIGURE 2.51

In Figure 2.51, you can see that the selected window element is removed from its original location and displayed at the new location in the drawing area.

This completes our discussion of how to copy, cut, and paste elements in Revit Architecture. Let's move on to the next section, which focuses on how to trim and extend an element.

2.14 TRIMMING AND EXTENDING AN ELEMENT

Autodesk Revit Architecture allows you to trim or extend one or more elements using the Trim and Extend tools. With these tools, you can cut an element or extend it to meet other elements at a boundary. You can define this boundary by selecting an element. The Trim and Extend tools can be used only with walls, lines, beams, and braces to create corners, and to trim or extend a reference line or a wall to another reference line or wall. To use these tools, first you need to select the tool and then operate on elements in the model.

Perform the following steps to trim and extend elements in Revit Architecture:

1. *Open* the **Autodesk Revit Architecture 2010** window.
2. *Open* the file in which you want to trim or extend an element—in this case, **Project1.**
3. *Select* the **Modify** tab on the ribbon, as shown in **Figure 2.52**.

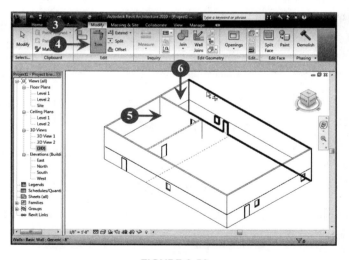

FIGURE 2.52

4. *Click* the **Trim** button under the **Edit** panel (Figure 2.52).
5. *Select* the first element that you want to trim (Figure 2.52).

6. *Select* the second element that is to be trimmed with the first element to create a corner (Figure 2.52).

Note: Ensure that you click the part of the element that you want to retain in the building model.

As you select the second element, the walls are trimmed and the corner is created, as shown in **Figure 2.53**.

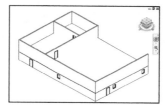

FIGURE 2.53

After trimming the element, continue with the following steps to extend the element.

7. *Click* the **Extend** drop-down button and then *select* the **Trim/Extend Single Element** option from the drop-down list, as shown in **Figure 2.54**.

FIGURE 2.54

Note: You can select Trim/Extend Multiple Elements to trim or extend multiple elements to a boundary defined by another element.

8. *Select* the first element to specify the reference for a boundary, as shown in **Figure 2.55**.

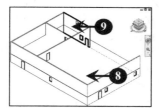

FIGURE 2.55

9. *Select* the second element that you want to extend to the boundary of the first element (Figure 2.55). When you select the second element, its boundary is extended, as shown in **Figure 2.56**.

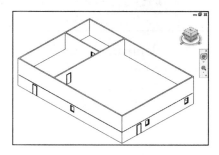

FIGURE 2.56

This completes our discussion about how to trim and extend elements. We next learn how to create an array of elements.

2.15 CREATING AN ARRAY OF ELEMENTS

You can create an array of elements using the Array tool to make the elements follow a line or an arc. The elements following a line are called a linear array of elements; the elements following an arc are called a radial array of elements. While creating a linear or radial array, you use the Array tool, which displays a number of options on the options bar. The Group And Associate check box on the options bar allows you to create a group of selected elements and then use all of these elements as a single entity, rather than as individual elements. The Move To option contains two radio buttons—2nd and Last—that allow you to specify the distance between elements. In this section, you learn how to create a linear and radial array of elements.

Creating a Linear Array

The linear array creates copies of the selected elements in a rectangular or linear pattern. When you select the Array tool, by default the **Linear** button is activated to create a linear array. While creating a linear array, you can enter the number of copies to be created for elements in the Number text box on the options bar. You can also view the dimensions of the elements using the **Activate Dimensions** button on the options bar. Selecting the Constrain check box enables you to restrict the movement of the mouse pointer in orthogonal direction only.

Let's perform the following steps to create a linear array:

1. *Open* the **Autodesk Revit Architecture 2010** window.
2. *Open* the file in which you want to create a linear array of elements—in this case, **Project1**.

3. *Select* the element(s) that you want to include in an array. In this case, we *select* the door element, as shown in **Figure 2.57**.

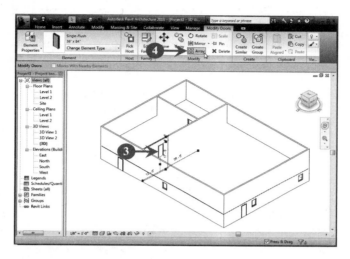

FIGURE 2.57

As you select the door element, the **Modify Doors** tab appears on the ribbon in the selected mode.

4. *Click* the **Array** button under the **Modify** panel (Figure 2.57). A number of options appear on the options bar, as shown in **Figure 2.58**.

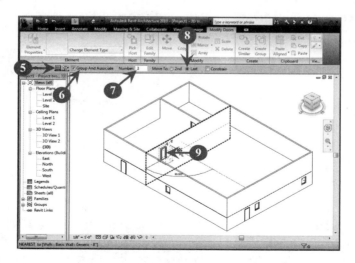

FIGURE 2.58

5. *Click* the **Linear** button on the options bar (Figure 2.58).

6. *Select* the **Group And Associate** check box to include each member of the array in a group (Figure 2.58).

7. *Enter* the number of copies to be created in the array in the **Number** text box. In this case, we *enter* **3** (Figure 2.58).

8. *Select* a radio button beside the **Move To** option to specify the distance between elements. In this case, we *select* the **Last** radio button (Figure 2.58).

9. *Click* at a location in the drawing area to specify the starting point where the first element of the array is placed (Figure 2.58).

10. *Move* the mouse pointer to the location where you want to place the last array element and then *click* the mouse button. A box appears to indicate the size of the selected elements, as shown in **Figure 2.59**.

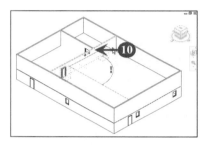

FIGURE 2.59

A number box appears in the drawing area indicating the total number of copies to be created in the array, as shown in **Figure 2.60**.

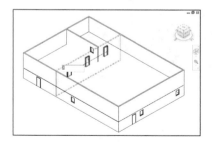

FIGURE 2.60

11. If required, *change* the number of copies and then *press* **ENTER**; otherwise, just *press* **ENTER**. The specified number of copies of the selected element(s) is created and placed using the appropriate spacing, as shown in **Figure 2.61**.

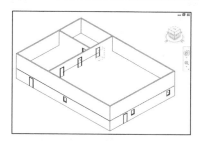

FIGURE 2.61

As you can see in Figure 2.61, the copies of elements are created in a linear pattern. Now, let's move on to the next section to learn how to create a radial array of elements.

Creating a Radial Array

A radial array arranges the elements using the arc representation. The options to create a radial array are similar to the options for the linear array, except that the radial array includes the Angle text box, which is used to specify an angle about which the curve is created to place the elements of the array. Let's perform the following steps to create a radial array of elements:

1. *Open* the **Autodesk Revit Architecture 2010** window.
2. *Open* the file in which you want to create a linear array of elements—in this case, **Project1**.
3. *Select* the element(s) that you want to include in an array. In this case, we *select* the wall element, as shown in **Figure 2.62**.

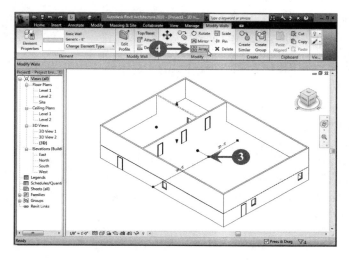

FIGURE 2.62

When you select the wall element, the **Modify Walls** tab appears on the ribbon in the selected mode.

4. *Click* the **Array** button under the **Modify** panel (Figure 2.62). A number of options associated with the Array tool appear on the options bar, as shown in **Figure 2.63**.

FIGURE 2.63

5. *Click* the **Radial** button on the options bar (Figure 2.63). The options associated with the radial array appear, as shown in **Figure 2.64**.

FIGURE 2.64

6. *Select* the **Group And Associate** check box to include each member of the array in a group (Figure 2.64).
7. *Enter* the number of copies to be created in the array in the **Number** text box. In this case, we *enter* **3** (Figure 2.64).
8. *Select* a radio button corresponding to the **Move To** option to specify the distance between elements. In this case, we *select* the **Last** radio button (Figure 2.64).
9. *Enter* the angle in the **Angle** text box about which you want to create an arc. In this case, we *enter* **60** (Figure 2.64).
10. *Move* the mouse pointer to the location where the arc of the radial array starts and then *click* the mouse button to set the first ray of rotation, as shown in **Figure 2.65**.

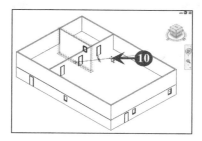

FIGURE 2.65

11. *Move* the mouse pointer to another location where you want to set the last member of the radial array and then *click* the mouse button to set the second ray of rotation, as shown in **Figure 2.66**.

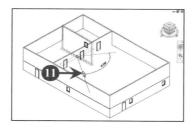

FIGURE 2.66

As you click the mouse button, the controls—such as text boxes and drag handles— appear on the radial array in the drawing area, as shown in **Figure 2.67**.

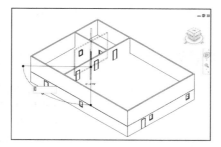

FIGURE 2.67

You can use the text box to change the number of copies of the elements to be created or use the start and end drag handles (which appear as points on the rotation ray) to resize the angle of the arc. The point at the center of the array elements is used to drag the entire array to a new location in the drawing area.

12. If required, *change* the number of copies and then *press* **ENTER**; otherwise, just *press* **ENTER**. The specified number of copies of the selected

element(s) are created and placed using the appropriate spacing, as shown in **Figure 2.68**.

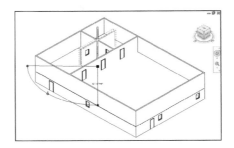

FIGURE 2.68

13. *Press* **ESC** to exit the Array tool. The final model appears, as shown in **Figure 2.69**.

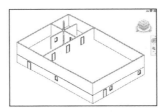

FIGURE 2.69

This completes our discussion about how to create array of elements. Let's move on to the next section to learn how to group elements in Autodesk Revit Architecture.

2.16 GROUPING ELEMENTS

While designing a building model, you can see a variety of elements in the drawing area. You can manage them by creating a group of similar elements. Grouping is a process of creating a group of more than one element. It enables you to treat multiple elements as a single entity. Revit Architecture provides two ways of creating a group: by selecting elements in the project view or by using the group editor. The group editor can be used for different grouping purposes, such as adding elements from the project view; placing additional elements in the view, which are then automatically added to the group; removing elements; creating attached detail groups; and viewing group properties.

Perform the following steps to group elements using the group editor:

1. *Open* the **Autodesk Revit Architecture 2010** window.
2. *Open* the file in which you want to group elements—in this case, **Project1**.

3. *Select* the **Home** tab on the ribbon, as shown in **Figure 2.70**.

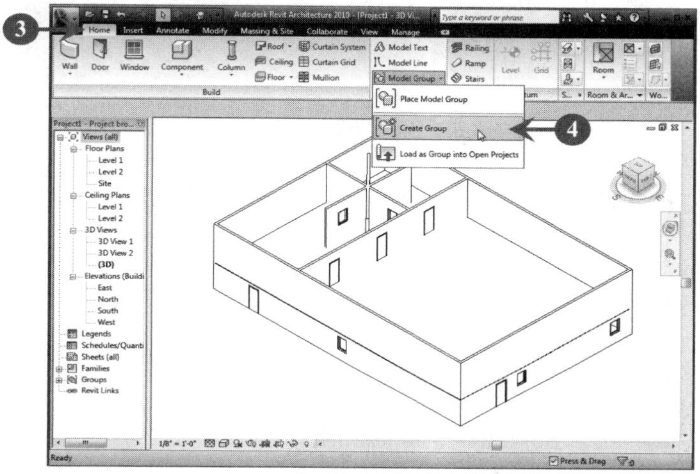

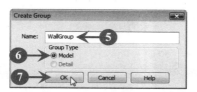

FIGURE 2.70

4. *Click* the **Model Group** drop-down button under the **Model** panel and then *select* the **Create Group** option from the drop-down list (Figure 2.70). The **Create Group** dialog box appears, as shown in **Figure 2.71**.

FIGURE 2.71

5. *Enter* the group name in the **Name** text box. In this case, we *enter* a group name of **Wall Group** (Figure 2.71).
6. *Select* a radio button under the **Group Type** group to specify the group type. In this case, we *select* the **Model** radio button (Figure 2.71).

Note: The Group Type includes two options: Model and Detail. In Figure 2.71, the Detail radio button is deactivated because the project does not have detail about any element.

7. *Click* the **OK** button (Figure 2.71). The **Edit Group** panel is added on the ribbon in the selected mode indicating that you are in group edit mode, as shown in **Figure 2.72**.

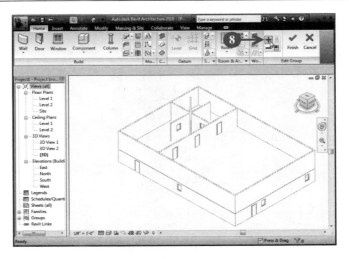

FIGURE 2.72

Note: When you are in group edit mode, the background color of the drawing area is changed.

8. *Click* the **Add** button under the **Edit Group** panel (Figure 2.72).
9. *Select* the elements that you want to include in the group, as shown in **Figure 2.73**.

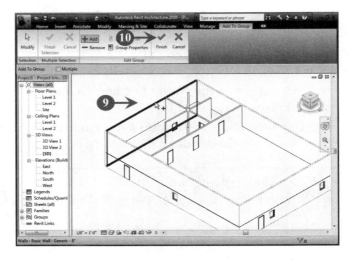

FIGURE 2.73

10. After you have completed adding elements to the group, *click* the **Finish** button under the **Edit Group** panel. All of the selected elements are grouped and displayed as a single entity, as shown in **Figure 2.74**.

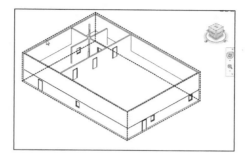

FIGURE 2.74

In Figure 2.74, you can see that when you move the mouse pointer over one element of the group, all of the elements in the group are selected at once.

Let's now move on to the next section to learn how to align elements in Revit Architecture.

2.17 ALIGNING ELEMENTS

Revit Architecture provides the Align tool so that you can align one or more elements according to the selected element. You can use this tool to align elements such as wall, beams, and lines. The Align tool can also be used to align other elements, although the alignment requires the elements to be of same type or from the different families. The elements can be aligned only in plan view or elevation view.

Perform the following steps to align elements in Autodesk Revit Architecture:

1. *Open* the **Autodesk Revit Architecture 2010** window.
2. *Open* the file in which you want to align elements—in this case, **Project1**.
3. *Select* the **Modify** tab on the ribbon, as shown in **Figure 2.75**.

FIGURE 2.75

4. *Click* the **Align** button under the **Edit** panel (Figure 2.75). A number of options appear on the options bar, as shown in **Figure 2.76**.

FIGURE 2.76

5. *Select* the **Multiple Alignment** check box to align multiple elements with a selected element (Figure 2.76).
6. *Select* an option from the **Prefer** drop-down list to specify the criteria according to which the walls are aligned. In this case, we *select* **Wall faces** (Figure 2.76).
7. *Select* the reference element about which you want to align other elements, as shown in **Figure 2.77**.

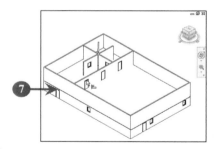

FIGURE 2.77

8. *Select* one or more elements that you want to align with the reference element, as shown in **Figure 2.78**.

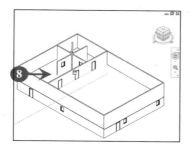

FIGURE 2.78

9. *Click* the padlock to lock the alignment so that if you later move the elements, the selected elements will stay aligned with the reference element. When you click the padlock, the alignment is locked (**Figure 2.79**).

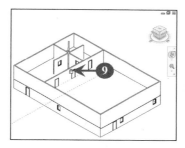

FIGURE 2.79

10. *Press* the **ESC** key twice to exit the Align tool.

This completes our discussion of aligning an element. We next learn how to delete an element in Revit Architecture.

2.18 DELETING AN ELEMENT

While designing a building model, you may need to remove some elements from the building model. For this purpose, Autodesk Revit Architecture provides the Delete tool, which removes the selected elements from the drawing area. The Delete tool is available only when you select an element in the drawing area. Once you delete the element, it is not stored on the clipboard; therefore, you need to be careful while deleting an element.

Perform the following steps to delete an element:

1. *Open* the **Autodesk Revit Architecture 2010** window.

2. *Open* the file from which you want to delete elements—in this case, **Project1**.

3. *Select* the elements in the drawing area that you want to delete, as shown in **Figure 2.80**.

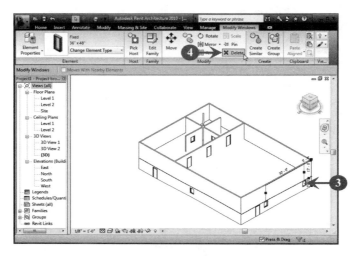

FIGURE 2.80

When you select the element, the **Modify <Element>** tab appears on the ribbon in the selected mode, where **Element** is the type of the selected element.

4. *Click* the **Delete** button under the **Modify** panel (Figure 2.80). The selected element is deleted, as shown in **Figure 2.81**.

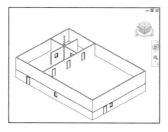

FIGURE 2.81

In Figure 2.81, you can see that the selected element is deleted and does not appear in the drawing area. This completes our discussion about deleting an element in Autodesk Revit Architecture.

3

WORKING WITH PROJECT VIEWS AND WORK PLANES

In This Chapter
◇ Working with Project Views
◇ Working with Work Planes

In Autodesk Revit Architecture, when you create a building model in a project, you may view the same building model in different project views, such as 2D view, 3D view, and plan view. A project view (view) represents a building model that contains a group of elements, such as walls, floors, doors, and windows. An Autodesk Revit Architecture project file stores information, such as components and elements used to design a building model, project views, and drawing of the building model. Autodesk Revit Architecture also provides the Project Browser, which contains lists of views available for a project. These views are floor plan (also called plan view), elevation, 3D view, and legend view. Each view in Autodesk Revit Architecture is associated with a work plane. A work plane is a planar surface used to add or sketch other elements, such as doors, walls, and windows, to a project. For example, when you start sketching a floor of a building model in the 3D view, the work plane is set to that floor associated with the 3D view.

This chapter covers project views, including how to display a building model in different project views, such as elevation view, section view, and 3D view. It also describes how to hide an element in a view, as well as how to crop and rotate a view. In the end, you learn how to set a work plane associated with a view.

3.1 WORKING WITH PROJECT VIEWS

A project view is a graphical way of representing a drawing or a model that you create in Autodesk Revit Architecture. The project views available in Autodesk Revit Architecture are 2D view, 3D view, plan view, and callout view.

When you create a project view in Autodesk Revit Architecture, you need to display this project view in different directions or angles, such as east and west, as well as different dimensions, such as 2D and 3D. Displaying a project view in different directions help the designer or architect to analyze and design the actual shape of a building model. Autodesk Revit Architecture provides the Project Browser so that you can display all your project views of a building model and access elements in a project view. All project views are stored in the Project Browser.

In this section, you will learn about the following topics in the context of project views:

- Different types of project views
- Visibility and graphic display of a project view
- Hiding elements in a view
- Cropping a project view
- Rotating a project view

Let's start the discussion by examining the types of project views available in Autodesk Revit Architecture 2010.

Exploring Project View Types

Project views are used to display a model or architecture of a house or building in different angles and directions, such as north, east, west, and south. You need to develop a building model before you can display a project view in different directions. You can add several elements (walls, doors, windows) of a building model in the drawing area by selecting various tools, such as the Wall, Door, and Window tools, from the Build panel under the Home tab, as shown in **Figure 3.1**.

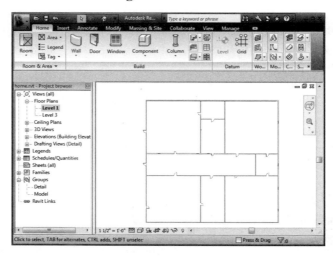

FIGURE 3.1

In Figure 3.1, the architecture of a building model is shown in the plan view. After designing a building model, you can save it. In our case, we have saved it with the name **home.rvt**.

> **Note:** Refer to Chapter 2, Working with Projects and Elements, for information on how to create a project, sketch elements (doors, windows, and walls) in the project, and save the project in Autodesk Revit Architecture.

In Autodesk Revit Architecture 2010, you can display a building model by using the following types of project views:

- Plan views
- Elevation views
- Section views
- Callout views
- 3D views
- Legend views
- Schedule views
- Duplicate dependent views

> **Note:** When you create the architecture of a building model, by default Autodesk Revit Architecture displays a building model in the plan view.

Let's discuss all of these project views in detail.

Plan Views

Plan views are used to display a building model in horizontal position. In Autodesk Revit Architecture, each plan view is associated with a level. A level is a horizontal view of floor-to-floor heights, such as first floor and second floor, of a building model. Perform the following steps to create a plan view:

1. *Click* **Start** > **All Programs** > **Autodesk** > **Autodesk Revit Architecture 2010** > **Autodesk Revit Architecture 2010** to open the **Autodesk Revit Architecture 2010** window.

2. *Open* the file in which you want to create a plan view. In our case, we *open* the **home.rvt** file.

3. *Select* the **View** tab from the ribbon; see **Figure 3.2**.

FIGURE 3.2

4. *Click* the **Plan Views** drop-down button from the **Create** panel and *select* the **Floor Plan** option from the drop-down list, as shown in Figure 3.2. The **New Plan** dialog box appears; see **Figure 3.3**.

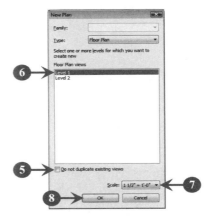

FIGURE 3.3

5. *Clear* the **Do not duplicate existing views** check box (Figure 3.3).

Note: To create a plan view for a level that already has an existing plan view, you are required to clear the Do not duplicate existing views check box.

6. *Select* the **Level1** option from the **Floor Plan views** list box (Figure 3.3).
7. *Select* an option from the **Scale** drop-down list to select the measurement unit of a building model. In our case, we *select* the **1 1/2" = 1'-0"** option (Figure 3.3).
8. *Click* the **OK** button (Figure 3.3). The new plan view is displayed, as shown in **Figure 3.4**.

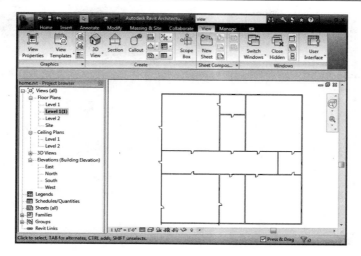

FIGURE 3.4

Figure 3.4 shows the name of the new plan view, Level 1(1), in the Project Browser. By default, in Autodesk Revit Architecture a new plan view is created with this name.

Elevation Views

Elevation views are used to display a building model in the north, south, east, and west directions. By default, Autodesk Revit Architecture creates four elevation views: East, North, South, and West in the Elevation (Building Elevation) node under the Project Browser. Each elevation view is represented by the elevation tag (◔). You can also create your own elevation view.

Perform the following steps to create an elevation view:

1. *Open* the **Autodesk Revit Architecture 2010** window.
2. *Open* the file in which you want to create an elevation view—in our case, **home.rvt**.
3. *Double-click* the **Level 1** plan view from the Project Browser to open it (See **Figure 3.5**).

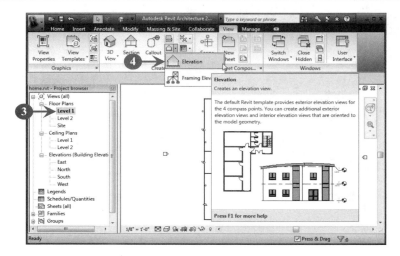

FIGURE 3.5

4. *Click* the **Elevation** split button from the **Create** panel under the **View** tab and *select* the **Elevation** option from the drop-down list, as shown in Figure 3.5. The **Elevation** tab and its panels (**Selection** and **Element**) appear on the ribbon (see **Figure 3.6**).

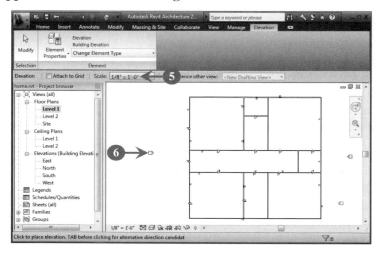

FIGURE 3.6

5. *Select* an option from the **Scale** drop-down list to select the measurement unit of a building model. In our case, we *select* the **1/8" = 1'-0"** option (Figure 3.6).

6. *Click* the mouse button near a wall of the building model to add the elevation tag (▷) in the drawing area, as shown in Figure 3.6. The new elevation view, **Elevation 1–a**, is added in the Project Browser (see **Figure 3.7**). By

default, in Autodesk Revit Architecture a new elevation view is created with this name.

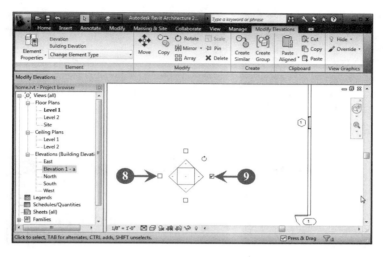

FIGURE 3.7

7. *Press* the **ESC** key to complete creating the elevation view.

8. *Select* the **square** shape of the elevation tag to set the interior elevation view (Figure 3.7).

9. *Select* the check box opposite to the building model to define a portion of the elevation view. In our case, we *select* the check box that is on the right-hand side of the square shape of the elevation tag, as shown in Figure 3.7.

10. *Click* the mouse button anywhere in your project to hide the check boxes (see **Figure 3.8**).

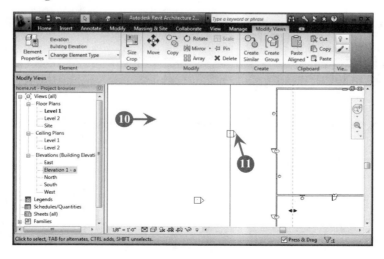

FIGURE 3.8

11. *Select* the **arrowhead** shape of the elevation tag to view the clip plane, as shown in Figure 3.8.

> **Note:** Clip plane is a vertical or horizontal plane that defines a boundary of the elevation view.

12. *Double-click* the **Elevation 1–a** elevation view from the Project Browser to display the **Elevation 1–a** elevation view in the drawing area, as shown in **Figure 3.9**.

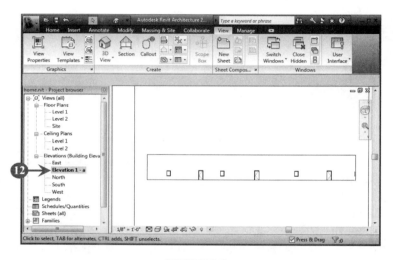

FIGURE 3.9

Section Views

A section view is a portion of a project that can be viewed by selecting a section of a building model. You can design a building model in the section view by using various elements, such as walls, doors, and windows, available in Autodesk Revit Architecture. Perform the following steps to create a section view:

1. *Open* the **Autodesk Revit Architecture 2010** window.
2. *Open* the file in which you want to create a section view—in our case, **home.rvt**.
3. *Double-click* the **Level 1** plan view from the Project Browser to open it (see **Figure 3.10**).

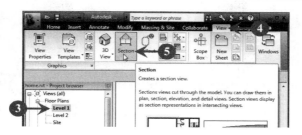

FIGURE 3.10

4. *Select* the **View** tab from the ribbon (Figure 3.10).
5. *Click* the **Section** button from the **Create** panel, as shown in Figure 3.10. The **Section** tab appears on the ribbon, as shown in **Figure 3.11**.

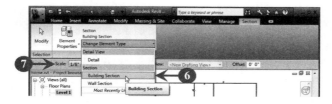

FIGURE 3.11

6. *Click* the **Change Element Type** (**Type Selector**) drop-down button from the **Element** panel to show a section of a building model and *select* an option from the drop-down list. In our case, we *select* the **Building Section** option (Figure 3.11).
7. *Select* an option from the **Scale** drop-down list of the options bar to select the measurement unit of a building model. In our case, we *select* the **1/8" = 1'-0"** option, as shown in Figure 3.11.
8. *Click* the mouse button at the starting point of the section of your building model (see **Figure 3.12**).

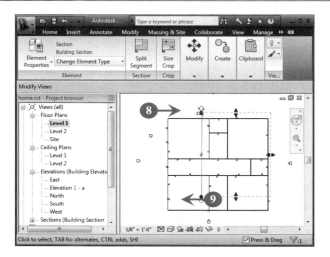

FIGURE 3.12

9. *Move* the mouse pointer and then *click* the mouse button at the end point of the section of your building model, as shown in Figure 3.12.
10. *Press* the **ESC** key to exit the creation of a section view.

Note: By default, in Autodesk Revit Architecture a new section view is created with the name **Section 1** (Figure 3.13).

11. *Double-click* the **Section 1** section view from the Project Browser to display the section view of a building model, as shown in **Figure 3.13**.

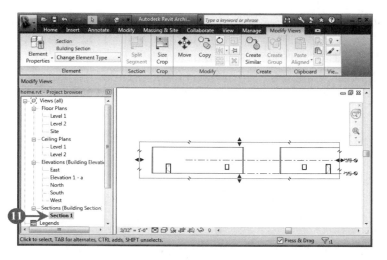

FIGURE 3.13

Callout Views

The callout view is used to display an enlarged view of a part or section of another view. You can create a callout view from a plan, section, detail, or an elevation view. This view provides more detailed information, such as types of elements used in a section of the building model. Perform the following steps to create a callout view:

1. *Open* the **Autodesk Revit Architecture 2010** window.
2. *Open* the file in which you want to create a callout view—in our case, **home.rvt**.
3. *Double-click* the **Level 1** plan view from the Project Browser to open it (see **Figure 3.14**).

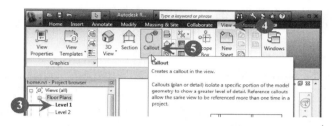

FIGURE 3.14

4. *Select* the **View** tab from the ribbon (Figure 3.14).
5. *Click* the **Callout** button from the **Create** panel, as shown in Figure 3.14. The **Callout** tab appears on the ribbon, as shown in **Figure 3.15**.

FIGURE 3.15

6. *Select* an option from the **Scale** drop-down list to select the measurement unit of a building model. In our case, we *select* the **1/64" = 1'-0"** option, as shown in Figure 3.15.
7. *Click* the mouse button in the drawing area to define the starting point of a callout view (see **Figure 3.16**).

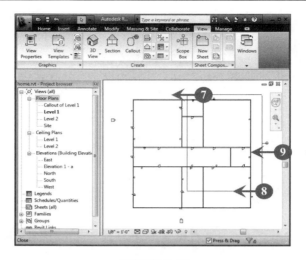

FIGURE 3.16

8. *Move* the mouse pointer and then *click* the mouse button in the drawing area to define the ending point of a callout view (Figure 3.16).

9. *Double-click* the callout head in the drawing area, as shown in Figure 3.16. The callout view is displayed in the drawing area, as shown in **Figure 3.17**.

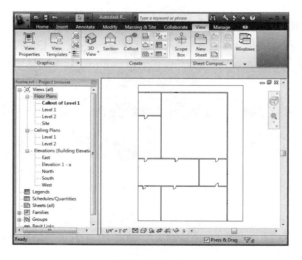

FIGURE 3.17

Figure 3.17 shows the **Callout of Level 1** callout view of your building model. By default, in Autodesk Revit Architecture a new callout view is created with this name.

3D Views

A three-dimensional view (3D view) is another important type of project view, which is used to display the architectural and interior design of a building model. Displaying the building model in all three dimensions (width, length, and depth) offers you extensive coverage of both the interior and exterior views of a building model. The exterior view is used to display the outer portion of the building model, whereas the interior view is used to display various interior elements, such as interior partitions, furniture, and plants.

Perform the following steps to create a 3D view:

1. *Open* the **Autodesk Revit Architecture 2010** window.
2. *Open* the file in which you want to create a 3D view—in our case, **home.rvt**.
3. *Double-click* the **Level 1** plan view from the Project Browser to open it (see **Figure 3.18**).

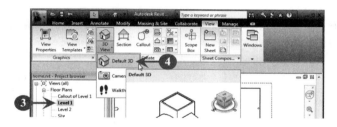

FIGURE 3.18

4. *Click* the **3D View** split button from the **Create** panel under the **View** tab and *select* the **Default 3D** option from the drop-down list, as shown in Figure 3.18. The design of your building model is displayed in 3D view, as shown in **Figure 3.19**.

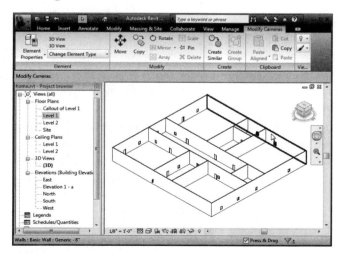

FIGURE 3.19

Figure 3.19 shows the design of your building model in the **{3D}** 3D view. By default, in Autodesk Revit Architecture a new 3D view is created with this name.

Legend Views

Legend views are used to display a list of various building components, such as doors, windows, ceramic tile, and brick constructed in a building model. The types of legends available in Autodesk Revit Architecture 2010 are as follows:

- **Annotation Legend:** Displays descriptive data or instructions usually added to each component of a building model. Examples of annotation legends include section heads, level markers, spot elevation marks, and element tags.
- **Model Symbol Legend:** Displays symbolic representations of a building model with some descriptive text. Some symbolic representations used in building models are electrical fixtures, plumbing fixtures, mechanical equipment, and site objects.
- **Line Styles Legend:** Displays a line in a selected line style to identify an element of a building model.
- **Phasing Legend:** Displays a section of a wall of a building model drawn with a selected graphic and text.

Perform the following steps to create a legend view:

1. *Open* the **Autodesk Revit Architecture 2010** window.
2. *Open* the file in which you want to create a legend view—in our case, **home.rvt**.
3. *Select* the **View** tab on the ribbon (see **Figure 3.20**).

FIGURE 3.20

4. *Double-click* the **Level 1** plan view from the Project Browser to open it (Figure 3.20).
5. *Click* the **Legends** drop-down button from the **Create** panel and *select* the **Legend** option from the drop-down list, as shown in Figure 3.20. The **New Legend View** dialog box appears, as shown in **Figure 3.21**.

FIGURE 3.21

6. *Enter* a name for a legend view in the **Name** text box. In our case, we *enter* the name **Legend Home 1** (Figure 3.21).

7. *Select* an option from the **Scale** drop-down list to select the measurement unit of a building model. In our case, we *select* the **1" = 1'-0"** option, as shown in Figure 3.21.

8. *Click* the **OK** button (Figure 3.21). The **Legend Home 1** legend view is added in the Project Browser, as shown in **Figure 3.22**.

FIGURE 3.22

9. *Select* **Families > Doors > Single–Flush > 30" × 80"** from the Project Browser (see **Figure 3.23**).

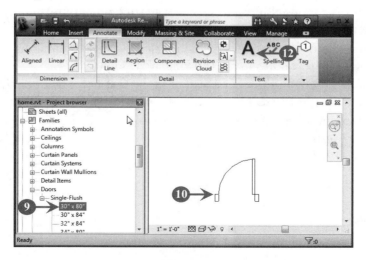

FIGURE 3.23

10. *Drag* and *drop* the selected door element (**30" × 80"**) in the drawing area (Figure 3.23).

11. *Press* the **ESC** key to exit from the door element (**30" × 80"**).

12. *Click* the **Text** button from the **Text** panel under the **Annotate** tab, as shown in Figure 3.23.

13. *Click* the **One Segment** button from the **Leader** panel under the **Place Text** tab (see **Figure 3.24**).

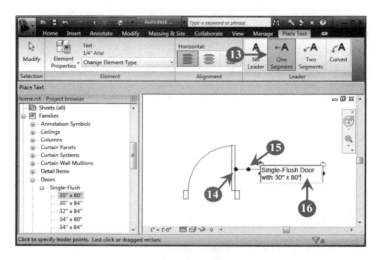

FIGURE 3.24

14. *Click* the mouse button to specify a starting point of text notes near the door element in the drawing area (Figure 3.24).

15. *Move* the mouse pointer and then *click* the mouse button to specify an ending point of a text notes in the drawing area (Figure 3.24).

16. *Enter* a name of the door element in the text notes text box. In our case, we *enter* **Single-Flush Door with 30" × 80"** (Figure 3.24).

17. *Select* **Families > Floors > Floor > Generic–12"** from the Project Browser (see **Figure 3.25**).

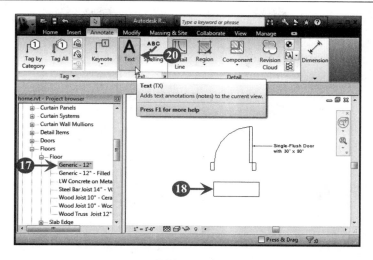

FIGURE 3.25

18. *Drag* and *drop* the selected floor element (**Generic–12"**) in the drawing area (Figure 3.25).

19. *Press* the **ESC** key to exit from the floor element (**Generic–12"**).

20. *Click* the **Text** button from the **Text** panel under the **Annotate** tab, as shown in Figure 3.25.

21. *Click* the **One Segment** button from the **Leader** panel under the **Place Text** tab (see **Figure 3.26**).

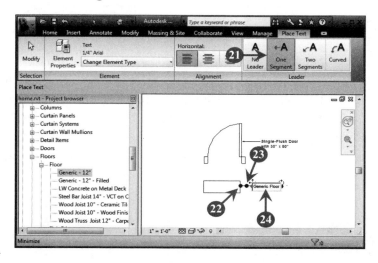

FIGURE 3.26

22. *Click* the mouse button to specify a starting point for a text note near the floor element in the drawing area (Figure 3.26).

23. *Move* the mouse pointer and *click* the mouse button to specify an ending point for a text note in the drawing area (Figure 3.26).

24. *Enter* a name of the floor element in the text notes text box. In our case, we *enter* **Generic Floor**, as shown in Figure 3.26.

25. *Select* **Families** > **Walls** > **Basic Wall** > **Generic–8"** from the Project Browser (see **Figure 3.27**).

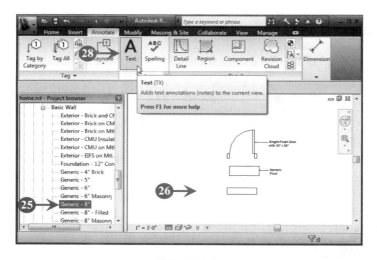

FIGURE 3.27

26. *Drag* and *drop* the selected wall element (**Generic–8"**) in the drawing area (Figure 3.27).

27. *Press* the **ESC** key to exit from the wall element (**Generic–8"**).

28. *Click* the **Text** button from the **Text** panel under the **Annotate** tab, as shown in Figure 3.27.

29. *Click* the **One Segment** button from the **Leader** panel under the **Place Text** tab (see **Figure 3.28**).

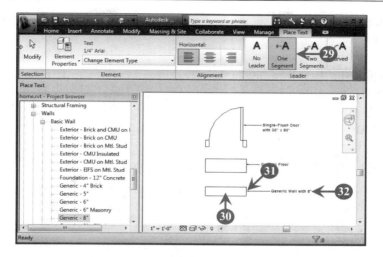

FIGURE 3.28

30. *Click* the mouse button to specify a starting point of text notes near the wall element in the drawing area (Figure 3.28).

31. *Move* the mouse pointer and then *click* the mouse button to specify an ending point of text notes in the drawing area (Figure 3.28).

32. *Enter* a name of the wall element in the text notes text box. In our case, we *enter* **Generic Wall with 8"**, as shown in Figure 3.28.

33. *Select* **Families > Windows > Fixed > 16" × 24"** from the Project Browser (see **Figure 3.29**).

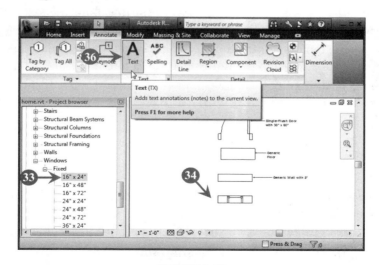

FIGURE 3.29

34. *Drag* and *drop* the selected window element (**16" × 24"**) in the drawing area (Figure 3.29).

35. *Press* the **ESC** key to exit from the window element (**16" × 24"**).

36. *Click* the **Text** button from the **Text** panel under the **Annotate** tab, as shown in Figure 3.29.

37. *Click* the **One Segment** button from the **Leader** panel under the **Place Text** tab (see **Figure 3.30**).

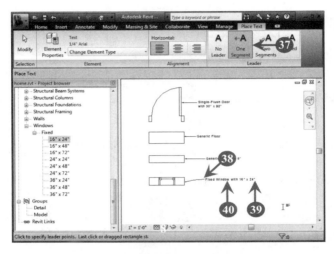

FIGURE 3.30

38. *Click* the mouse button to specify a starting point of text notes near the window element in the drawing area (Figure 3.30).

39. *Move* the mouse pointer and then *click* the mouse button to specify an ending point of text notes in the drawing area (Figure 3.30).

40. *Enter* a name of the window element in the text notes text box. In our case, we *enter* **Fixed Window with 16" × 24"**, as shown in Figure 3.30.

Figure 3.30 shows different elements, such as doors, windows, floors, and walls of a building model in the **Legend Home 1** legend view.

Schedule Views

A schedule view is used to display information that is extracted from the properties of the elements used in a project, such as their area, volume, height, and width, and is stored in a tabular format. Perform the following steps to create a schedule view:

1. *Open* the **Autodesk Revit Architecture 2010** window.

2. *Open* the file in which you want to create a schedule view—in our case, **home.rvt**.

3. *Select* the **View** tab from the ribbon (see **Figure 3.31**).

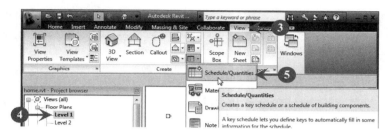

FIGURE 3.31

4. *Double-click* the **Level 1** plan view from the Project Browser to open it (Figure 3.31).
5. *Click* the **Schedules** drop-down button from the **Create** panel and *select* the **Schedule/Quantities** option from the drop-down list, as shown in Figure 3.31. The **New Schedule** dialog box appears, as shown in **Figure 3.32**.

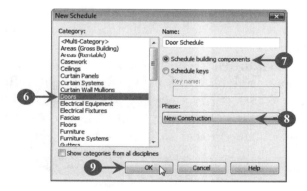

FIGURE 3.32

6. *Select* the **Doors** option from the **Category** list to display the description of the door element (Figure 3.32).
7. *Select* the **Schedule building components** radio button (Figure 3.32).
8. *Select* the **New Construction** option from the **Phase** drop-down list (Figure 3.32).
9. *Click* the **OK** button, as shown in Figure 3.32. The **Schedule Properties** dialog box appears, as shown in **Figure 3.33**.

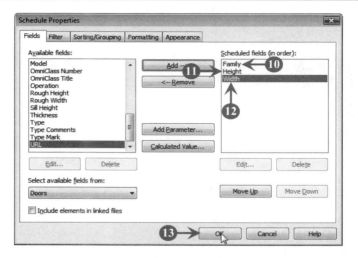

FIGURE 3.33

10. *Select* the **Family** field from the **Available fields** list box and *click* the **Add** button to add the **Family** field in the **Scheduled fields (in order)** list box (Figure 3.33).

11. *Select* the **Height** field from the **Available fields** list box and *click* the **Add** button to add the **Height** field in the **Scheduled fields (in order)** list box (Figure 3.33).

12. *Select* the **Width** field from the **Available fields** list box and *click* the **Add** button to add the **Width** field in the **Scheduled fields (in order)** list box (Figure 3.33).

13. *Click* the **OK** button, as shown in Figure 3.33. The **Door Schedule** schedule view is added in the Project Browser, as shown in **Figure 3.34**.

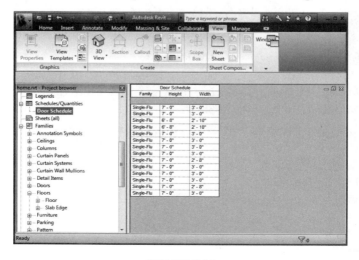

FIGURE 3.34

Figure 3.34 shows a list of height and width of doors used in the project, in a tabular format.

Duplicate Dependent Views

You can create multiple copies of a view by copying the original view. All of the various copies of a view are known as dependent views. The duplicate dependent views are synchronous with the original views, which means that any changes made in the original views will be reflected in all copies of the views.

Perform the following steps to create a duplicate dependent view:

1. *Open* the **Autodesk Revit Architecture 2010** window.
2. *Open* the file in which you want to create a duplicate dependent view—in our case, **home.rvt**.
3. *Select* the **Level 1** plan view from the Project Browser to open it (see **Figure 3.35**).

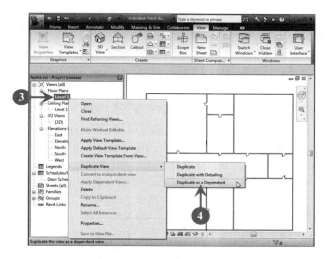

FIGURE 3.35

4. *Right-click* the **Level 1** plan view and *select* **Duplicate View > Duplicate as a Dependent** from the context menu, as shown in Figure 3.35.

The **Dependent on Level 1** duplicate plan view is created, as shown in **Figure 3.36**. By default, in Autodesk Revit Architecture a new duplicate dependent view is created with this name.

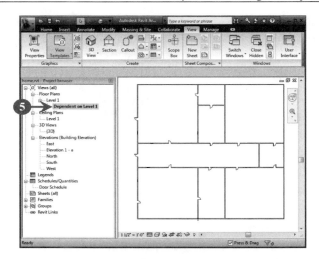

FIGURE 3.36

5. *Double-click* the **Dependent on Level 1** plan view to display the copy of the **Level 1** plan view in the Project Browser, as shown in Figure 3.36.

After learning about different types of views, we are now ready to learn how to use visibility and graphic display in project views.

Using Visibility and Graphic Display in Project Views

Autodesk Revit Architecture allows you to control the visibility and graphic display of a single element or a category of various elements in a project view. You can modify the line type (dotted line, solid line) and pattern (fill color) of an element in a building model. For example, you can display an element (wall) in a green color and with a red outline.

In this section, you learn about the following topics in the context of visibility and graphic display of elements used in a project view:

- Modifying the visibility and graphic display of an element
- Modifying the graphic display of an element category

Modifying the Visibility and Graphic Display of an Element

To modify the visibility and graphic display of a single element, perform the following steps:

1. *Open* the **Autodesk Revit Architecture 2010** window.
2. *Open* the file in which you want to modify the visibility and graphic display of an element. In our case, we *open* the **home.rvt** file.
3. *Double-click* the **{3D}** 3D view from the Project Browser to open the **{3D}** view (see **Figure 3.37**).

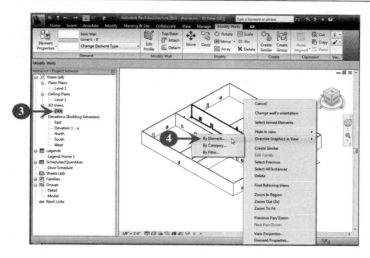

FIGURE 3.37

4. *Right-click* the wall element from the drawing area and *select* **Override Graphics in View > By Element** from the context menu, as shown in Figure 3.37. The **View-Specific Element Graphics** dialog box appears, as shown in **Figure 3.38**.

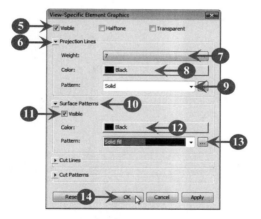

FIGURE 3.38

5. *Select* the **Visible** check box (Figure 3.38).
6. *Expand* the **Projection Lines** group (Figure 3.38).
7. *Select* an option to change the width of the outline of the wall element from the **Weight** drop-down list. In our case, we *select* **7** (Figure 3.38).
8. *Click* the **Color** button to set the outline color of the wall element. In our case, we *set* the outline color to **Black** (Figure 3.38).

> **Note:** When you click the **Color** button, the **Color** dialog box appears. Select the appropriate color and then click the **OK** button to choose the color.

9. *Select* the **Solid** option from the **Pattern** drop-down list (Figure 3.38).
10. *Expand* the **Surface Patterns** group (Figure 3.38).
11. *Select* the **Visible** check box (Figure 3.38).
12. *Click* the **Color** button to set the fill color of the wall element. In our case, we *set* the fill color to **Black** (Figure 3.38).
13. *Select* an option to change the fill pattern of the wall element from the **Pattern** drop-down list. In our case, we *select* the **Solid fill** option (Figure 3.38).
14. *Click* the **OK** button (see **Figure 3.38**).

The visibility and graphic display of the element are modified, as shown in **Figure 3.39**. Specifically, a single element (wall) of a building model is shaded with black color.

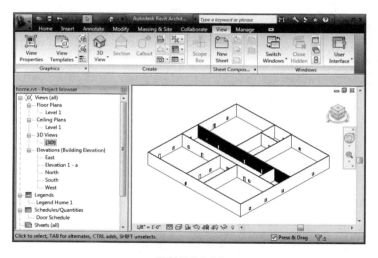

FIGURE 3.39

Modifying the Graphic Display of an Element Category

Autodesk Revit Architecture allows you to shade and use a fill color in a group of the same elements of a building model. For example, you can change the color of all walls in a building model. Perform the following steps to display all walls filled with a green color and having a red outline:

1. *Open* the **Autodesk Revit Architecture 2010** window.
2. *Open* the file in which you want to modify graphic display of an element category—in our case, **home.rvt**.

3. *Double-click* the **{3D}** 3D view from the Project Browser to open it (see **Figure 3.40**).

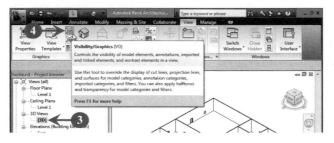

FIGURE 3.40

4. *Click* the **Visibility/Graphics** (▥) button from the **Graphics** panel under the **View** tab, as shown in Figure 3.40. The **Visibility/Graphic Overrides for 3D View: {3D}** dialog box appears, as shown in **Figure 3.41**.

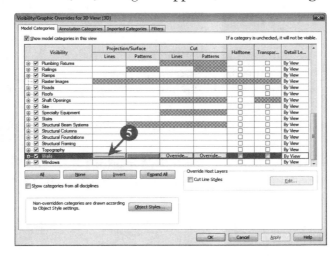

FIGURE 3.41

5. *Double-click* the **Lines** button corresponding to the **Walls** check box (Figure 3.41). The **Line Graphics** dialog box appears, as shown in **Figure 3.42**.

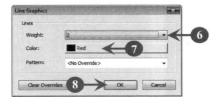

FIGURE 3.42

6. *Select* an option to change the width of the outline of the wall element from the **Weight** drop-down list. In our case, we *select* **2** (Figure 3.42).
7. *Click* the **Color** button to set the outline color of the wall element. In our case, we *set* the outline color to **Red** (Figure 3.42).
8. *Click* the **OK** button (Figure 3.42).
9. *Click* the **Patterns** button corresponding to the **Walls** check box in the **Visibility/Graphic Overrides for 3D View: {3D}** dialog box (Figure 3.41). The **Fill Pattern Graphics** dialog box appears, as shown in **Figure 3.43**.

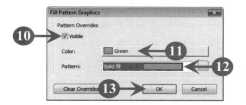

FIGURE 3.43

10. *Select* the **Visible** check box (Figure 3.43).
11. *Click* the **Color** button to set the fill color of the wall element. In our case, we *set* the **Green** color (Figure 3.43).
12. *Select* an option to modify the pattern of the wall element from the **Pattern** drop-down list. In our case, we *select* the **Solid fill** option (Figure 3.43).
13. *Click* the **OK** button (**Figure 3.43**). The **Fill Pattern Graphics** dialog box closes.
14. *Click* the **OK** button in the **Visibility/Graphic Overrides for 3D View: {3D}** dialog box (Figure 3.41). The wall element of a building model is modified and displayed in the drawing area, as shown in **Figure 3.44**.

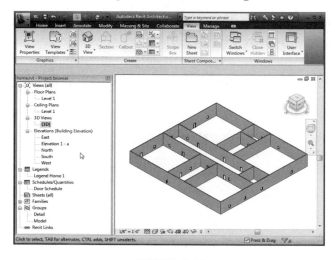

FIGURE 3.44

In Figure 3.44, you can see on your computer screen that the walls element of the building model is filled with green color and has a red outline.

Hiding Elements in a View

You can hide a single element or list of same categories of elements in a view. When you hide an element, the dimension and text related to that element is also hidden. Perform the following steps to hide an element:

1. *Open* the **Autodesk Revit Architecture 2010** window.
2. *Open* the file in which you want to hide elements in a view—in our case, **home.rvt**.
3. *Double-click* the **{3D}** 3D view from the Project Browser to open it (see **Figure 3.45**).

FIGURE 3.45

4. *Right-click* the wall element in the drawing area and select **Hide in view** >**Elements** from the context menu, as shown in Figure 3.45. The selected wall element of the building model is hidden, as shown in **Figure 3.46**.

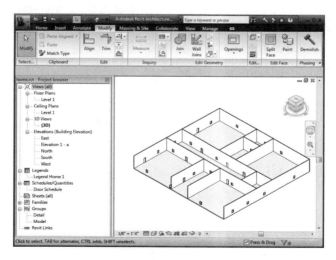

FIGURE 3.46

Now that we know how to hide elements in views, let's learn how to crop a view.

Cropping a View

You can trim or crop a section of a view. Perform the following steps to crop a view:

1. *Open* the **Autodesk Revit Architecture 2010** window.
2. *Open* the file in which you want to crop a view—in our case, **home.rvt**.
3. *Double-click* the **Level 1** plan view from the Project Browser to open it (see **Figure 3.47**).

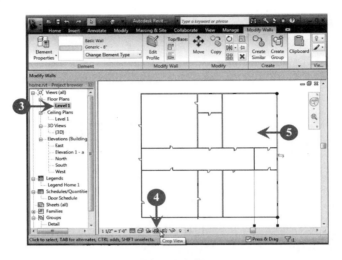

FIGURE 3.47

4. *Click* the **Crop View** (⊞) button from the view control bar (Figure 3.47).
5. *Select* an element (wall) of a view and *drag* the wall element to the desired size, as shown in Figure 3.47. The **Autodesk Revit Architecture 2010** message box appears, as shown in **Figure 3.48**.

FIGURE 3.48

6. *Click* the **Delete Instance(s)** button (Figure 3.48). All elements (instances) related to the wall element are deleted, as shown in **Figure 3.49**.

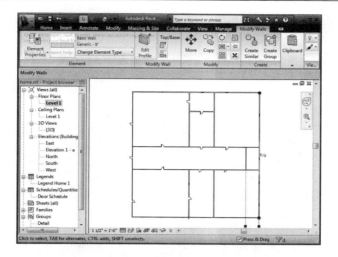

FIGURE 3.49

In Figure 3.49, you can see that the selected side of a building model is cropped.

Rotating a View

You can also rotate a portion of a view. Perform the following steps to rotate a view:

1. *Open* the **Autodesk Revit Architecture 2010** window.
2. *Open* the file in which you want to rotate a view—in our case, **home.rvt**.
3. *Double-click* the **Level 1** plan view from the Project Browser to open it (see **Figure 3.50**).

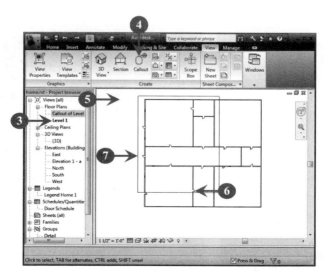

FIGURE 3.50

4. *Click* the **Callout** button from the **Create** panel under the **View** tab (Figure 3.50).

5. *Click* the mouse button in the drawing area to specify a starting point for the callout view (Figure 3.50).

6. *Move* the mouse pointer and then *click* the mouse button in the drawing area to specify an endpoint for the callout view (Figure 3.50).

7. *Select* the **rectangle** area of the **Level 1** plan view, as shown in Figure 3.50. After selecting the section of the **Level 1** plan view, the **Callout of Level 1** callout view is created in the Project Browser. By default, in Autodesk Revit Architecture a new callout view has this name.

8. *Click* the **Rotate** button from the **Modify** panel under the **Modify Views** tab (see **Figure 3.51**).

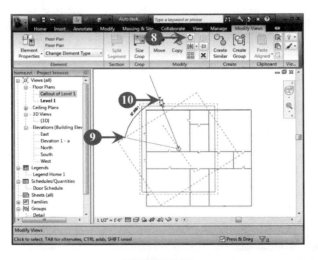

FIGURE 3.51

9. *Click* the mouse button in the drawing area to define a starting point for rotating a portion of a building model (Figure 3.51).

10. *Move* the mouse pointer and then *click* the mouse button in the drawing area to define an ending point for rotating a portion of a building model, as shown in Figure 3.51.

11. *Double-click* the **Callout of Level 1** callout view to see the rotation of the selected portion of the building model, as shown in **Figure 3.52**.

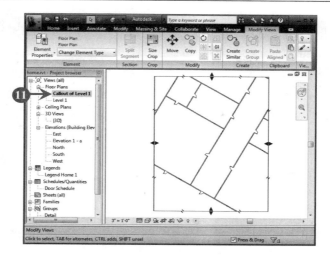

FIGURE 3.52

In Figure 3.52, you can see that the **Callout of Level 1** callout view is rotated and displayed in the drawing area.

3.2 WORKING WITH WORK PLANES

A work plane is a planar surface on which you can add or sketch lines, walls, and other elements in a project. In Autodesk Revit Architecture, each view is associated with a work plane. A work plane is automatically associated in some views, such as the plan and 3D views. In other views, such as the elevation and section views, you need to explicitly associate a work plane. A work plane is used to sketch operations, such as creating an extruded roof in a project.

Perform the following steps to create a work plane in a project view:

1. *Open* the **Autodesk Revit Architecture 2010** window.
2. *Open* the file in which you want to set a work plane—in our case, **home.rvt**.
3. *Double-click* the **{3D}** 3D view from the Project Browser to open it (see **Figure 3.53**).

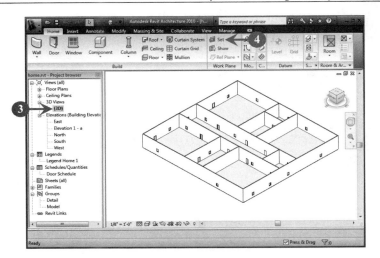

FIGURE 3.53

4. *Click* the **Set** button from the **Work Plane** panel under the **Home** tab, as shown in Figure 3.53. The **Work Plane** dialog box appears, as shown in **Figure 3.54**.

FIGURE 3.54

5. *Select* the **Pick a plane** radio button (Figure 3.54).
6. *Click* the **OK** button, as shown in Figure 3.54.
7. *Select* an element that you want to set for a work plane in the drawing area. In our case, we *select* the wall element, as shown in **Figure 3.55**.

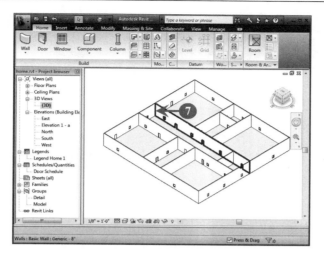

FIGURE 3.55

8. *Click* the **Show** button from the **Work Plane** panel under the **Home** tab, as shown in **Figure 3.56**.

FIGURE 3.56

In Figure 3.56, you can see the wall element of a building model is set for a work plane.

WORKING WITH BASIC BUILDING COMPONENTS

A building model consists of several components, such as walls, floors, ceilings, roofs, railings, and ramps, as well as furniture items, trees, and curtain elements to decorate the building site. Creating a building model requires you to model the objects in the 3D view. It also requires you to understand the construction of objects at various levels, the interaction of various building elements with one another, and the dependencies of elements. In addition, it is important to know which materials the elements are made of, and how they are constructed and assembled. To meet all these needs, Autodesk Revit

Architecture includes a set of tools that may be used to create a final building model according to your requirements.

This chapter focuses first on the workflow of a building project. Next, you learn to work with walls, add doors and windows to the wall, add free-standing components, and create a floor, roof, and ceiling. You then learn to cut openings in elements, such as walls, floors, and roofs, and attach other elements to walls. In addition, you learn to create stairs, railings, ramps, and architectural columns. Finally, you learn to use curtain elements, create a model text, and use rooms in Autodesk Revit Architecture.

Let's start by exploring the workflow of the building project.

4.1 UNDERSTANDING THE WORKFLOW OF A BUILDING PROJECT

In Autodesk Revit Architecture, a project refers not only to the building model, but also to the associated documentation, such as drawings, views, schedules, and areas. A schedule displays the element information in a tabular format.

While you are designing a building model, the sequence of using the building elements also varies depending on various parameters, such as the building type you want to design, the building volume, and building shape. In most cases, however, the following sequence of steps is followed to design a building model:

1. Add the exterior walls of the building on Level 1, which is the lowest level of the building model, and then add the interior walls as required in the building model.

2. Add doors and windows to the exterior and interior walls at appropriate locations in the building model.

3. Add the floor and then the roof to the building model.

4. Add the structural or architectural grid and structural elements, such as structural walls and structural beams in the building model.

5. Add independent components, such as furniture items and plumbing fixtures. Then add text and annotations to the various spaces.

6. Specify the dimensions for the parameters of the project and create project details and documentation.

7. Create rendered 3D views and perform a walkthrough.

Let's look at the first step in this sequence—creating walls in Autodesk Revit Architecture.

4.2 WORKING WITH WALLS

Walls are the basic building blocks of a building model. They are used to create boundaries for rooms and the complete building model. Similar to the real-world walls in the building architecture, the walls in Autodesk Revit Architecture are built from individual materials where one material is layered on the top of the other. Each layer of wall has important roles in building construction, which are represented by a hierarchy of labels and numbers, such as Core, Substrate, Thermal/Air Layer, Finish 1, and Finish 2, to determine how they should put in order with adjoining walls.

Walls are used as hosts for elements, such as doors and windows that are created on the walls. A wall is created by sketching the location line of the wall in any one of the views, such as the plan view, ceiling plan view, or 3D view. The location line is a plane in the wall that does not change even if you change the type of the wall. The walls are categorized into different types, as discussed in the next section.

Exploring Wall Types

Walls in Revit Architecture are of different types. The most frequently used wall types are described here:

- **Interior Wall:** Contains a dry wall construction with a metal stud framing and varying thickness to create interior partition in a building project.
- **Exterior Wall:** Creates the outside surface of the building model. The predefined wall types in Revit Architecture include walls such as Brick on CMU, Brick on Mtl. Stud, and CMU Insulated.
- **Retaining Wall:** Retains soil or rock from a building, structure, or area.
- **Foundation Wall:** Forms the basis of the main building architecture. Foundation–12" Concrete is the predefined foundation wall included in Revit Architecture.
- **Arc Wall:** Creates a wall in a curved shape. Such walls have a temporary angular dimension so that you can precisely place them in the project.
- **Curtain Wall:** Creates a building façade that does not carry any load. Such walls may include any exterior walls that are attached to the building structure without carrying the load of the floor or the roof of the building. The curtain walls are usually thin or aluminum-framed walls containing in-fills of glass, metal panels, or thin stone.

Apart from the preceding list of wall types, you can create custom walls. However, Autodesk Revit Architecture also provides you with the flexibility to change the basic functioning of the preceding walls, depending on the project requirements. Now that you have become familiar with the different types of walls in Autodesk Revit Architecture, let's move on to the next section and learn to create interior and exterior walls.

Creating Interior and Exterior Walls

The interior walls provide partitions in the building model at desired locations; the exterior walls provide the outer shield of the building structure. The interior walls are non-load-bearing elements and are completely different from the exterior walls. Perform the following steps to create the interior and exterior walls for a building model:

1. *Open* the **Autodesk Revit Architecture 2010** window.
2. *Create* a new project and save it with the name **Walls**.
3. *Select* the **Home** tab on the ribbon, as shown in **Figure 4.1**.

FIGURE 4.1

4. *Click* the lower part of the **Wall** split button under the **Build** panel. *Select* the **Wall** option from the drop-down list (Figure 4.1). The **Place Wall** tab containing a number of options related to the Wall tool appears on the ribbon in the selected mode, as shown in **Figure 4.2**.

FIGURE 4.2

5. *Select* an exterior wall type from the **Type Selector** drop-down list under the **Element** panel. In this case, we select **Exterior—CMU Insulated** (Figure 4.2).
6. *Select* the height of the wall from the **Height** drop-down list on the options bar. By default, the **Unconnected** option is selected, which enables you to specify the height of the wall in the text box next to the **Height** drop-down list. In this case, we select **Level 2**, as shown in **Figure 4.3**.

FIGURE 4.3

7. *Select* a location line from the **Location Line** drop-down list. In this case, we select **Finish Face: Exterior**, as shown in **Figure 4.4**.

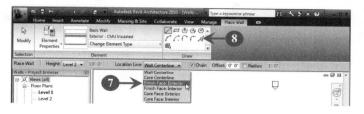

FIGURE 4.4

> **Note:** The position of the location line can vary based on the way you draw the wall.

8. *Select* a tool under the **Draw** panel that you want to use to sketch the wall. By default, the **Line** tool is selected (Figure 4.4).

9. *Click* at a location in the drawing area to specify the starting point of the wall, as shown in **Figure 4.5**.

FIGURE 4.5

10. *Move* the mouse pointer away from the starting point and then *click* to fix the second point of the wall (Figure 4.5). The wall appears, as shown in **Figure 4.6**.

> **Note:** You can also set the endpoint of the wall by just entering the length via the keyboard immediately after specifying the first point of the wall.

FIGURE 4.6

11. Similarly *create* the points for the other wall, as required. In this case, we *create* two more points to construct a wall in a rectangular shape. The final model for the wall appears, as shown in **Figure 4.7**.

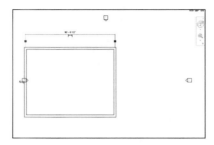

FIGURE 4.7

12. *Press* the **ESC** key.

The exterior wall is created. Now, to create the interior walls, continue with the following steps:

13. *Select* an interior wall type from the **Type Selector** drop-down list under the **Element** panel. In this case, we select **Interior—5 1/2" Partition (1-hr)**, as shown in **Figure 4.8**.

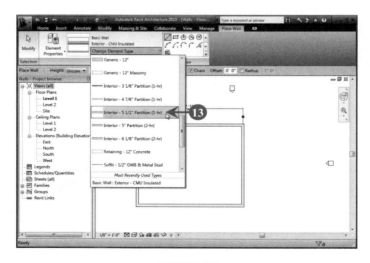

FIGURE 4.8

14. *Click* at a location in the drawing area from where you want to start creating the partition, as shown in **Figure 4.9**.

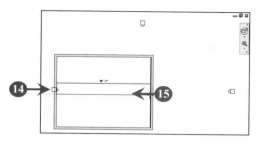

FIGURE 4.9

15. *Move* the mouse pointer away from the starting point and then *click* to set the ending point, where you want to end the partition (Figure 4.9). The final model of the wall appears, as shown in **Figure 4.10**.

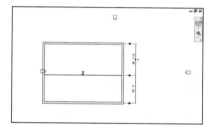

FIGURE 4.10

Note: Select the View tab and then click the upper part of the **3D View** button to view the model in 3D.

16. *Press* the **ESC** key twice to exit the Wall tool.

After learning to create exterior and interior walls, we can now add doors to a wall.

4.3 ADDING DOORS TO A WALL

Autodesk Revit Architecture provides the Door tool to add doors to a building model. A door can be added only to a host element, such as a wall in a plan, elevation, or 3D view. You can add a door to any type of wall, such as arc walls, in-place walls, and face-based walls. When you add the door on a wall, Autodesk Revit Architecture automatically cuts an opening in the wall to place the door.

Perform the following steps to add doors to a wall:

1. *Open* the **Autodesk Revit Architecture 2010** window.
2. *Open* the file containing the wall to which you want to add a door. In this case, we open the **Walls** file that we created earlier.
3. *Select* the **Home** tab on the ribbon, if not already selected, as shown in **Figure 4.11**.

FIGURE 4.11

4. *Click* the **Door** button under the **Build** panel (Figure 4.11). The **Place Door** tab appears on the ribbon in the selected mode, as shown in **Figure 4.12**.

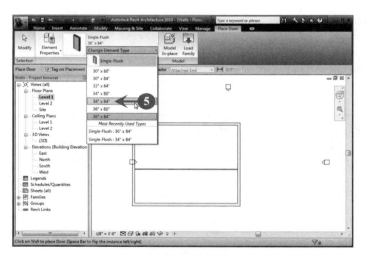

FIGURE 4.12

5. *Select* a door type from the **Type Selector** drop-down list under the **Element** panel. In this case, we select the **34" × 84"** door type (Figure 4.12).
6. *Select* the **Tag on Placement** check box on the options bar to automatically tag the door, as shown in **Figure 4.13**.

FIGURE 4.13

Note: A tag is an annotation to identify the elements in a drawing.

7. *Select* the **Leader** check box to include a tag leader line for the door (Figure 4.13).

Note: A leader line is a line that connects the tag head to the tag bubble.

8. *Enter* the length of the tag in the text box next to the ⊢ icon. In this case, we *enter* the length **1/2"** (Figure 4.13).
9. *Move* the mouse pointer at a location over a wall where you want the door to appear. *Click* to place the door, as shown in **Figure 4.14**.

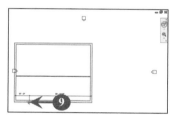

FIGURE 4.14

The final model including the door appears, as shown in **Figure 4.15**.

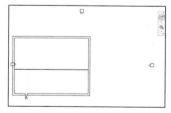

FIGURE 4.15

10. *Press* the **ESC** key twice to exit the Door tool.

With this, we have learned to add doors to a wall. Let's now learn to add windows, in the next section.

4.4 ADDING WINDOWS TO A WALL

Similar to doors, windows require a host element where you can place the window. To add windows to a host element such as a wall, you use the Window tool. You can add windows to a wall in a plan, elevation, or 3D view. Windows can be placed on any type of walls, such as arc walls, in-place walls, and face-based walls, by cutting an opening automatically and placing the window in the wall.

Perform the following steps to add windows to a wall:

1.   *Open* the **Autodesk Revit Architecture 2010** window.
2.   *Open* the file containing the wall to which you want to add a window—in this case, **Walls**.
3.   *Select* the **Home** tab (if not already selected), as shown in **Figure 4.16**.

FIGURE 4.16

4.   *Click* the **Window** button under the **Build** panel (Figure 4.16). The **Place Window** tab appears on the ribbon, as shown in **Figure 4.17**.

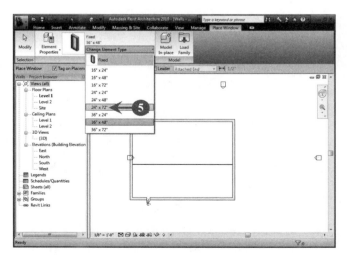

FIGURE 4.17

5. *Select* a window type from the **Type Selector** drop-down list under the **Element** panel. In this case, we select the **24" × 72"** window type (Figure 4.17).

6. *Select* the **Tag on Placement** check box on the options bar to automatically tag the window, as shown in **Figure 4.18**.

FIGURE 4.18

7. *Select* the **Leader** check box to include a tag leader for the window (Figure 4.18).

8. *Enter* the length of the tag in the text box next to the ⊢⊣ icon. In this case, we enter the length **1/2"** (Figure 4.18).

9. *Move* the mouse pointer at a location over a wall where you want the window to appear and *click* to place the window, as shown in **Figure 4.19**.

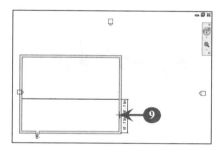

FIGURE 4.19

The final model including the window appears, as shown in **Figure 4.20**.

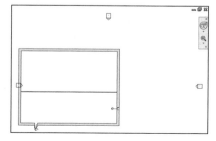

FIGURE 4.20

10. *Press* the **ESC** key twice to exit the Window tool.

This completes our discussion about adding a window element to a wall. Let's move on to the next section and learn to add free-standing components in Revit Architecture.

4.5 ADDING FREE-STANDING COMPONENTS

Autodesk Revit Architecture includes a wide range of free-standing components, such as furniture items, plumbing fixtures, electrical fittings, and trees that can be placed in a building model. The free-standing components are independent and do not have any associativity with other elements in Autodesk Revit Architecture. You can add these components to a building model by using the Component tool.

Perform the following steps to add a free-standing component in the building model:

1. *Open* the **Autodesk Revit Architecture 2010** window.

2. *Open* the file having a building model to which you want to add a free-standing component—in this case, **Walls**.

3. *Select* the **Home** tab, if not selected, as shown in **Figure 4.21**.

FIGURE 4.21

4. *Click* the lower part of the **Component** split button under the **Build** panel and then *select* the **Place a Component** option from the drop-down list (Figure 4.21). The **Place Component** tab appears on the ribbon in the selected mode, as shown in **Figure 4.22**.

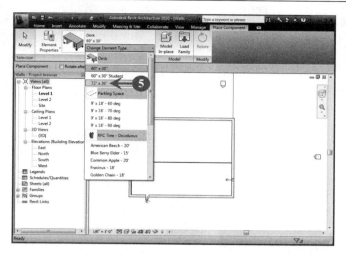

FIGURE 4.22

5. *Select* a component type from the **Type Selector** drop-down list under the **Element** panel. In this case, we select **72" × 36"** desk (Figure 4.22).

6. *Move* the mouse pointer to a location in the drawing area where you want the selected component to appear and then *click* to place the component, as shown in **Figure 4.23**.

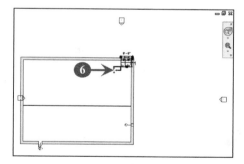

FIGURE 4.23

7. *Press* the **ESC** key twice to exit the Component tool.

When you select a component after placing it in the drawing area, the Moves With Nearby Elements check box appears on the options bar. You can select this check box to move the component with its nearby element. For example, suppose you place the desk just next to the wall. When you move the wall, the desk will also move accordingly.

Now that we know how to add a free-standing component to the building model, let's now move on and learn how to create a floor in Autodesk Revit Architecture.

4.6 CREATING A FLOOR

You can create a floor in the building model by using the Floor tool. The Floor tool allows you to create (sketch) the floor in two ways: by selecting the walls in the drawing area or by using the Line tool. When you sketch floors, they are offset downward from the level on which they are sketched.

Perform the following steps to create a floor in Autodesk Revit Architecture:

1. *Open* the **Autodesk Revit Architecture 2010** window.
2. *Open* the file containing the building model in which you want to create a floor—in this case, **Walls**.
3. *Select* the **Home** tab, if not selected, as shown in **Figure 4.24**.

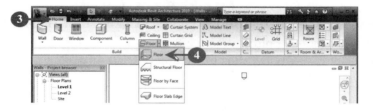

FIGURE 4.24

4. *Click* the right part of the **Floor** split button under the **Build** panel and then *select* the **Floor** option from the drop-down list (Figure 4.24). The **Create Floor Boundary** tab appears on the ribbon in the selected mode, as shown in **Figure 4.25**.

FIGURE 4.25

5. *Click* the **Pick Walls** button under the **Draw** panel, if not active (Figure 4.25).

Note: By default, the **Pick Walls** button under the Draw panel is activated.

6. *Select* the walls in the drawing area that you want to use as floor boundaries, as shown in **Figure 4.26**.

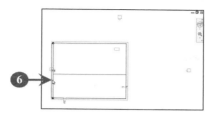

FIGURE 4.26

Note: You can use any of the sketching tools to draw the profile of the floor boundary, which must be a closed loop. In addition, to create openings in a floor, you can draw another closed loop to a location where you want the opening to appear.

7. *Enter* an offset value in the **Offset** text box on the options bar. In this case, we enter the offset value **3' 6"**, as shown in **Figure 4.27**.

FIGURE 4.27

8. *Select* the **Extend into wall (to core)** check box on the options bar to measure the offset from the core of the wall (Figure 4.27).
9. *Click* the **Finish Floor** button under the **Floor** panel to complete the floor creation (Figure 4.27). The floor is created, as shown in **Figure 4.28**.

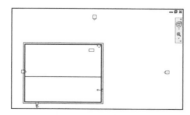

FIGURE 4.28

After creating a floor, you can change the type of the floor by selecting a floor type from the Type Selector drop-down list under the Element panel in the Modify Floors tab. Autodesk Revit Architecture creates the floor of Generic–12" type.

After creating a floor, we need to create the roof.

4.7 CREATING A ROOF

Autodesk Revit Architecture includes the Roof tool, with which you create roofs in the building model. Similar to the floor element, the roof is a sketched element that can be created by using any of the three methods: footprint, extrusion, or mass instances.

The footprint method uses the Roof By Footprint tool, which allows you to create a roof by specifying the footprint or outline of the roof in the plan view. You can define the slopes of the roof by using the lines in the footprint. These lines are the edges of sloping roof planes.

The extrusion method uses the Roof By Extrusion tool, which allows you to create a roof by sketching the profile of the roof in the elevation view and then extruding the roof. The depth of the extrusion can be specified by setting the starting and ending points of the roof.

You can also create a roof from the mass instances by using the Roof By Face tool. This tool allows you to create roofs on any nonvertical faces of a mass. The faces from different masses for the same roof cannot be selected.

> **Note:** The mass floors are used to divide a mass and are displayed graphically as a slice through the mass at a defined level. They provide geometric information about the dimensions of the mass up to the top of the mass.

Let's learn how to add a roof by footprint.

Adding a Roof by Footprint

You use the Roof By Footprint tool to add a roof by footprint. This tool allows you to create a standard roof that follows the outline of the building model. These roofs are based on a sketched shape, which is defined at the soffit level and can be edited at any time during the development of the building model. You can create a roof by using the Line tool and creating a loop of lines. Alternatively, you can use the Pick Wall tool to create a roof based on the walls that you select in the drawing area.

Perform the following steps to add a roof by footprint in Autodesk Revit Architecture:

1. *Open* the **Autodesk Revit Architecture 2010** window.
2. *Open* the file containing the building model to which you want to add a roof—in this case, **Walls**.
3. *Open* a floor plan view or a reflected ceiling plan view by using the Project Browser.
4. *Select* the **Home** tab, if not selected, as shown in **Figure 4.29**.

FIGURE 4.29

5. *Double-click* a level in the Project Browser on which you want to create a roof to open it. In this case, we open **Level 2** (Figure 4.29).

Note: If you select the lowest level, a dialog box appears asking you to move the level to a higher level. If you do not move the level to a higher level, Autodesk Revit Architecture notifies you later if the roof is too low.

6. *Click* the right part of the **Roof** split button under the **Build** panel and then *select* the **Roof By Footprint** option from the drop-down list (Figure 4.29). The **Create Roof Footprint** tab appears on the ribbon in the selected mode, as shown in **Figure 4.30**.

FIGURE 4.30

7. *Click* the **Pick Walls** button under the **Draw** panel (Figure 4.30).
8. *Select* the walls in the drawing area to create a closed loop for roof boundaries, as shown in **Figure 4.31**.

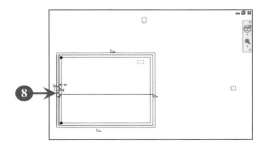

FIGURE 4.31

9. *Select* the **Extend to wall core** check box to measure the overhang from the core of the wall, as shown in **Figure 4.32**.

FIGURE 4.32

10. *Enter* a value in the **Overhang** text box. In this case, we enter **2' 6"** (Figure 4.32).

11. *Click* the **Finish Roof** button under the **Roof** panel (Figure 4.32). The roof is created, as shown in **Figure 4.33**.

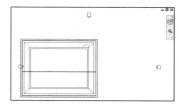

FIGURE 4.33

The roof is added by footprint. Now let's learn how to add a roof by extrusion.

Adding a Roof by Extrusion

You use the Roof By Extrusion tool to create a roof by using the extrusion method. This method is best suited for the roof shapes that are generated by extrusion of a profile, such as sawtooth roofs, barrel vaults, and waveform roofs. Similar to the footprint method, in this method you also need to sketch the roof. However, the sketch of the roof is drawn in elevation or section view and then extruded along the plan of the building.

Unlike the footprint method, which follows the footprint of the building, the extrusion method uses a special tool called Cut Plan Profile for this purpose. The Cut Plan Profile tool appears on the options bar once you select a roof created by using the Roof By Extrusion tool.

Perform the following steps to add a roof by extrusion in Autodesk Revit Architecture:

1. *Open* the **Autodesk Revit Architecture 2010** window.

2. *Open* the file containing the building model to which you want to add a roof—in this case, **Walls**.

3. *Open* an elevation, 3D, or section view by using the Project Browser. In this case, we open the 3D view, as shown in **Figure 4.34**.

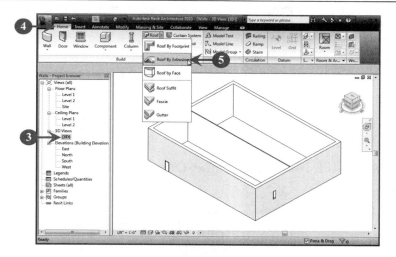

FIGURE 4.34

Note: The elevation, 3D, and section views appear in the Project Browser only when you have already created them. Refer to Chapter 3, Working with Project Views and Work Planes, to learn how to create various project views.

4. *Select* the **Home** tab on the ribbon, if not selected (Figure 4.34).
5. *Click* the right part of the **Roof** split button and then *select* the **Roof By Extrusion** option from the drop-down list (Figure 4.34). The **Work Plane** dialog box appears, as shown in **Figure 4.35**.

FIGURE 4.35

6. *Select* a radio button under the **Specify a new Work Plane** group to specify a work plane for the building model. In this case, we select the **Pick a plane** radio button (Figure 4.35).
7. *Click* the **OK** button (Figure 4.35).
8. *Select* a vertical plane in the drawing area, as shown in **Figure 4.36**.

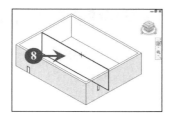

FIGURE 4.36

The **Roof Reference Level and Offset** dialog box appears, as shown in **Figure 4.37**.

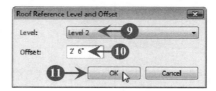

FIGURE 4.37

9. *Select* a level in the building model from the **Level** drop-down list. In this case, we select **Level 2** (Figure 4.37).

10. *Enter* the offset value in the **Offset** text box. In this case, we *enter* **2' 6"** (Figure 4.37).

11. *Click* the **OK** button (Figure 4.37). The **Create Extrusion Roof Profile** tab appears on the ribbon in the selected mode, as shown in **Figure 4.38**.

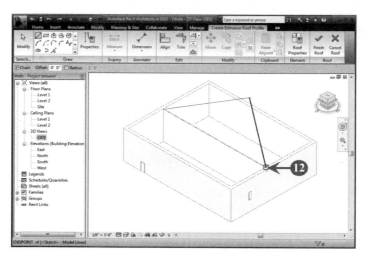

FIGURE 4.38

12. *Draw* the profile of the roof in the drawing area (Figure 4.38).

13. *Press* the **ESC** key twice to exit the Line tool as you complete drawing the profile of the roof.

14. *Click* the **Finish Roof** button under the **Roof** panel, as shown in **Figure 4.39**.

FIGURE 4.39

The roof is created and the final building model appears, as shown in **Figure 4.40**.

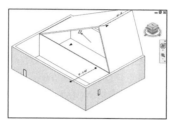

FIGURE 4.40

Let's now move on to the next section to learn how to create a ceiling.

4.8 CREATING A CEILING

Ceilings are level-based elements; that is, they are sketched at a specified distance above the level in which they reside. For example, if you want to create a ceiling on Level 1, you should place it 3 meters above the Level 1. You can use the Ceiling tool to create a ceiling in the building model. Ceilings can be automatically created in a project view or you can sketch one in the drawing area. Let's learn how to create a ceiling automatically in Autodesk Revit Architecture.

Creating an Automatic Ceiling

You can create an automatic ceiling by using the Ceiling tool and then selecting the ceiling type from the Type Selector drop-down list. Autodesk Revit Architecture includes various ceiling types, such as Generic and 2' × 2' ACT System, that can be used in the building model.

Perform the following steps to create a ceiling automatically in Autodesk Revit Architecture:

1. *Open* the **Autodesk Revit Architecture 2010** window.
2. *Open* the file containing the building model to which you want to add a ceiling—in this case, **Walls**.
3. *Open* a ceiling plan view. In this case, we open the **Level 2** view, as shown in **Figure 4.41**.

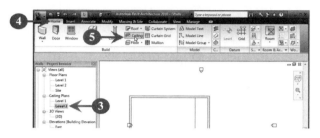

FIGURE 4.41

4. *Select* the **Home** tab, if not selected (Figure 4.41).
5. *Click* the **Ceiling** button under the **Build** panel (Figure 4.41). The **Place Ceiling** tab appears on the ribbon in the selected mode, as shown in **Figure 4.42**.

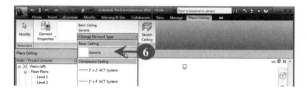

FIGURE 4.42

6. *Select* a ceiling type from the **Type Selector** drop-down list under the **Element** panel. In this case, we select the **Generic** ceiling type (Figure 4.42).
7. *Move* the mouse pointer to the location in drawing area where you want the ceiling to appear and then *click* the mouse button, as shown in **Figure 4.43**.

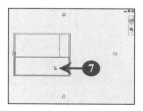

FIGURE 4.43

The ceiling is created and appears in the 3D view, as shown in **Figure 4.44**.

FIGURE 4.44

8. *Press* the **ESC** key twice to exit the Ceiling tool.

Notice that when you click the mouse button at the location where you want to place the ceiling, the ceiling is created automatically. After creating a ceiling, you can modify it at any time, such as by changing the ceiling type, applying a surface pattern, and editing a ceiling sketch. Alternatively, you can sketch a ceiling in the drawing area. Let's now learn how to sketch a ceiling.

Sketching a Ceiling

Sketching a ceiling requires you to sketch the boundaries of the ceiling. You can enable the sketch mode by first using the Ceiling tool and then using the Sketch Ceiling tool under the Ceiling panel of the Place Ceiling tab. You can also sketch a ceiling by using the Line tool or the Pick Walls tool.

Perform the following steps to sketch a ceiling by picking walls in Autodesk Revit Architecture:

1. *Open* the **Autodesk Revit Architecture 2010** window.
2. *Open* the file containing the building model to which you want to add a ceiling—in this case, **Walls**.
3. *Open* a ceiling plan view by using the Project Browser. In this case, we open the **Level 2** view, as shown in **Figure 4.45**.

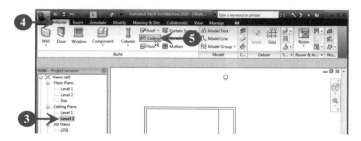

FIGURE 4.45

4. *Select* the **Home** tab on the ribbon, if not selected (Figure 4.45).

5. *Click* the **Ceiling** button under the **Build** panel (Figure 4.45). The **Place Ceiling** tab appears on the ribbon in the selected mode, as shown in **Figure 4.46**.

FIGURE 4.46

6. *Click* the **Sketch Ceiling** button under the **Ceiling** panel (Figure 4.46). The **Create Ceiling Boundary** tab appears on the ribbon in the selected mode, as shown in **Figure 4.47**.

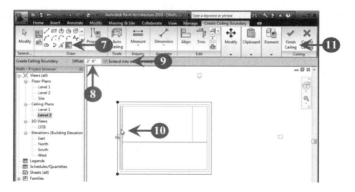

FIGURE 4.47

7. *Click* the **Pick Walls** button under the **Draw** panel (Figure 4.47).
8. *Enter* the offset value in the **Offset** text box on the options bar. In this case, we enter **2′ 6″** (Figure 4.47).
9. *Select* the **Extend into wall (to core)** check box on the options bar to measure the offset from the core of the wall (Figure 4.47).
10. *Select* the walls that you want to use as boundaries for the ceiling (Figure 4.47).

Note: You can change the properties of the ceiling by clicking the **Properties** button under the Draw panel and then specifying the ceiling type and its associated properties in the **Instance Properties** dialog box.

---

11. *Click* the **Finish Ceiling** button under the **Ceiling** panel (Figure 4.47). The ceiling is created, as shown in **Figure 4.48**.

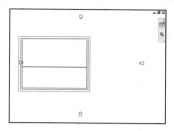

FIGURE 4.48

Now that we know how to create ceilings, let's learn how to cut openings in the elements, such as walls, floors, and ceilings.

4.9 CUTTING OPENINGS

Openings are used to create holes in the elements, such as walls, floors, roofs, slabs, ceilings, beams, braces, and columns. You can use the Opening tool to cut an opening in the Autodesk Revit Architecture elements. You can cut an opening in a floor, ceiling, or roof vertically or perpendicular to the surface. In the case of walls, you can cut a rectangular opening in a straight or arc wall. However, Autodesk Revit Architecture does not allow you to cut round or polygon shapes in walls.

Perform the following steps to cut openings in the wall element:

1. *Open* the **Autodesk Revit Architecture 2010** window.
2. *Open* the file containing the wall in which you want to cut an opening—in this case, **Walls**.
3. *Open* an elevation or section view by using the Project Browser. In this case, we open the **North** elevation view, as shown in **Figure 4.49**.

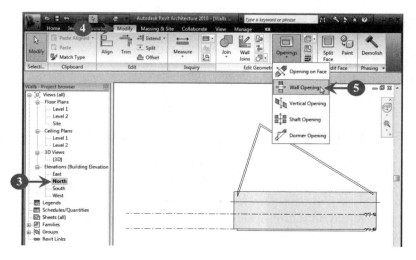

FIGURE 4.49

4. *Select* the **Modify** tab on the ribbon (Figure 4.49).

5. *Click* the **Openings** drop-down button under the **Edit Geometry** panel and then *select* the **Wall Opening** option from the drop-down list (Figure 4.49).

Note: You can create openings in roofs, ceilings, and floors by using the Opening on Face and Vertical Opening options.

6. *Select* the wall on which you want to cut an opening, as shown in **Figure 4.50**.

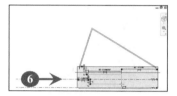

FIGURE 4.50

7. *Draw* an opening on the selected wall, as shown in **Figure 4.51**.

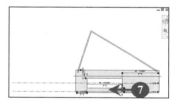

FIGURE 4.51

8. *Press* the **ESC** key twice to exit the Openings tool.

When you move the mouse pointer over the wall to highlight it, the opening is instantly highlighted. In the next section, we learn how to attach the wall element to other elements in Autodesk Revit Architecture.

4.10 ATTACHING THE WALL TO OTHER ELEMENTS

Walls are independent elements in Revit Architecture. That is, when you create a wall, it is not attached to the roof, ceiling, floor, and other modeling components automatically. Instead, you need to manually attach the wall to other modeling components in the building model. While attaching walls to other components, you should comply with the following rules of thumb:

- The wall tops can be attached to nonvertical reference planes.
- The walls can be attached to in-place roofs or floors.
- When a wall top is already attached to a reference plane, if you attach the wall top to another reference plane, the wall top is detached from the earlier reference plane.
- Walls that are parallel and directly above or below each other can be attached together.

Perform the following steps to attach the wall element to other elements in Revit Architecture:

1. *Open* the **Autodesk Revit Architecture 2010** window.
2. *Open* the file containing the building model in which you want to attach a wall to other elements of the building model. In this case, we open the **Walls** file.
3. *Open* a view in which you want to attach the wall to other building elements. In this case, we open the **3D** view, as shown in **Figure 4.52**.

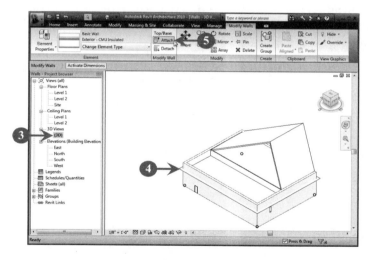

FIGURE 4.52

4. *Select* the walls to which you want to attach other elements of the building model in the drawing area (Figure 4.52). When you select the walls, the **Modify Walls** tab appears on the ribbon in the selected mode.
5. *Click* the **Attach** button under the **Modify Wall** panel (Figure 4.52). The **Attach Wall** option appears on the options bar, as shown in **Figure 4.53**.

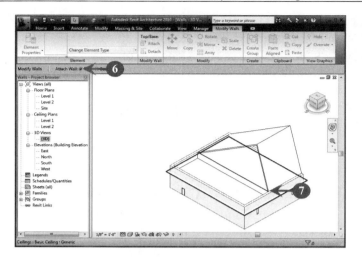

FIGURE 4.53

6. *Select* a radio button beside the **Attach Wall** option on the options bar to determine how you want to attach a wall: from the top or from the base. In this case, we *select* the **Top** radio button (Figure 4.53).

7. *Select* an element, such as the roof, floor, or ceiling, to attach to the wall. In this case, we select the ceiling (Figure 4.53). The selected walls are attached to the ceiling, as shown in **Figure 4.54**.

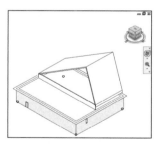

FIGURE 4.54

Note: After attaching the selected walls to the selected elements, the Modify Walls tab appears again on the ribbon in the selected mode. You can repeat steps 4 to 6 to attach other elements to the walls.

Let's move on to the next section, where we learn how to create stairs in Autodesk Revit Architecture.

4.11 CREATING STAIRS

Stairs are used in a building model to connect two or more floors. You can use the Stairs tool to create stairs in the building model. Stairs can be created in a plan or 3D view either by defining the run of stairs or by sketching riser lines and boundaries. The run of stairs refers to a single set of stairs, or a section of a stairway, from one platform to the next. You can define runs, such as straight runs and L-shaped runs, with a platform, which can be U-shaped stairs or spiral stairs. When you create stairs, the railings for the stairs are created automatically. The stairs are restricted within the specified boundaries, which can be modified by modifying the sketch of the stairs. When you modify the boundaries, the risers and runs are updated accordingly.

Autodesk Revit Architecture allows you to create stairs by either of two methods: by sketching the stair runs or by sketching the stair boundaries and riser lines. In both methods, the number of treads is automatically calculated depending on the distance between the two floors and the maximum riser height. The stairs can be created from inside the building model or from outside the building model. While creating stairs from inside, you need to cut an opening of an appropriate size in the roof. In the case of stairs outside the building model, you just sketch the stairs at the desired location. This section discusses how to create stairs by sketching runs and by sketching boundaries and riser lines, as well as how to create spiral stairs. We begin by creating stairs by sketching runs.

Creating Stairs by Sketching Runs

Stairs can be created in either plan or 3D views, although it is especially easy to sketch them in plan view. You can sketch stairs by specifying the starting and ending points of the stairs. After you specify the starting point, move the mouse pointer to another location; the number of risers created in the corresponding distance and the remaining number of risers are displayed. To set the ending point, click the mouse button once you approach the ending point.

Perform the following steps to create stairs by sketching runs in Revit Architecture:

1. *Open* the **Autodesk Revit Architecture 2010** window.
2. *Open* the file containing the building model in which you want to create stairs—in this case, **Walls**.
3. *Open* a plan view by using the Project Browser. In this case, we open the **Level 1** view under the **Floor Plans** view, as shown in **Figure 4.55**.

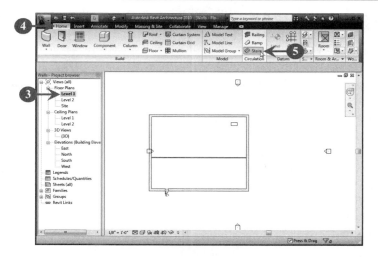

FIGURE 4.55

4. *Select* the **Home** tab on the ribbon, if not selected (Figure 4.55).
5. *Click* the **Stairs** button under the **Circulation** panel (Figure 4.55). The **Create Stairs Sketch** tab appears on the ribbon in the selected mode, as shown in **Figure 4.56**.

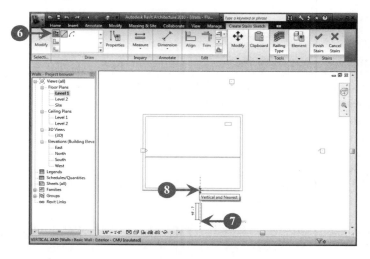

FIGURE 4.56

6. *Click* the **Run** button under the **Draw** panel (Figure 4.56).
7. *Click* at a location in the drawing area where you want to place the starting point of the stairs (Figure 4.56).
8. *Move* the mouse pointer to a location in the drawing area where you want to end the stairs and then *click* to fix the ending point (Figure 4.56).

> **Note:** When you move the mouse pointer, a rectangular box appears. One end of the box is attached to the starting point, and the other end is attached to the mouse pointer. The rectangular box also contains a number of risers that can be created at a specified distance.

9. *Click* the boundary of the stairs and then *move* the mouse pointer away from the stairs to increase the width of the stairs, as shown in **Figure 4.57**.

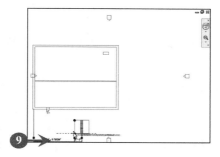

FIGURE 4.57

10. *Click* and *drag* the risers to the locations where you want to place them in the drawing area, as shown in **Figure 4.58**.

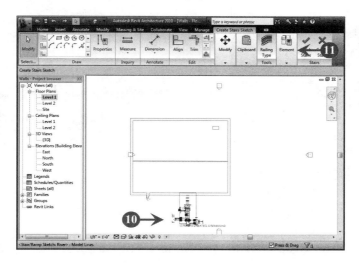

FIGURE 4.58

11. *Click* the **Finish Stairs** button under the **Stairs** panel (Figure 4.58). The stairs are created, as shown in **Figure 4.59**.

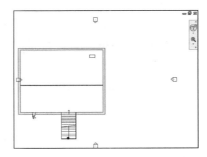

FIGURE 4.59

Let's now learn how to create stairs by sketching boundaries and riser lines.

Creating Stairs by Sketching Boundaries and Risers

In addition to creating stairs by sketching runs, you can create stairs by sketching boundaries and risers. To create boundaries and risers, you use the Boundary and Riser tools, respectively, which are found under the Draw panel of the Create Stairs Sketch tab.

Perform the following steps to create stairs by sketching boundaries and riser lines:

1. *Open* the **Autodesk Revit Architecture 2010** window.
2. *Open* the file containing the building model in which you want to create stairs—in this case, **Walls**.
3. *Open* a plan view by using the Project Browser. In this case, we open the **Level 1** view under the floor plan view, as shown in **Figure 4.60**.

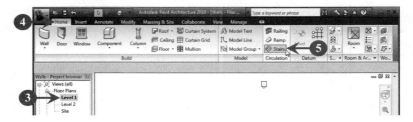

FIGURE 4.60

4. *Select* the **Home** tab on the ribbon, if not selected (Figure 4.60).
5. *Click* the **Stairs** button under the **Circulation** panel (Figure 4.60). The **Create Stairs Sketch** tab appears on the ribbon in the selected mode, as shown in **Figure 4.61**.

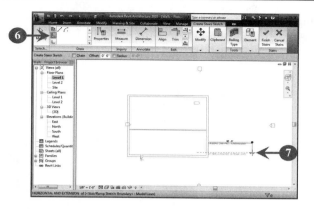

FIGURE 4.61

6. *Click* the **Boundary** button under the **Draw** panel (Figure 4.61).
7. *Draw* the boundaries of stairs (Figure 4.61).
8. *Click* the **Riser** button under the **Draw** panel, as shown in **Figure 4.62**.

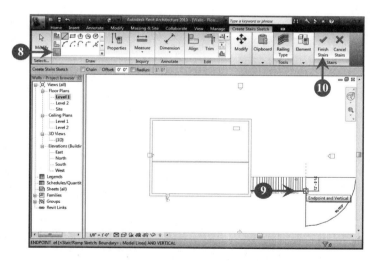

FIGURE 4.62

9. *Draw* the risers between the specified boundaries (Figure 4.62).

Note: When you use the Riser tool, the Line tool is active to sketch risers by default. You can also use other tools, such as Start-End-Radius-Arc, Center-End Arc, and Tangent-End Arc, to sketch the curved risers.

10. *Click* the **Finish Stairs** button under the **Stairs** panel (Figure 4.62). The stairs are created, as shown in **Figure 4.63**.

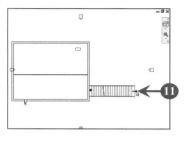

FIGURE 4.63

11. *Click* the arrow at the end of the stairs to flip the direction of the stairs up and down (Figure 4.63). The direction of the stairs flips, as shown in **Figure 4.64**.

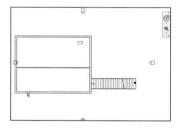

FIGURE 4.64

Let's now learn how to create spiral staircases.

Creating Spiral Staircases

In a manner similar to that used to create straight stairs, you can create spiral staircases. The only difference lies in the selection of the tool that you select to sketch the stairs. When you create spiral staircases, you should note that the spiral of the staircases is limited to less than 360 degrees, which means that you cannot overlap the spiral runs. If you intersect spiral runs, a warning message appears to inform you that the stringers and railings are not placed accurately.

Perform the following steps to create spiral staircases:

1. *Open* the **Autodesk Revit Architecture 2010** window.
2. *Open* the file containing the building model in which you want to create stairs—in this case, **Walls**.

3. *Open* the 3D view by using the Project Browser, as shown in **Figure 4.65**.

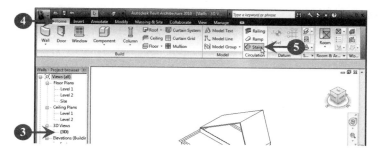

FIGURE 4.65

4. *Select* the **Home** tab on the ribbon, if not selected (Figure 4.65).

5. *Click* the **Stairs** button under the **Circulation** panel (Figure 4.65). The **Create Stairs Sketch** tab appears on the ribbon in the selected mode, as shown in **Figure 4.66**.

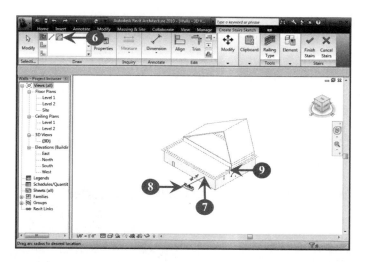

FIGURE 4.66

6. *Click* the **Center-ends Arc** button under the **Draw** panel (Figure 4.66).

7. *Click* at the location in the drawing area where you want to set a center point for the spiral (Figure 4.66).

8. *Move* the mouse pointer away from the center point and then *click* at a location in the drawing area to set a starting point for the stairs (Figure 4.66).

9. *Move* the mouse pointer away from the starting point and then *click* at a location in the drawing area to set the ending points for the stairs (Figure 4.66).

10. *Select* the boundary of the stair and then *drag* its **Drag Line End** point to the specified ending point, as shown in **Figure 4.67**.

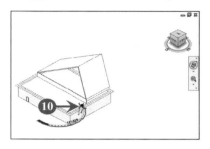

FIGURE 4.67

11. *Click* the **Drag End Line** point of one boundary and *drag* it away from the other boundary, as shown in **Figure 4.68**.

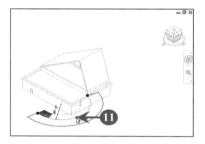

FIGURE 4.68

12. *Click* the **Split** button under the **Edit** panel to split the stairs at the point where you want to create a landing of the stairs, as shown in **Figure 4.69**.

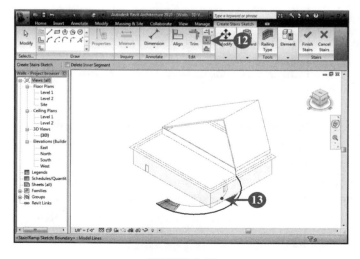

FIGURE 4.69

Note: A landing is the flat surface between the two runs of a stair.

13. *Click* the points on the boundaries from where you want to split the stairs (Figure 4.69).

14. *Press* the **ESC** key twice to exit the Split tool.

15. *Click* and *drag* the risers to the locations where you want to place them between the stairs' boundaries in the drawing area, as shown in **Figure 4.70**.

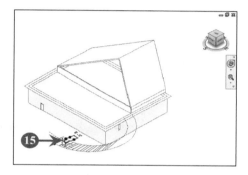

FIGURE 4.70

16. *Click* the **Riser** button under the **Draw** panel to create risers above the landing of the stairs, as shown in **Figure 4.71**.

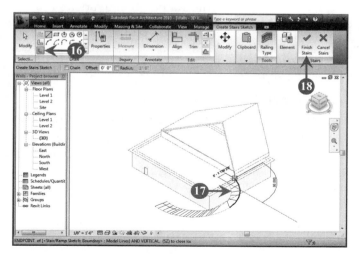

FIGURE 4.71

17. *Draw* the risers between the specified boundaries (Figure 4.71).

18. *Click* the **Finish Stairs** button under the **Stairs** panel (Figure 4.71). The stairs are created, as shown in **Figure 4.72**.

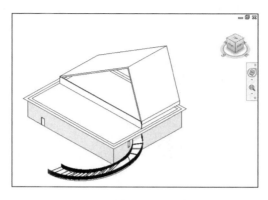

FIGURE 4.72

In the next section, we learn how to create a railing in Revit Architecture.

4.12 CREATING A RAILING

Railings in Autodesk Revit Architecture work as free-standing components. Nevertheless, you can attach them to host elements, such as floors, ramps, or stairs. After you sketch the railing, the rails and balusters are automatically placed on the railing, at equal intervals. You can use the Railing tool to create railings in the building model. Railings are generally created automatically with the stairs, but you can also create them for other locations, such as terraces, passages, gardens, and balconies, in the building model.

Perform the following steps to create a railing in Autodesk Revit Architecture:

1. *Open* the **Autodesk Revit Architecture 2010** window.
2. *Open* the file containing the building model in which you want to create a railing—in this case, **Walls**.
3. *Open* a plan or 3D view by using the Project Browser. In this case, we open the 3D view, as shown in **Figure 4.73**.

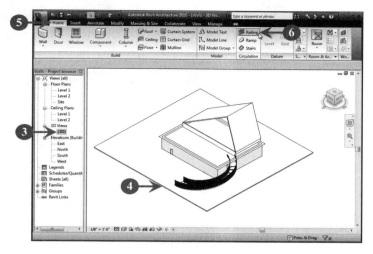

FIGURE 4.73

4. *Create* a host object, such as a floor, stairs, or ramp, on which you want to create a railing, if the building model does not have any host object. In this case, we create the floor (Figure 4.73).

5. *Select* the **Home** tab on the ribbon, if not selected (Figure 4.73).

6. *Click* the **Railing** button under the **Circulation** panel (Figure 4.73). The **Create Railing Path** tab appears on the ribbon in the selected mode, as shown in **Figure 4.74**.

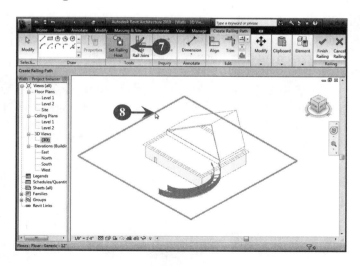

FIGURE 4.74

7. *Click* the **Set Railing Host** button under the **Tools** panel (Figure 4.74).

8. *Select* an element in the drawing area on which you want to create a railing (Figure 4.74). The sketch mode is automatically activated when you *select* the **Line** tool under the **Draw** panel, as shown in **Figure 4.75**.

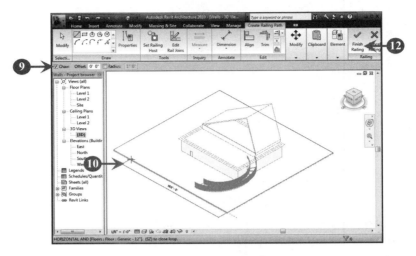

FIGURE 4.75

9. *Select* the **Chain** check box on the options bar to draw a chain of railings (Figure 4.75).

10. *Draw* a line on the host object where you want to create the railing (Figure 4.75).

11. *Press* the **ESC** key twice to exit the Line tool.

12. *Click* the **Finish Railing** button under the **Railing** panel (Figure 4.75). The railing is created, as shown in **Figure 4.76**.

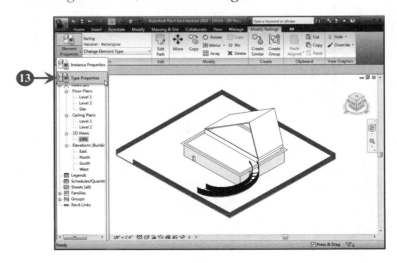

FIGURE 4.76

Simultaneously, the **Modify Railings** tab appears on the ribbon in the selected mode. Now, continue with the following steps to change the parameters, such as type and height of the railing.

13. *Click* the lower part of the **Element Properties** split button and then *select* the **Type Properties** option from the drop-down list (Figure 4.76). The **Type Properties** dialog box appears, as shown in **Figure 4.77**.

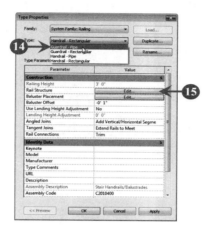

FIGURE 4.77

14. *Select* a railing type from the **Type** drop-down list to change the railing type. In this case, we select the **GuardRail–Pipe** railing type (Figure 4.77).

15. *Click* the **Edit** button adjacent to the **Rail Structure** parameter (Figure 4.77). The **Edit Rails** dialog box appears, as shown in **Figure 4.78**.

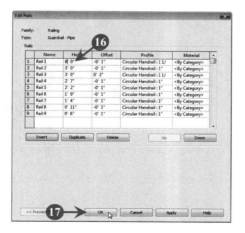

FIGURE 4.78

16. *Change* the height of the railing to a new value. In this case, we *enter* **8' 0"** (Figure 4.78).

17. *Click* the **OK** button (Figure 4.78). The height of the railing is changed and the **Edit Rails** dialog box is closed. The **Type Properties** dialog box appears with the newly specified height of the railing, as shown in **Figure 4.79**.

FIGURE 4.79

18. *Click* the **OK** button (Figure 4.79). The **Type Properties** dialog box is closed and the railing appears, as shown in **Figure 4.80**.

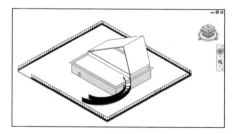

FIGURE 4.80

Let's now move on to the next section, which focuses on how to create a ramp.

4.13 CREATING A RAMP

Ramps are inclined shapes that are used to create a slope. The creation of ramps in Revit Architecture is similar to stairs. You can create ramps in a plan view or a 3D view by using the Ramp tool. Once you access the Ramp tool, Revit Architecture enables the sketch mode, allowing you to draw the sketch of a ramp.

Perform the following steps to create a ramp:

1. *Open* the **Autodesk Revit Architecture 2010** window.
2. *Open* the file containing the building model in which you want to create a ramp—in this case, **Walls**.
3. *Set* the thickness of the floor so that the slope of the ramp matches the level of the floor. In this case, we *set* the thickness of the floor to **10' 0"**. The building model appears with increased floor's thickness, as shown in **Figure 4.81**.

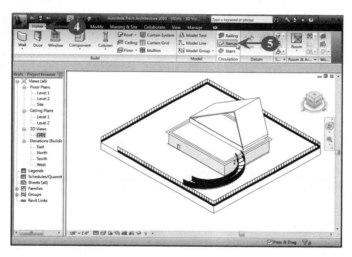

FIGURE 4.81

Note: You can change the thickness of the floor by using the **Type Properties** dialog box.

4. *Select* the **Home** tab on the ribbon, if not selected (Figure 4.81).
5. *Click* the **Ramp** button under the **Circulation** panel (Figure 4.81). The **Create Ramp Sketch** tab appears on the ribbon in the selected mode wherein the **Run** tool is automatically activated, as shown in **Figure 4.82**.

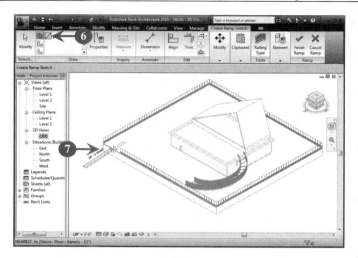

FIGURE 4.82

6. *Click* the **Line** tool or the **Center-ends Arc** tool to draw the run for the ramp. In this case, we *click* the **Line** tool (Figure 4.82).
7. *Draw* the ramp run in the drawing area (Figure 4.82).
8. *Press* the **ESC** key twice to exit the Line tool.
9. *Click* and *drag* the boundaries of the ramp away from each other to increase the width of the ramp, as shown in **Figure 4.83**.

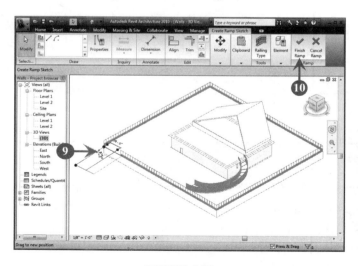

FIGURE 4.83

10. *Click* the **Finish Ramp** button under the **Ramp** panel (Figure 4.83). The ramp is created, as shown in **Figure 4.84**.

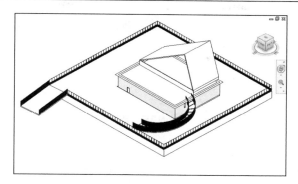

FIGURE 4.84

After creating ramps, we are ready to move on to the next section and learn how to create architectural columns.

4.14 CREATING ARCHITECTURAL COLUMNS

Architectural columns are used to model column boxes around structural columns, which are themselves used to model vertical load-bearing elements in a building. You can also use architectural columns for decoration purposes in the building model. Architectural columns inherit the material of other elements to which they are joined. For example, if an architectural column is joined to the roof, it uses the material applied to the roof. The architectural columns are added in a plan view.

When you place the architectural columns in the building model, they are not attached automatically to the elements, such as roofs, floors, and ceilings. However, you can select a column and then easily attach its base or top to other elements, such as roofs, floors, ceilings, reference planes, and structural framing members.

In this section, you learn how to create a column and attach and detach columns with other elements in Revit Architecture.

Creating a Column

Columns are created in plan view; therefore, you need to open the plan view to create a column. When you create a column, its height is defined through its properties after you select it from the Type Selector drop-down list.

Perform the following steps to create an architectural column in Autodesk Revit Architecture:

1. *Open* the **Autodesk Revit Architecture 2010** window.
2. *Open* the file containing the building model in which you want to create a column—in this case, **Walls**.
3. *Select* the **Home** tab on the ribbon, if it is not selected, as shown in **Figure 4.85**.

FIGURE 4.85

4. *Click* the lower part of the **Column** split button under the **Build** panel
   and then *select* the **Architectural Column** option from the drop-down list
   (Figure 4.85). The **Place Column** tab appears on the ribbon in the selected
   mode, as shown in **Figure 4.86**.

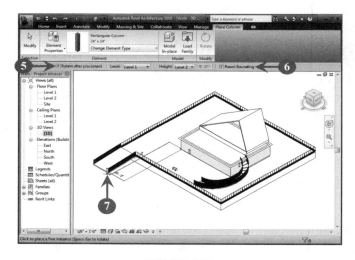

FIGURE 4.86

5. *Select* the **Rotate after placement** check box on the options bar to rotate
   the column after placing it in the drawing area (Figure 4.86).
6. *Select* the **Room Bounding** check box to assign the column as a room-
   bounding element before adding it to the building model (Figure 4.86).

Note: The room-bounding element defines the boundary of the room, which helps
in calculating the area and volume of the room.

7. *Move* the mouse pointer to the location in the drawing area where you want
   the column to appear and then *click* to place the column (Figure 4.86).

8. *Move* the mouse pointer left or right to rotate the column and then *click* to fix the column, as shown in **Figure 4.87**.

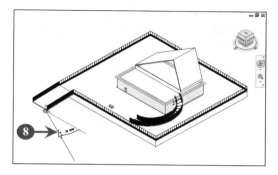

FIGURE 4.87

9. *Repeat* steps 7 and 8 to place more columns. In this case, we place another column adjacent to the column that we previously placed, as shown in **Figure 4.88**.

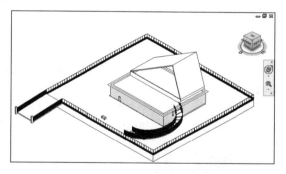

FIGURE 4.88

10. *Press* the **ESC** key twice to exit the Architectural Column tool.

Let's now learn how to attach and detach columns in Revit Architecture.

Attaching and Detaching Columns

After creating a column, you can attach it to other elements, such as floors, roofs, and ceilings. Similarly, after attaching a column, you can detach it from an element to which it is attached.

Perform the following steps to attach and detach columns in Revit Architecture:

1. *Open* the **Autodesk Revit Architecture 2010** window.
2. *Open* the file containing the columns that you want to attach. In this case, we open the **Walls** file that we used in the previous section.

3. *Create* a floor below the ramp, which you can use as a target for the columns, as shown in **Figure 4.89**.

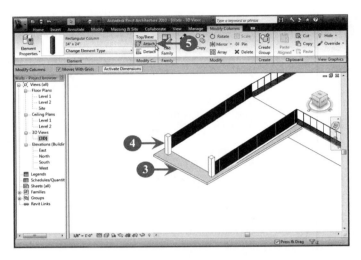

FIGURE 4.89

4. *Select* one or more columns in the drawing area (Figure 4.89). The **Modify Columns** tab appears on the ribbon in the selected mode.
5. *Click* the **Attach** button under the **Modify** panel (Figure 4.89). Different options, such as **Attach Column** and **Attachment Style**, appear on the options bar with which you can modify the selected columns, as shown in **Figure 4.90**.

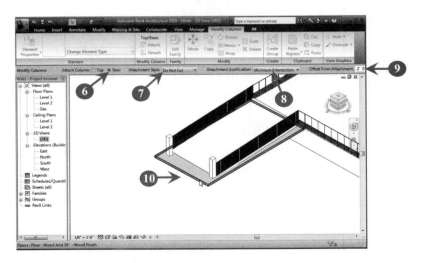

FIGURE 4.90

6. *Select* a radio button beside the **Attach Column** option to specify which part of columns you want to attach. In this case, we *select* the **Base** radio button (Figure 4.90).

7. *Select* a style from the **Attachment Style** drop-down list. In this case, we *select* the **Do Not Cut** attachment style (Figure 4.90).

8. *Select* an option from the **Attachment Justification** drop-down list to specify the attachment justification. In this case, we *select* the **Minimum Intersection** option (Figure 4.90).

9. *Enter* an offset value in the **Offset From Attachment** text box, which determines the offset from the target. In this case, we *enter* **2' 0"** (Figure 4.90).

10. *Click* the target element, such as a floor or a roof to which you want to attach the selected columns. In this case, we *click* the floor (Figure 4.90).

The selected columns are attached to the specified floor. Continue with the following steps to learn how to detach the columns from the target element:

11. *Select* one or more columns in the drawing area that you want to detach, as shown in **Figure 4.91**. The **Modify Columns** tab appears on the ribbon in the selected mode.

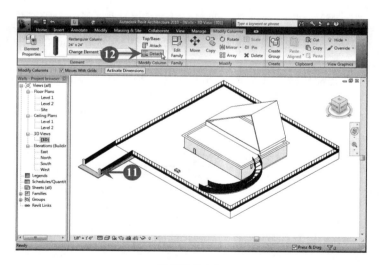

FIGURE 4.91

12. *Click* the **Detach** button under the **Modify Column** panel (Figure 4.91).

13. *Click* the target element in the drawing area from which you want to detach the selected columns, as shown in **Figure 4.92**.

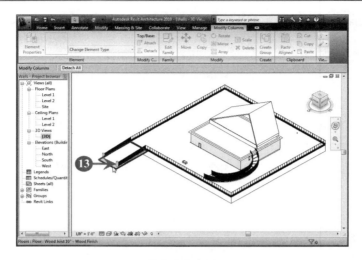

FIGURE 4.92

The columns are detached from the specified target element.

> **Note:** If the column is attached to the target by its top and bottom, you can click the **Detach All** button on the options bar to detach the top and bottom of the column from the target simultaneously.

Now that we know how to create, attach, and detach columns, we can move on to learn how to use curtain elements in Autodesk Revit Architecture.

4.15   USING CURTAIN ELEMENTS

Curtain elements are the elements that do not carry the floor or roof loads of the building. They consist of curtain walls, curtain grids, mullions, and curtain systems. Curtain walls are thin, aluminum-framed walls filled with glass, metal panels, or thin stone.

When you draw a curtain wall, a single panel is extended to the entire length of the wall. In contrast, when you create a curtain wall with automatic curtain grids, the wall is subdivided into numbers of panels. Curtain grids define the geometry of a curtain system or curtain wall and form a grid line where you can add mullions. Mullions are nonstructural vertical strips between the panels of a wall.

A curtain system consists of panels, curtain grids, and mullions. Curtain systems are created by selecting element faces. Once you create a curtain system, it is easy to add curtain grids and mullions by using a similar technique as used with curtain walls. While creating curtain systems, you should note that a wall or a roof cannot be created as a curtain system.

Let's learn how to create a curtain wall and add curtain grids to the curtain wall.

Creating a Curtain Wall

A curtain wall is a type of exterior wall that is attached to the building model but does not carry the loads of the roof and floor. As stated earlier, these are thin, aluminum-framed walls having in-fills of glass, metal panels, or thin stone; you can use them to create the decorated front of the building.

Perform the following steps to create a curtain wall in Autodesk Revit Architecture:

1. *Open* the **Autodesk Revit Architecture 2010** window.
2. *Create* a new file and save it with the name **CurtainWalls**.
3. *Select* the **Home** tab on the ribbon, if it is not already selected, as shown in **Figure 4.93**.

FIGURE 4.93

4. *Click* the lower part of the **Wall** split button and then *select* the **Wall** option from the drop-down list (Figure 4.93). The **Place Wall** tab appears on the ribbon in the selected mode, as shown in **Figure 4.94**.

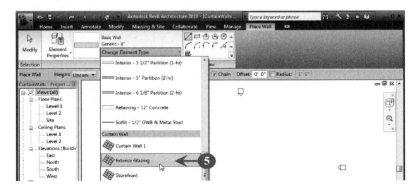

FIGURE 4.94

5. *Select* a curtain wall type from the **Type Selector** drop-down list under the **Element** panel. In this case, we *select* **Exterior Glazing** (Figure 4.94).

6. *Select* a draw tool from the **Draw** panel that you want to use to sketch the wall. In this case, we *select* the **Line** tool, which is the default draw tool, as shown in **Figure 4.95**.

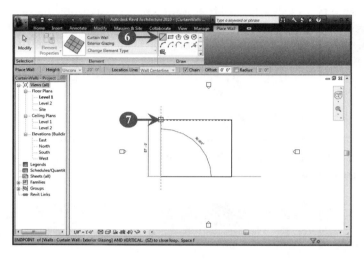

FIGURE 4.95

Note: You can specify the vertical and horizontal layout properties of the wall type to create a wall with automatic horizontal and vertical curtain grids. Remember that after drawing the wall, you cannot move the automatic curtain grids until and unless you make them independent.

7. *Draw* the curtain wall in the drawing area (Figure 4.95).

8. *Press* the **ESC** key twice to exit the Wall tool.

Now you can change the panel type of the curtain wall by performing the following steps:

9. *Open* a view where you can see the panels of the curtain wall. In this case, we *open* the 3D view, as shown in **Figure 4.96**.

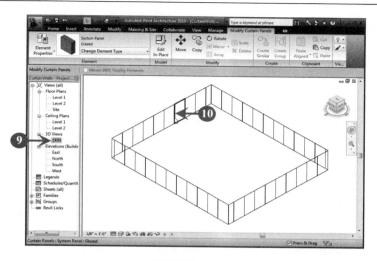

FIGURE 4.96

10. *Select* a panel of the curtain wall in the drawing area (Figure 4.96).

Note: You can select a panel by placing the mouse pointer over the grid line of the panel and then pressing the **TAB** key multiple times until the panel is selected. When you select a panel, the Modify Curtain Panels tab appears on the ribbon in the selected mode.

11. *Select* an appropriate panel type from the **Type Selector** drop-down list under the **Element** panel. In this case, we *select* the **Solid** system panel, as shown in **Figure 4.97**. The panel type of the selected panel is changed to the panel type that you have selected from the Type Selector drop-down list.

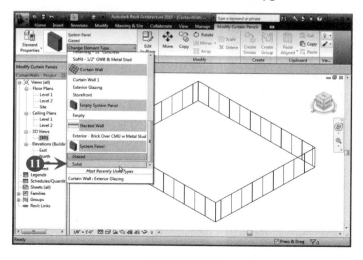

FIGURE 4.97

Let's learn how to add curtain grids to the curtain wall.

Adding Curtain Grids

Curtain grids create a grid line in the curtain walls or curtain systems. When you place curtain grids in the curtain walls or curtain systems, the grids snap to equal intervals on the curtain wall and to visible levels, grids, or reference planes. However, when you select a common corner edge, curtain grids snap to other curtain grids.

Perform the following steps to add curtain grids to the curtain wall:

1. *Open* the **Autodesk Revit Architecture 2010** window.
2. *Open* the file containing the curtain wall to which you want to add curtain grids. In this case, we open the **CurtainWalls** file (which we created in the previous section).
3. *Open* a 3D view or an elevation view. In this case, we *open* the 3D view, as shown in **Figure 4.98**.

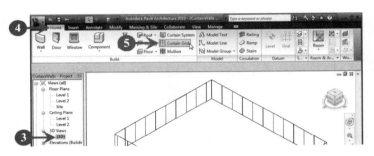

FIGURE 4.98

4. *Select* the **Home** tab on the ribbon, if it is not already selected (Figure 4.98).
5. *Click* the **Curtain Grid** button under the **Build** panel (Figure 4.98). The **Place Curtain Grid** tab appears on the ribbon in the selected mode, as shown in **Figure 4.99**.

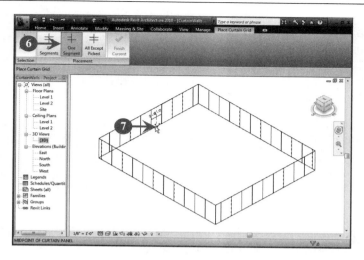

FIGURE 4.99

6.   *Click* a placement type under the **Placement** panel. In this case, we *click* the **One Segment** placement type (Figure 4.99).

The different placement types are briefly described here:

- **All Segments:** Places grid segments on all panels where the preview appears
- **One Segment:** Places one grid segment on one panel where the preview appears
- **All Except Picked:** Places a grid segment on all panels except the selected panels

7.   *Move* the mouse pointer along wall edges. A temporary grid line appears (Figure 4.99).

8.   *Click* the mouse button to place the curtain grid, as shown in **Figure 4.100**.

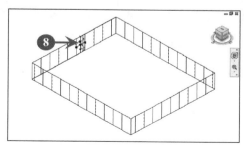

FIGURE 4.100

Note: If you click the **All Except Picked** button, then after placing each grid, click the **Finish Current** button to place the curtain grids.

9. *Click* the **Modify** button under the **Selection** panel to exit the One Segment tool, as shown in **Figure 4.101**.

FIGURE 4.101

After adding curtain grids to the curtain wall, we are ready to learn how to create a model text in Autodesk Revit Architecture.

4.16 CREATING A MODEL TEXT

Model texts in Autodesk Revit Architecture are used for many purposes, such as placing signage on a building or letters on a wall. You can also use them for hoardings. Model texts are available only for those families that are represented in 3D, such as walls, floors, doors, and windows. They are not available for families that are represented in 2D, such as annotations, detail components, and profiles.

Perform the following steps to create a model text:

1. *Open* the **Autodesk Revit Architecture 2010** window.
2. *Open* the file containing the building model in which you want to create a model text. In this case, we open the **Walls** file.
3. *Select* the **Home** tab on the ribbon, if it is not already selected, as shown in **Figure 4.102**.

FIGURE 4.102

4. *Click* the **Set Work Plane** button under the **Work Plane** panel to set the work plane where you want the text to appear (Figure 4.102). The **Work Plane** dialog box appears, as shown in **Figure 4.103**.

FIGURE 4.103

5. *Select* a radio button under the **Specify a new Work Plane** group to specify how you want to create a work plane. In this case, we *select* the **Pick a plane** radio button (Figure 4.103).

6. *Click* the **OK** button (Figure 4.103).

7. *Select* a plane that you want to set as a work plane. In this case, we *select* the wall, as shown in **Figure 4.104**.

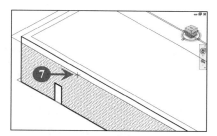

FIGURE 4.104

8. *Click* the **Model Text** button under the **Model** panel, as shown in **Figure 4.105**.

FIGURE 4.105

The **Edit Text** dialog box appears, as shown in **Figure 4.106**.

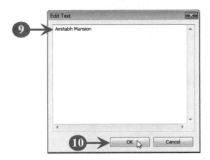

FIGURE 4.106

9. *Enter* the text that you want to display on the wall. In this case, we *enter* the text **Amitabh Mansion** (Figure 4.106).

10. *Click* the **OK** button (Figure 4.106).

11. *Move* the mouse pointer to the location in the drawing area where you want the text to appear, as shown in **Figure 4.107**.

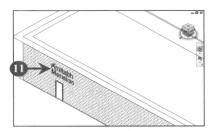

FIGURE 4.107

Note: When you move the mouse pointer, a preview image of the model text appears.

12. *Click* to place the model text, as shown in **Figure 4.108**.

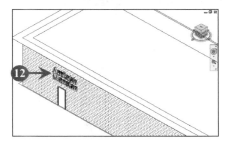

FIGURE 4.108

After learning about creating a model text, let's move on to the next section to learn about rooms.

4.17 USING ROOMS

Rooms are included in Autodesk Revit Architecture so that you can perform a basic analysis of a design and plan occupancy and usage of a building. In simple words, a room is a subdivision of space in a building model created by using the elements, such as walls, floors, roofs, and ceilings, which are termed room-bounding elements. These room-bounding elements are used when you want to calculate the different dimensions of a room, such as its perimeter, volume, and area. In this section, you learn how to create a room and compute the volume and area of a room.

Creating and Tagging a Room

You can create rooms by using the Room tool. Rooms are created only in the plan and schedule views. When you access the Room tool, an option to create a room tag automatically appears on the options bar to allow you to tag the room instantly. If you do not want to tag the room at the time of its creation, you can tag it later.

Perform the following steps to create a room in Autodesk Revit Architecture:

1. *Open* the **Autodesk Revit Architecture 2010** window.
2. *Create* a new file and save it with the name **Rooms**.
3. *Create* an enclosed region by using the **Wall** tool where you want to create a room.
4. *Open* a plan view.
5. *Select* the **Home** tab on the ribbon, if it is not already selected, as shown in **Figure 4.109**.

FIGURE 4.109

6. *Click* the lower part of the **Room** split button under the **Room & Area** panel and then *select* the **Room** option from the drop-down list (Figure 4.109). The **Place Room** tab appears on the ribbon in the selected mode, as shown in **Figure 4.110**.

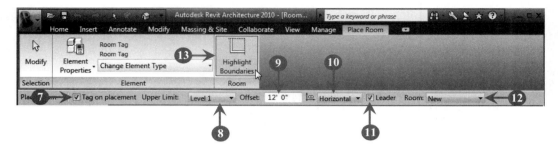

FIGURE 4.110

7. *Select* the **Tag on placement** check box on the options bar to display a room tag with the room (Figure 4.110).

8. *Select* an upper limit level of the room from the **Upper Limit** drop-down list. In this case, we *select* the **Level 1** option (Figure 4.110).

9. *Enter* an offset value in the **Offset** text box, which is measured from the upper limit level to the distance of the upper boundary of the room. In this case, we *enter* **12' 0"** (Figure 4.110).

Note: You can enter a positive value to go beyond the upper limit level and a negative value to go below the upper limit level.

10. *Select* an option from the drop-down list immediate next to the 🔳 icon to specify the orientation of the room tag. In this case, we *select* the **Horizontal** option (Figure 4.110).

11. *Select* the **Leader** check box to include a leader line with the room tag (Figure 4.110).

12. *Select* an option from the **Room** drop-down list to specify whether you want to create a new room or to use an existing room. In this case, we *select* the **New** option (Figure 4.110).

13. *Click* the **Highlight Boundaries** button under the **Room** panel to view the room-bounding elements (Figure 4.110). Autodesk Revit Architecture highlights all room-bounding elements and displays a warning message box, as shown in **Figure 4.111**.

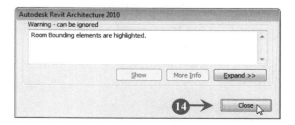

FIGURE 4.111

14. *Click* the **Close** button to close the warning message box (Figure 4.111).

15. *Move* the mouse pointer to the location in the drawing area where you want to create the room and then *click* the mouse button to place the room, as shown in **Figure 4.112**.

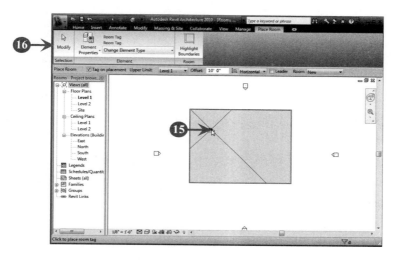

FIGURE 4.112

> **Note:** The room is placed only if the available space in the building is greater than 1' or 306 mm wide.

16. *Click* the **Modify** button under the **Selection** panel (Figure 4.112).

17. *Select* the room in the drawing area and then *click* the room text within the room tag, as shown in **Figure 4.113**.

FIGURE 4.113

> **Note:** When you select the room, the Modify Room Tags tab appears on the ribbon in the selected mode.

A text box appears in which you can enter the new tag name for the room, as shown in **Figure 4.114**.

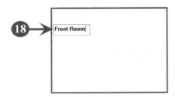

FIGURE 4.114

18. *Enter* a new name for the room tag. In this case, we *enter* the name **Front Room** (Figure 4.114).
19. *Click* outside the room tag to finish tagging the room.

Let's move on to the next section, where we learn how to compute the area and volume of a room.

Computing the Room Area and Volume

While creating a room in the building model, it is important to know about the area and volume of the room. In Autodesk Revit Architecture, the area of a room is computed by using one of two methods. The first method requires the room boundaries, whereas the second method uses the computation height.

The volume of the room appears in the Instance Properties dialog box, tags, and schedules for rooms.

> **Note:** By default, room volumes are not calculated automatically, and room tags and schedules display the text "Not Calculated" for the Volume parameter.

Perform the following steps to compute the room area in Revit Architecture:

1. *Open* the **Autodesk Revit Architecture 2010** window.
2. *Open* the file containing the room for which you want to compute the area and volume. In this case, we open the **Rooms** file.
3. *Select* the **Home** tab on the ribbon, if it is not already selected, as shown in **Figure 4.115**.

FIGURE 4.115

4. *Click* the drop-down button on the **Room & Area** panel and then *select* the **Area and Volume Computations** option from the drop-down list (Figure 4.115). The **Area and Volume Computations** dialog box appears, as shown in **Figure 4.116**.

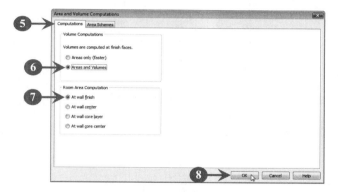

FIGURE 4.116

5. *Select* the **Computations** tab (Figure 4.116).
6. *Select* a radio button under the **Volume Computations** group to specify whether you want to calculate only the area of the room or both the area and volume of the room. In this case, we *select* the **Areas and Volumes** radio button (Figure 4.116).
7. *Select* a radio button under the **Room Area Computation** group to specify how you want to calculate the room area, such as at the wall finish, at the wall center, at the wall core layer, or at the wall core center. In this case, we *select* the **At wall finish** radio button (Figure 4.116).
8. *Click* the **OK** button (Figure 4.116). The **Area and Volume Computations** dialog box closes.
9. *Select* the room in the drawing area, as shown in **Figure 4.117**. The **Modify Room Tags** tab appears on the ribbon.

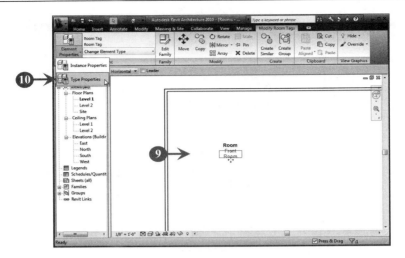

FIGURE 4.117

10. *Click* the lower part of the **Element Properties** split button and then *select* the **Type Properties** option from the drop-down list (Figure 4.117). The **Type Properties** dialog box appears, as shown in **Figure 4.118**.

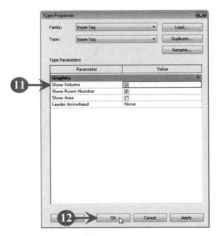

FIGURE 4.118

11. *Select* the **Show Volume** check box under the **Type Parameters** list box to display the volume of the room (Figure 4.118).

12. *Click* the **OK** button (Figure 4.118). The **Type Properties** dialog box closes and the volume of the room appears, as shown in **Figure 4.119**.

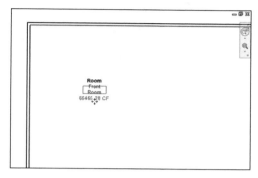

FIGURE 4.119

13. *Open* the **Type Properties** dialog box and then *select* the **Show Area** check box under the **Type Parameters** list box to display the area of the room, as shown in **Figure 4.120**.

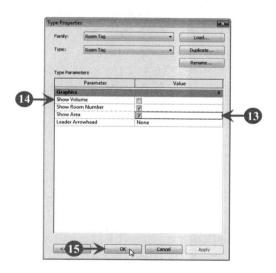

FIGURE 4.120

14. *Clear* the **Show Volume** check box (Figure 4.120).

15. *Click* the **OK** button (Figure 4.120). The area of the room appears, as shown in **Figure 4.121**.

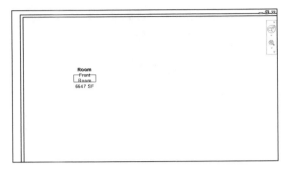

FIGURE 4.121

5 WORKING WITH SITE DESIGN

In This Chapter

◊ Using Toposurfaces
◊ Using Property Lines
◊ Creating a Building Pad
◊ Adding Parking Components
◊ Adding Site Components

A site is a location or plot of a ground that is used for designing a project. Autodesk Revit Architecture provides a feature known as site design that helps you to design a site. After designing a site, you can create a 3D view of that site in more realistic way; that is, you can create a toposurface in a site. A toposurface is an area of a land that is used to create building models and add different site components, such as parking areas, trees, building pads, and ponds.

In this chapter, you learn about toposurfaces, including how to create, split, and merge toposurfaces. Next, you learn how to create a boundary line in a toposurface by using the Property Line tool. You also learn how to create a building pad, which serves as the base of a building block. Next, you learn how to add parking components in toposurfaces. Finally, you learn how to add site components in toposurfaces.

Let's start by learning how to create toposurfaces in Autodesk Revit Architecture 2010.

5.1 USING TOPOSURFACES

A toposurface is a graphical representation of a land or terrain that is used to create a building site or plot. Autodesk Revit Architecture provides the Toposurface tool to create a topological surface. You can create a topological surface in the 3D or site plan view.

In this section, you learn how to complete the following tasks:

- Create a toposurface
- Add a toposurface region
- Split a toposurface
- Merge toposurfaces

Creating a Toposurface

You can create a toposurface by using any of the following methods:

- Picking points
- Points file

Let's first learn how to create a toposurface by using the picking points method.

Using Picking Points

In this method, you place different points of a toposurface by clicking the mouse button in the drawing area to define an area of the toposurface. The toposurface is created in the 3D or plan view; thus, you need to create a 3D or plan view before creating a toposurface in your project.

> **Note:** To discover how to create a 3D or plan view, refer to the "Working with Project Views" section of Chapter 3.

Perform the following steps to create a toposurface by using the picking points method:

1. *Click* **Start > All Programs > Autodesk > Autodesk Revit Architecture 2010 > Autodesk Revit Architecture 2010** to open the **Autodesk Revit Architecture 2010** window.
2. *Create* a new project.
3. *Double-click* the {**3D**} 3D view from the Project Browser to open the {3D} view, as shown in **Figure 5.1**.

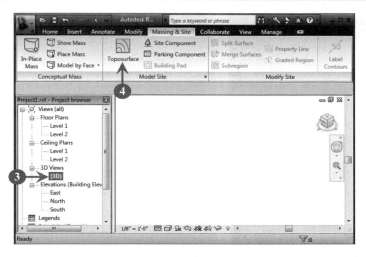

FIGURE 5.1

4. *Click* the **Toposurface** button from the **Model Site** panel under the **Massing & Site** tab (Figure 5.1).

5. *Select* an option beside the **Edit Surface** drop-down list of the options bar to display points of a toposurface at the specified location in the drawing area. In our case, we have selected the **Absolute Elevation** option from the drop-down list, as shown in **Figure 5.2**.

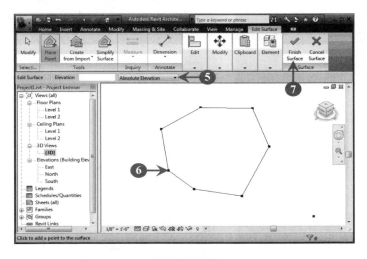

FIGURE 5.2

6. *Click* at different points in the drawing area (Figure 5.2).

7. *Click* the **Finish Surface** button from the **Surface** panel under the

Edit Surface tab (Figure 5.2). The toposurface is created, as shown in **Figure 5.3**.

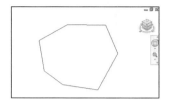

FIGURE 5.3

Figure 5.3 shows the toposurface that you have created. You can use this toposurface to design a building model and add components such as parks, roads, and trees.

Using a Points File

You can also create a toposurface from a points file. A points file is a text file that contains numeric values for the x, y, and z coordinates that specify the starting point from which to create a toposurface. The values of these coordinates must be separated with commas.

Perform the following steps to create a toposurface by using the points file method:

1. *Open* the **Notepad** editor and *create* a text file. In our case, we *create* a text file named **test.txt** and save it on the Windows desktop, as shown in **Figure 5.4**.

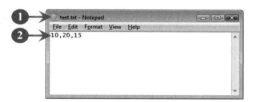

FIGURE 5.4

2. *Enter* the values for the x, y, and z coordinates in the points file. In our case, we have entered **10**, **20**, and **15** (Figure 5.4). After entering these values, *save* the changes in the **test.txt** file and *exit* the Notepad editor.

3. *Open* the **Autodesk Revit Architecture 2010** window and then *create* a new Autodesk Revit Architecture project.

4. *Double-click* the {**3D**} 3D view from the Project Browser to open the {3D} view, as shown in **Figure 5.5**.

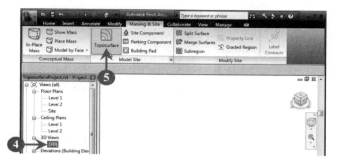

FIGURE 5.5

5. *Click* the **Toposurface** button from the **Model Site** panel under the **Massing & Site** tab (Figure 5.5).
6. *Click* the **Create from Import** drop-down button from the **Tools** panel under the **Edit Surface** tab and *select* the **Specify Points File** option from the drop-down list, as shown in **Figure 5.6**.

FIGURE 5.6

The **Open** dialog box appears, as shown in **Figure 5.7**.

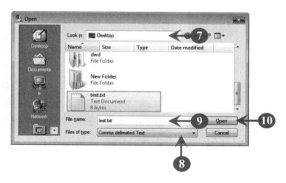

FIGURE 5.7

7. *Select* the location where you saved the **test.txt** file from the **Look in** drop-down list. In our case, we *select* the **Desktop** (Figure 5.7).

8. *Select* the **Comma delimited Text** option from the **Files of type** drop-down list to view all the text files (Figure 5.7).

9. *Select* the text file that you have created from the **File name** combo box. In our case, we *select* the **test.txt** file (Figure 5.7).

10. *Click* the **Open** button (Figure 5.7). The **Format** dialog box appears, as shown in **Figure 5.8**.

FIGURE 5.8

11. *Select* an option from the **One unit in the file equals one** drop-down list to specify the measurement of the toposurface area. In our case, we *select* the **Decimal feet** option (Figure 5.8).

12. *Click* the **OK** button (Figure 5.8).

13. *Click* the mouse button at different points in the drawing area to define an area of a toposurface, as shown in **Figure 5.9**.

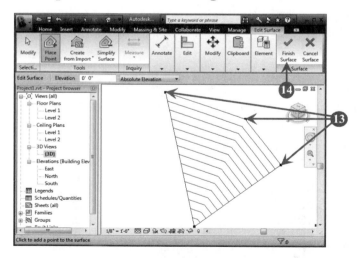

FIGURE 5.9

14. *Click* the **Finish Surface** button from the **Surface** panel under the **Edit Surface** tab (Figure 5.9).

The toposurface is created, as shown in **Figure 5.10**. Figure 5.10 shows that the toposurface is created by using the values of the x, y, and z coordinates that you entered in the **test.txt** points file.

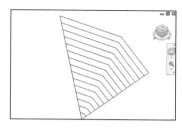

FIGURE 5.10

Adding a Toposurface Subregion in a Toposurface

In Autodesk Revit Architecture, toposurface subregions are surfaces that you sketch inside an existing toposurface. Toposurface subregions are used to add site components such as parking lots, roads, or ponds inside a toposurface.

Perform the following steps to add a toposurface subregion:

1. *Open* the **Autodesk Revit Architecture 2010** window.
2. *Create* a new project.
3. *Create* a 3D view in a project.

Note: Refer to the "3D Views" section of Chapter 3 for instructions on how to create a 3D view.

4. *Double-click* the **{3D}** 3D view from the Project Browser to open the {3D} view, as shown in **Figure 5.11**.

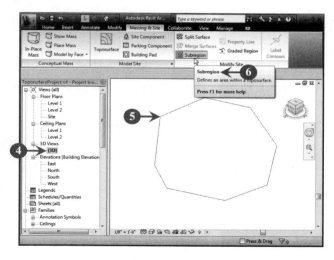

FIGURE 5.11

5. *Create* a toposurface in the drawing area by using picking points (Figure 5.11).

6. *Click* the **Subregion** button from the **Modify Site** panel under the **Massing & Site** tab (Figure 5.11).

After creating toposurface by using picking points, you can save it. In our case, we *save* it with the name **ToposurfaceProject.rvt**.

> **Note:** Refer to the section "Using Picking Points" in this chapter for instructions on how to create a toposurface.

7. *Click* the **Ellipse** (⬭) button from the **Draw** panel under the **Create Subregion Boundary** tab, as shown in **Figure 5.12**.

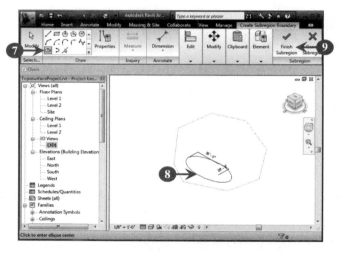

FIGURE 5.12

8. *Sketch* a toposurface subregion in the drawing area (Figure 5.12).
9. *Click* the **Finish Subregion** button from the **Subregion** panel to exit from the Subregion tool (Figure 5.12).

Figure 5.12 shows that the toposurface subregion is created in the toposurface.

Splitting a Toposurface

You can split a toposurface into two distinct surfaces and modify each split toposurface as per your requirements. You can add site components such as roads, lakes, plazas, or ponds in these split toposurfaces. You can also delete an entire portion of a split toposurface.

> **Note:** A toposurface cannot be split into more than two parts.

Perform the following steps to split a toposurface:

1. *Open* the **Autodesk Revit Architecture 2010** window.

2. *Open* the project that we created in the previous section.

3. *Double-click* the **{3D}** 3D view from the Project Browser, as shown in **Figure 5.13**.

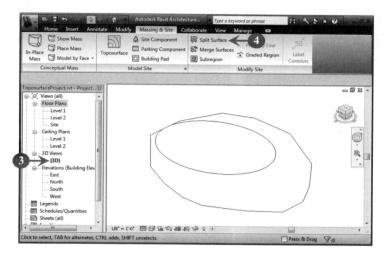

FIGURE 5.13

4. *Click* the **Split Surface** button from the **Modify Site** panel under the **Massing & Site** tab (Figure 5.13).

5. *Select* the toposurface that you want to split. In our case, we *select* the toposurface that we created earlier, as shown in **Figure 5.14**.

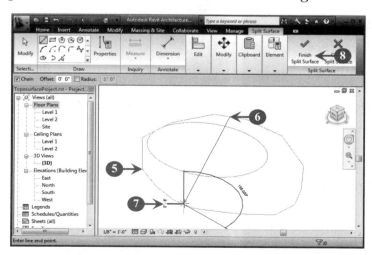

FIGURE 5.14

6. *Click* the mouse button in the drawing area to specify the starting point of the toposurface area that you want to split (Figure 5.14).

7. *Click* the mouse button in the drawing area to specify the ending point of the toposurface area that you want to split (Figure 5.14).

8. *Click* the **Finish Split Surface** button from the **Split Surface** panel under the **Split Surface** tab to exit from the Split Surface tool (Figure 5.14). Now the toposurface is divided into two portions.

9. *Select* one portion of the split toposurface and *move* it to another location in the drawing area, as shown in **Figure 5.15**. Figure 5.15 shows the two split surfaces of the toposurface.

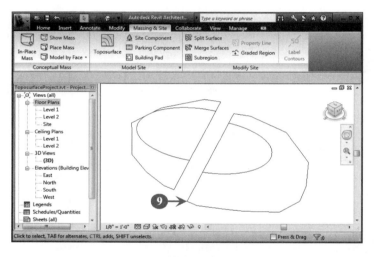

FIGURE 5.15

Merging Toposurfaces

You can merge two toposurfaces into one toposurface. The toposurfaces that you want to merge should be connected to each other.

Perform the following steps to merge two toposurfaces:

1. *Open* the **Autodesk Revit Architecture 2010** window.

2. *Create* a new project.

3. *Double-click* the **{3D}** 3D view from the Project Browser, as shown in **Figure 5.16**.

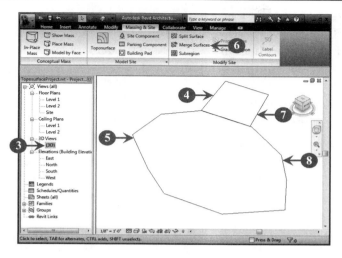

FIGURE 5.16

4. *Create* a toposurface in the drawing area. In our case, we *create* a rectangular toposurface (Figure 5.16).

5. *Create* another toposurface in the drawing area. In our case, we *create* a polygonal toposurface (Figure 5.16).

6. *Click* the **Merge Surfaces** button from the **Modify Site** panel under the **Massing & Site** tab (Figure 5.16).

7. *Select* the rectangle toposurface (Figure 5.16).

8. *Select* the polygon toposurface (Figure 5.16).

The selected toposurfaces are merged into one toposurface, as shown in **Figure 5.17**.

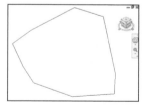

FIGURE 5.17

After creating, adding subregions to, merging, and splitting toposurfaces, let's create a boundary of a land in a toposurface.

5.2 USING PROPERTY LINES

Property lines are a boundary of a land or the site of a building project. You can use property lines to design a boundary of a building model or components, such as parking areas and ponds. Autodesk Revit Architecture provides sketching tools, such as line, rectangle, inscribed polygon, and circle tools, with which you can create the property lines of a toposurface.

Perform the following steps to create property lines:

1. *Open* the **Autodesk Revit Architecture 2010** window.
2. *Open* the project that we created in the previous section.
3. *Double-click* the **Site** plan view from the Project Browser, as shown in **Figure 5.18**.

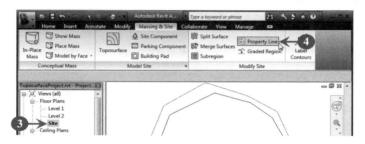

FIGURE 5.18

4. *Click* the **Property Line** button from the **Modify Site** panel under the **Massing & Site** tab (Figure 5.18). The **Create Property Line** dialog box appears, as shown in **Figure 5.19**.

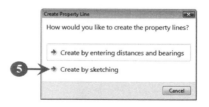

FIGURE 5.19

5. *Select* the **Create by sketching** option from the **Create Property Line** dialog box (Figure 5.19).
6. *Select* the ☐ button from the **Draw** panel under the **Create Property Line Sketch** tab, as shown in **Figure 5.20**.

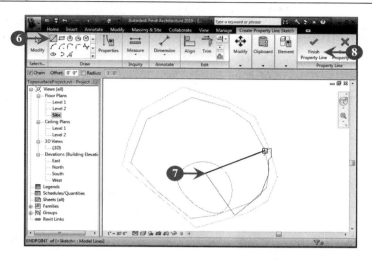

FIGURE 5.20

7. *Sketch* the property lines in the drawing area (Figure 5.20).
8. *Click* the **Finish Property Line** button from the **Property Line** panel under the **Create Property Line Sketch** tab (Figure 5.20). The property lines are created in the toposurface, as shown in **Figure 5.21**.

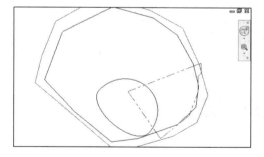

FIGURE 5.21

After creating property lines in the toposurface, we are ready to create a building pad in a toposurface.

5.3 CREATING A BUILDING PAD

A building pad is a flat surface that is used to create the base of a building block at the appropriate location in a toposurface. This toposurface element is created by grading and excavating a land surface or filling of materials, such as bricks in a land surface. You can add a building pad in a toposurface and also modify the structure and depth of the building pad.

Perform the following steps to create a building pad in a toposurface:

1. *Open* the **Autodesk Revit Architecture 2010** window.

2. *Open* the project that we created in the previous section.

3. *Double-click* the **Site** plan view from the Project Browser, as shown in **Figure 5.22**.

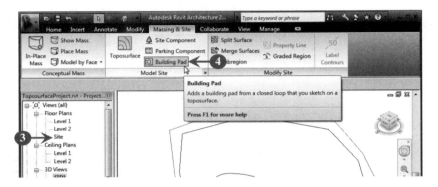

FIGURE 5.22

4. *Click* the **Building Pad** button from the **Model Site** panel under the **Massing & Site** tab (Figure 5.22).

5. *Select* the **Line** (✏) tool from the **Draw** panel under the **Create Pad Boundary** tab, as shown in **Figure 5.23**.

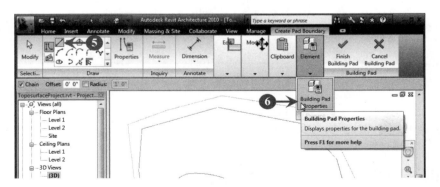

FIGURE 5.23

6. *Click* the **Element** drop-down button from the **Element** panel under the **Create Pad Boundary** tab and *select* the **Building Pad Properties** option from the drop-down list (Figure 5.23). The **Instance Properties** dialog box appears, as shown in **Figure 5.24**.

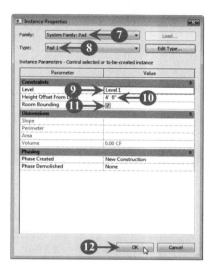

FIGURE 5.24

7. *Select* an option from the **Family** drop-down list to define the type of building pad. In our case, we *select* the **System Family: Pad** option (Figure 5.24).

8. *Select* an option from the **Type** drop-down list to define the name of the building pad. In our case, we *select* the **Pad 1** option (Figure 5.24).

9. *Select* an option from the **Level** drop-down list to set the level of the building pad. In our case, we *select* the **Level 1** option (Figure 5.24).

Note: Levels are finite horizontal planes of a building model that are divided into different floors, such as the first floor and second floor.

10. *Enter* the height of the building pad in the **Height Offset From Level** text box. In this case, we *enter* **4' 0"** (Figure 5.24).

11. *Select* the **Room Bounding** check box (Figure 5.24).

12. *Click* the **OK** button (Figure 5.24).

13. *Sketch* the building pad in the drawing area, as shown in **Figure 5.25**.

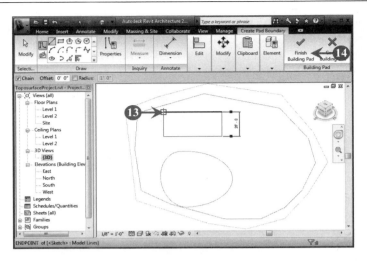

FIGURE 5.25

14. *Click* the **Finish Building Pad** button from the **Building Pad** panel under the **Create Pad Boundary** tab (Figure 5.25). The building pad is created in the toposurface, as shown in **Figure 5.26**.

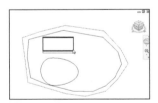

FIGURE 5.26

Let's now learn to create parking components, which are used to park vehicles in a toposurface.

5.4 ADDING PARKING COMPONENTS

Parking components are used to add parking spaces in a toposurface. Autodesk Revit Architecture provides the Parking Component tool with which you can create parking spaces in a toposurface.

Perform the following steps to add parking components in toposurfaces:

1. *Open* the **Autodesk Revit Architecture 2010** window.
2. *Open* the project that we created in the previous section.

3. *Double-click* the {3D} 3D view from the Project Browser, as shown in **Figure 5.27**.

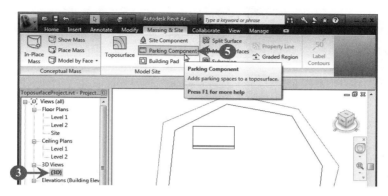

FIGURE 5.27

4. *Load* the **Parking Space–ADA** family in the project.

> **Note:** To load a family in the project, *click* the **Load** family button under the **Load from Library** panel of the **Insert** tab and then *select* the appropriate family by browsing the location of the family in the **Load Family** dialog box. Then *click* the **Open** button.

5. *Click* the **Parking Component** button from the **Model Site** panel of the **Massing & Site** tab (Figure 5.27).

6. *Click* the **Change Element Type** (also called **Type Selector**) drop-down button from the **Element** panel under the **Parking Component** tab and *select* an option from the drop-down list. In our case, we *select* the **9' × 18' (5' Aisle)** option, as shown in **Figure 5.28**.

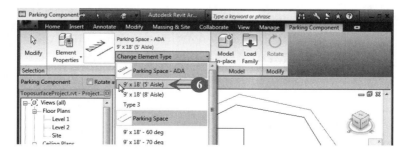

FIGURE 5.28

7. *Add* the parking components in the toposurfaces, as shown in **Figure 5.29**.

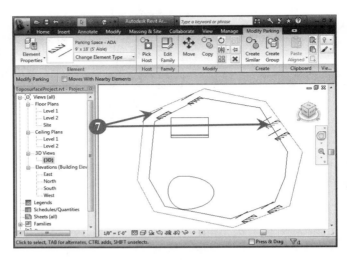

FIGURE 5.29

8. *Press* the **ESC** key twice to finish the insertion of parking components in toposurfaces. In Figure 5.29, you can see the different parking components are added in toposurfaces.

Let's now learn how to add site components in toposurfaces.

5.5 ADDING SITE COMPONENTS

Site components are used to place items, such as trees, utility poles, and fire hydrants (fireplugs) in a site plan. A site plan is an area on which a building is located; it includes components such as building pads, parking lots, sidewalks, and trees.

Perform the following steps to add site components in a toposurface:

1. *Open* the **Autodesk Revit Architecture 2010** window.
2. *Open* the project that we created in the previous section.
3. *Double-click* the **{3D}** 3D view from the Project Browser, as shown in **Figure 5.30**.

FIGURE 5.30

4. *Click* the **Site Component** button from the **Model Site** panel under the **Massing & Site** tab (Figure 5.30).

5. *Click* the **Change Element Type** drop-down button from the **Element** panel under the **Site Component** tab and *select* an option from the drop-down list. In our case, we *select* the **Japanese Cherry–15'** option, as shown in **Figure 5.31**.

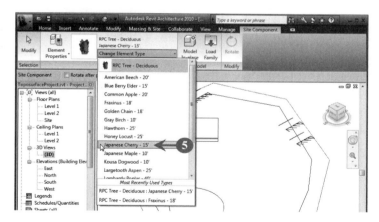

FIGURE 5.31

6. *Click* the mouse button at different locations in the toposurface to add the **Japanese Cherry–15'** trees (site component), as shown in **Figure 5.32**.

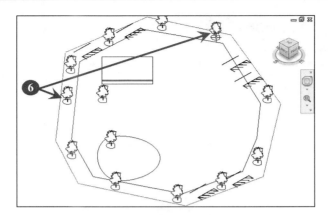

FIGURE 5.32

7. *Press* the **ESC** key twice to finish the addition of the **Japanese Cherry–15'** trees site component. In Figure 5.32, you can see that the **Japanese Cherry–15'** trees (site component) have been added in different locations of the toposurface.

6 WORKING WITH MASSING STUDIES

In This Chapter

◇ Exploring Massing Studies
◇ Using a Mass Family
◇ Creating a Mass Floor
◇ Creating a Wall from a Mass Face
◇ Creating a Floor from a Mass Floor
◇ Creating a Curtain System from a Mass Instance
◇ Creating a Roof from a Mass Instance

In Autodesk Revit Architecture, you can explore designing ideas and conceptualized shapes of building through massing studies. After finalizing the conceptual design of a building model, you can add elements such as walls, floors, and doors in the building model.

In Autodesk Revit Architecture 2010, when you design a building model, you can use a mass family to construct various mass instances (masses)—such as a polygon, rectangle, circle, sphere, cylinder, cone, and dome—and thereby design a building model. You can construct floors, walls, curtain systems, and roofs of a building model by using mass instances, such as a mass face and a mass floor. A mass floor is a horizontal surface of a mass that represents a floor of the building model. A mass face is the surface of an element, such as a wall, floor, or roof of a building model.

In this chapter, you learn about massing studies and discover terms that will help you construct a building model. You also learn how to construct mass instances, such as a cone and a sphere, so that you can design a building model. Further, you learn how a mass floor is used to divide a mass instance into slices. Next, you learn how to create a wall by using a mass face and how to create a floor by using a mass floor. You also learn how to create a curtain system of a building model by using a mass instance. In the end, you learn how to create a roof from a mass instance.

Let's start by exploring the terms used in massing studies.

6.1 EXPLORING MASSING STUDIES

Massing studies help you to explore the process of designing ideas and conceptualized shapes to build a building model. Once the conceptual design of a building model is completed, you can add needed elements such as walls, doors, and floors in the building model. You need to know various terms used in massing studies to understand the concept of massing studies. Table 6.1 describes various terms used in massing studies.

Term	Description
Massing	The process of visualizing, studying, and analyzing building models using mass instances.
Mass family	A list of shapes that belong to the mass elements, such as polygon, sphere, cylinder, and dome.
Mass instance or mass	A three-dimensional shape used in the initial design of a building model.
Conceptual design environment	A type of family editor that creates a conceptual design of a building model. A family editor is a tool that allows you to make changes to existing families or to create new families.
Mass form	The whole surface of each mass family.
Mass face	A surface of a mass instance that is used to create a building element, such as a wall or roof.
Mass floor	A horizontal surface of a mass.
Building elements	Elements, such as walls, roofs, floors, and curtains, that are used to create a building model.
Zoning envelope	Constraints of a building model, such as the maximum height of a building as well as the rear and side views of a wall or a building.

TABLE 6.1   **Terms used in massing studies**

Let's learn how a mass family is used to design a building model.

6.2 USING A MASS FAMILY

A mass family contains lists of three-dimensional and solid shapes or elements that are used to create the initial design of a building model. Some important shapes within a mass family are the cone, dome, pyramid, sphere, and cylinder.

In this section, you learn about the following topics, which enable you to create or design mass instances of a building model:

- Create an in-place mass
- Add a mass instance by using a mass family
- Merge two mass instances

We start by creating an in-place mass in Autodesk Revit Architecture.

Creating an In-Place Mass

The masses (e.g., cone, sphere, rectangle, and polygon) that are created within a project are known as in-place masses; those created outside a project are known as loadable masses. An in-place mass is created within the current project and exists only within the current project. In addition, in-place mass cannot be loaded into other projects.

Perform the following steps to create in-place masses:

1. *Click* **Start > All Programs > Autodesk > Autodesk Revit Architecture 2010 > Autodesk Revit Architecture 2010** to open the Autodesk Revit Architecture 2010 window.
2. *Create* a new project and *save* it with the name **Project1**.
3. *Create* a 3D view in the **Project1.rvt** file.

Note: Refer to the section "3D Views" in Chapter 3 for instructions on how to create a 3D view.

---

4. *Double-click* the {**3D**} view from the Project Browser to open the 3D view, as shown in **Figure 6.1**.

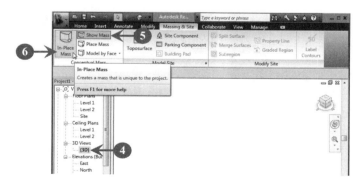

FIGURE 6.1

5. *Click* the **Show Mass** button from the **Conceptual Mass** panel under the **Massing & Site** tab (Figure 6.1).

6. *Click* the **In-Place Mass** button from the **Conceptual Mass** panel under the **Massing & Site** tab (Figure 6.1). The **Name** dialog box appears, as shown in **Figure 6.2**.

FIGURE 6.2

7. *Enter* a name of a mass in the **Name** text box. In our case, we *enter* the name **MyMass 1** (Figure 6.2).

8. *Click* the **OK** button (Figure 6.2). The **Model In-Place Mass** contextual tab appears, as shown in **Figure 6.3**.

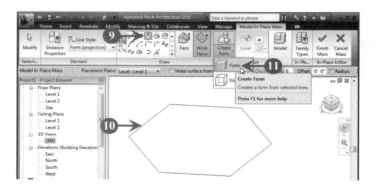

FIGURE 6.3

9. *Click* the **Inscribed Polygon** (⊙) button from the **Draw** panel under the **Model In-Place Mass** tab (Figure 6.3).

10. *Draw* the inscribed polygon mass in the drawing area (Figure 6.3).

11. *Click* the **Create Form** split button in the **Form** panel and *select* the **Form** option from drop-down list (Figure 6.3).

12. *Click* the **Finish Mass** button from the **In-Place Editor** panel under the **Modify Form** tab, as shown in **Figure 6.4**.

FIGURE 6.4

13. *Navigate* to **Families > Mass > MyMass 1** from the Project Browser to display the **MyMass 1** mass, as shown in **Figure 6.5**. In Figure 6.5, you can see that the inscribed polygon mass is created in the drawing area.

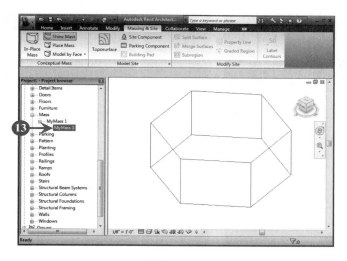

FIGURE 6.5

Adding a Mass Instance from a Mass Family

As you know, mass instances are three-dimensional shapes, such as a cone, cylinder, and dome, that are used to design a building model. These mass instances are stored in a mass family. Perform the following steps to add a mass instance in your project from a mass family:

1. *Open* the **Autodesk Revit Architecture 2010** window.
2. *Open* the file in which you want to add a mass instance from a mass family. In this case, we *open* the **Project1** file that we created in the previous section.

3. *Click* the **Load Family** button from the **Load from Library** panel under the **Insert** tab, as shown in **Figure 6.6**.

FIGURE 6.6

4. *Select* the **Mass** folder from the **Look in** drop-down list, as shown in **Figure 6.7**.

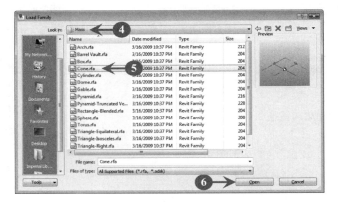

FIGURE 6.7

5. *Select* the desired mass instance file from the **Mass** folder. In our case, we *select* the **Cone.rfa** file (Figure 6.7).
6. *Click* the **Open** button (Figure 6.7).
7. *Click* the **Show Mass** button from the **Conceptual Mass** panel under the **Massing & Site** tab, as shown in **Figure 6.8**.

FIGURE 6.8

8. *Click* the **Place Mass** button from the **Conceptual Mass** panel under the **Massing & Site** tab (Figure 6.8).

9. *Click* the **Change Element Type** (also called **Type Selector**) drop-down button from the **Element** panel under the **Place Mass** tab and *select* the **Cone** option from the drop-down list, as shown in **Figure 6.9**.

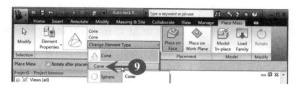

FIGURE 6.9

10. *Click* the **Place on Work Plane** button from the **Placement** panel under the **Place Mass** tab, as shown in **Figure 6.10**.

FIGURE 6.10

11. *Click* the mouse button in the drawing area to add the cone mass, as shown in **Figure 6.11**.

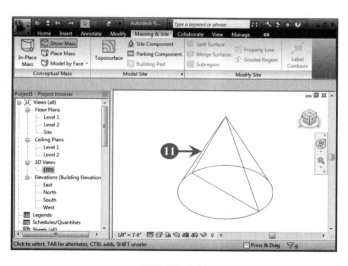

FIGURE 6.11

12. *Press* the **ESC** key twice to exit from the Cone tool.

Figure 6.11 shows that the cone mass is created in the drawing area.

Merging Mass Instances

You can merge mass instances, such as rectangles, inscribed and circumscribed polygons, circles, and ellipses, in a project. Perform the following steps to merge two mass instances:

1. *Open* the **Autodesk Revit Architecture 2010** window.
2. *Create* a new project.
3. *Draw* two mass instances in the drawing area. In our case, we *draw* two rectangles, as shown in **Figure 6.12**.

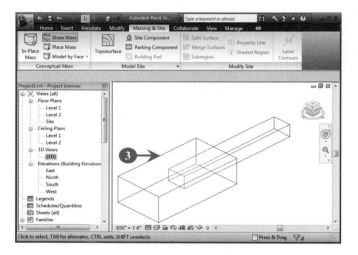

FIGURE 6.12

Note: You can create rectangle mass instances by performing the steps outlined in the "Creating an In-Place Mass" section of this chapter.

4. *Click* the **Join** split button in the **Edit Geometry** panel under the **Modify** tab and *select* the **Join Geometry** option from the drop-down list, as shown in **Figure 6.13**.

FIGURE 6.13

5. *Select* the first rectangle mass instance from the drawing area, as shown in **Figure 6.14**.

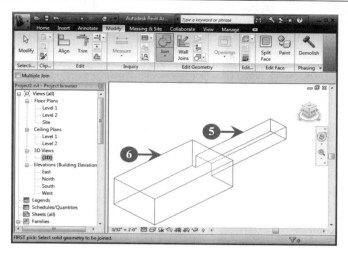

FIGURE 6.14

6. *Select* the second rectangle mass instance from the drawing area (Figure 6.14).

Figure 6.14 shows that the two rectangle mass instances are merged with each other.

We next learn how to create a mass floor from an in-place mass instance.

6.3 CREATING A MASS FLOOR

In Autodesk Revit Architecture, a mass floor is a horizontal surface of a floor in a building model. Each surface displays the geometric information for a mass, such as its dimensions, volume, and perimeter. Perform the following steps to create a mass floor in Autodesk Revit Architecture:

1. *Open* the **Autodesk Revit Architecture 2010** window.
2. *Create* a new project and *save* it. In our case, we *save* the project with the name **Project1**.
3. *Click* the **Section** button from the **Create** panel under the **View** tab, as shown in **Figure 6.15**.

FIGURE 6.15

4. *Click* the mouse button in the drawing area to specify the starting point of a section view, as shown in **Figure 6.16**.

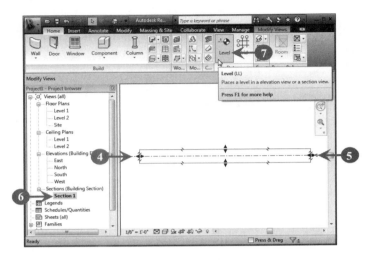

FIGURE 6.16

5. *Click* the mouse button in the drawing area to specify the ending point of a section view (Figure 6.16).

6. *Double-click* the **Section 1** section view from the Project Browser (Figure 6.16).

7. *Click* the **Level** button from the **Datum** panel under the **Home** tab (Figure 6.16).

8. *Click* the mouse button at different locations to define levels in the **Section 1** section view, as shown in **Figure 6.17**.

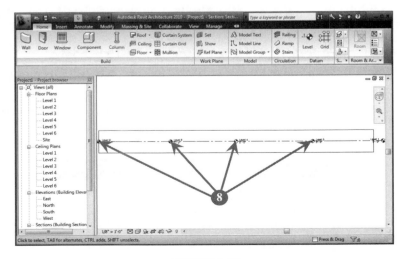

FIGURE 6.17

9. *Click* the **Show Mass** button from the **Conceptual Mass** panel under the **Massing & Site** tab, as shown in **Figure 6.18**.

FIGURE 6.18

10. *Click* the **In-Place Mass** button from the **Conceptual Mass** panel under the **Massing & Site** tab (Figure 6.18). The **Name** dialog box appears, as shown in **Figure 6.19**.

FIGURE 6.19

11. *Enter* the name of a mass floor in the **Name** text box. In our case, we *enter* **Building Mass 1** (Figure 6.19).
12. *Click* the **OK** button (Figure 6.19).
13. *Click* the **Inscribed Polygon** button from the **Draw** panel under the **Model In-Place Mass** tab, as shown in **Figure 6.20**.

FIGURE 6.20

The **Work Plane** dialog box appears, as shown in **Figure 6.21**.

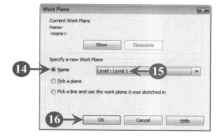

FIGURE 6.21

14. *Select* the **Name** radio button (Figure 6.21).

15. *Select* the **Level: Level 1** option from the drop-down list beside the Name radio button (Figure 6.21).

16. *Click* the **OK** button (Figure 6.21). The **Go To View** dialog box appears, as shown in **Figure 6.22**.

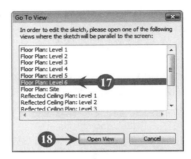

FIGURE 6.22

17. *Select* an option to define the levels of a mass floor from the **Go To View** dialog box. In our case, we *select* the **Floor Plan: Level 6** option (Figure 6.22).

18. *Click* the **Open View** button (Figure 6.22).

19. *Click* the **Work Plane** button from the **Draw** panel under the **Model In-Place Mass** tab, as shown in **Figure 6.23**.

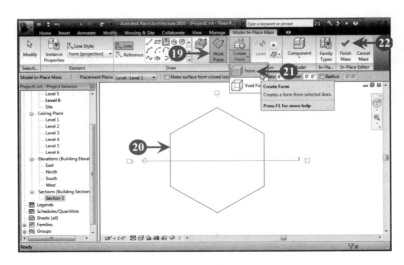

FIGURE 6.23

20. *Draw* the inscribed polygon mass instance in the drawing area (Figure 6.23).

21. *Click* the **Create Form** split button and *select* the **Form** option from the drop-down list (Figure 6.23).

22. *Click* the **Finish Mass** button from the **In-Place Editor** panel under the **Model In-Place Mass** tab (Figure 6.23).

23. *Select* the inscribed polygon mass instance from the drawing area, as shown in **Figure 6.24**.

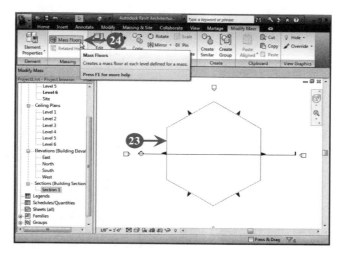

FIGURE 6.24

24. *Click* the **Mass Floors** button from the **Massing** panel under the **Modify Mass** tab (Figure 6.24). The **Mass Floors** dialog box appears, as shown in **Figure 6.25**.

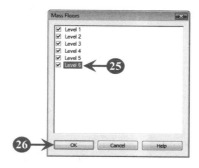

FIGURE 6.25

25. *Select* the **Level 1**, **Level 2**, **Level 3**, **Level 4**, **Level 5**, and **Level 6** check boxes from the **Mass Floors** dialog box (Figure 6.25).

26. *Click* the **OK** button (Figure 6.25).

27. *Click* the **3D View** split button in the **Create** panel under the **View** tab and *select* the **Default 3D** option from the drop-down list, as shown in **Figure 6.26**.

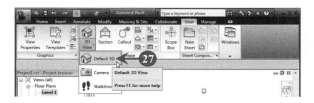

FIGURE 6.26

The inscribed polygon mass floor is created, as shown in **Figure 6.27**.

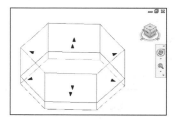

FIGURE 6.27

Let's now learn how to create a wall from a mass face.

6.4 CREATING A WALL FROM A MASS FACE

A mass face is a surface of an element or a mass, such as a wall, floor, or roof of a building model. Autodesk Revit Architecture provides the Model by Face tool with which you can create walls from a mass face. Perform the following steps to create a wall from a mass face:

1. *Open* the **Autodesk Revit Architecture 2010** window.

2. *Create* a new project.

3. *Click* the **3D View** split button from the **Create** panel of the **View** tab and *select* the **Default 3D** option from the drop-down list, as shown in **Figure 6.28**.

FIGURE 6.28

4. *Double-click* the **{3D}** view from the Project Browser to open the 3D view, as shown in **Figure 6.29**.

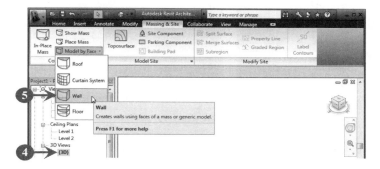

FIGURE 6.29

5. *Click* the **Model by Face** drop-down button of the **Conceptual Mass** panel under the **Massing & Site** tab and *select* the **Wall** option from the drop-down list (Figure 6.29).

6. *Click* the **Line** button from the **Draw** panel of the **Place Wall** tab, as shown in **Figure 6.30**.

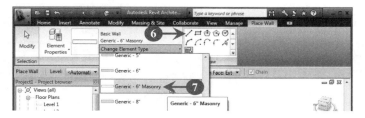

FIGURE 6.30

7. *Click* the **Change Element Type** drop-down button from the **Element** panel under the **Place Wall** tab and *select* the **Generic–6" Masonry** option from the drop-down list (Figure 6.30).

8. *Draw* the wall mass instance of a building model in the drawing area, as shown in **Figure 6.31**.

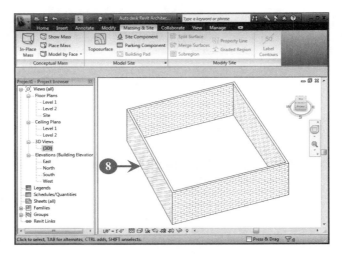

FIGURE 6.31

9. *Press* the **ESC** key twice to exit the Model by Face tool. In Figure 6.31, you can see that a wall has been created by using the Model by Face tool.

Let's now learn how to create a floor of a building model by using in-place mass instances.

6.5 CREATING A FLOOR FROM A MASS FLOOR

As you know, a mass floor is a horizontal surface of a mass that can be divided into slices (surfaces) that provide geometric information (e.g., area, perimeter, and volume) for the horizontal surface. Autodesk Revit Architecture provides the Model by Face tool with which you can create a floor from a mass floor.

> **Note:** To create a floor from a mass floor, first you need to create a mass floor. Perform all the steps outlined in the "Creating a Mass Floor" section of this chapter to create a mass floor.

Perform the following steps to create a floor from a mass floor:

1. *Create* a mass floor.
2. *Click* the **Model by Face** drop-down button from the **Conceptual Mass** panel under the **Massing & Site** tab and *select* the **Floor** option from the drop-down list, as shown in **Figure 6.32**.

FIGURE 6.32

3. *Select* the mass floor that you have created from the drawing area, as shown in **Figure 6.33**.

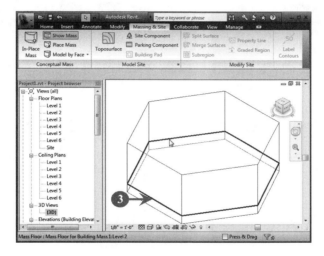

FIGURE 6.33

4. *Click* the **Change Element Type** drop-down button from the **Element** panel under the **Place Floor by Face** tab and *select* the **Steel Bar Joist 14"—VCT on Concrete** option from the drop-down list, as shown in **Figure 6.34**.

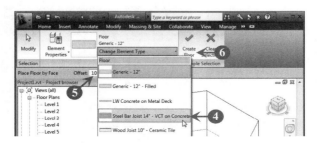

FIGURE 6.34

5. *Enter* a value for the edge of the mass floor in the options bar. In our case, we *enter* **10' 0"** (Figure 6.34).
6. *Click* the **Create Floor** button from the **Multiple Selection** panel under the **Place Floor by Face** tab (Figure 6.34).
7. *Click* the **Modify** button to exit the **Model by Face** tool, as shown in **Figure 6.35**. Figure 6.35 shows the floor mass instance.

FIGURE 6.35

Let's now learn how to create a curtain system from a mass instance of a building model.

6.6 CREATING A CURTAIN SYSTEM FROM A MASS INSTANCE

A curtain system is a component or element of a building model that contains panels and mullions. A panel is a small area of a curtain system that is made of glass, brick, or other materials. Each panel is connected to the structure by a joint known as mullion. Autodesk Revit Architecture 2010 provides the Curtain System tool with which you can create a curtain system in any exterior or interior part, such as a wall or dome of a building model. **Figure 6.36** shows a curtain system that contains 25 panels and 12 mullions.

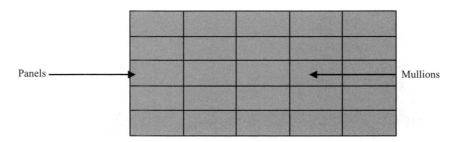

FIGURE 6.36

Note: Before creating a curtain system from a mass instance, you need to create the mass instance of a building model. You can create any mass instance, such as a line, rectangle, circle, or arc, and then circumscribe a polygon by performing the steps mentioned in the "Creating an In-Place Mass" section of this chapter.

Perform the following steps to create a curtain system from a mass instance:

1. *Double-click* the **{3D}** view from the Project Browser to open the 3D view, as shown in **Figure 6.37**.

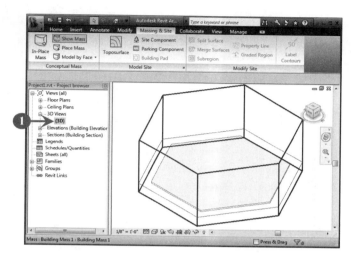

FIGURE 6.37

2. *Click* the **Model by Face** drop-down button from the **Conceptual Mass** panel under the **Massing & Site** tab and *select* the **Curtain System** option from the drop-down list, as shown in **Figure 6.38**.

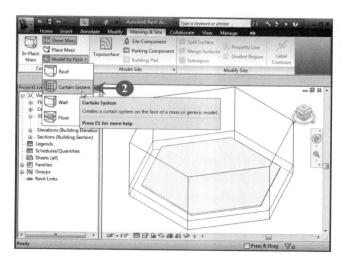

FIGURE 6.38

3. *Click* the **Change Element Type** drop-down button from the **Element** panel under the **Place Curtain System by Face** tab and *select* an option to define the size of the curtain system from the drop-down list. In our case, we *select* the **5' × 10'** option, as shown in **Figure 6.39**.

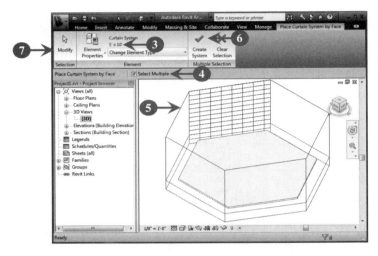

FIGURE 6.39

4. *Select* the **Select Multiple** check box from the options bar (Figure 6.39).
5. *Select* the wall element in the drawing area (Figure 6.39).
6. *Click* the **Create System** button from the **Multiple Selection** panel under the **Place Curtain System by Face** tab (Figure 6.39).
7. *Click* the **Modify** button from the **Selection** panel under the **Place Curtain System by Face** tab to exit the Curtain System tool (Figure 6.39). The wall element is covered with the curtain system in a building model, as shown in **Figure 6.40**. That is, the curtain system is created on the wall element, which contains mullions and panels.

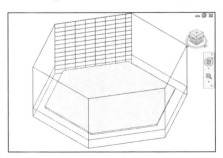

FIGURE 6.40

Let's now learn how to create a roof from a mass instance.

6.7 CREATING A ROOF FROM A MASS INSTANCE

Autodesk Revit Architecture 2010 provides the Roof by Face tool with which you can create roofs on nonvertical surfaces of a building model. Perform the following steps to create a roof from a mass instance:

1. *Open* the **Autodesk Revit Architecture 2010** window.
2. *Open* the project that we created in the previous section.
3. *Click* the **Model by Face** drop-down button from the **Conceptual Mass** panel under the **Massing & Site** tab and *select* the **Roof** option from the drop-down list, as shown in **Figure 6.41**.

FIGURE 6.41

4. *Clear* the **Select Multiple** check box from the options bar, as shown in **Figure 6.42**.

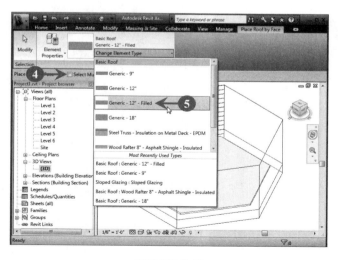

FIGURE 6.42

5. *Click* the **Change Element Type** drop-down button from the **Element** panel under the **Place Roof by Face** tab and *select* an option to define the type of roof from the drop-down list. In our case, we *select* the **Generic–12"– Filled** option (Figure 6.42).

6. *Select* a face of the mass instance, as shown in **Figure 6.43**.

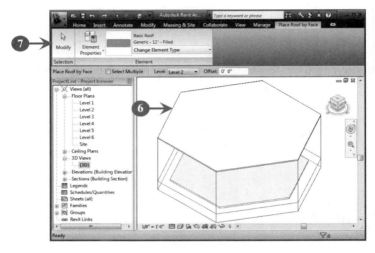

FIGURE 6.43

7. *Click* the **Modify** button from the **Selection** panel under the **Place Roof by Face** tab (Figure 6.43).

The roof element is created from the polygon mass instance, as shown in **Figure 6.44**.

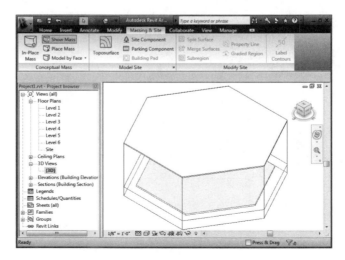

FIGURE 6.44

Chapter 7 ANNOTATION AND DETAILING

In This Chapter

◇ Creating Text Notes
◇ Creating Grids
◇ Creating Levels
◇ Creating a Keynote
◇ Adding a Tag
◇ Adding a Symbol
◇ Adding an Insulation
◇ Working with Labels
◇ Working with Detailing

In Autodesk Revit Architecture, elements such as text notes, symbols, tags, keynotes, dimensions, and labels are used to document a building model. These elements are known as annotations or annotation elements. In Autodesk Revit Architecture, the process known as detailing provides the information, such as types of material to be used in a building model, needed by the constructor to construct or design a final building model.

In this chapter, you learn how to create text notes that represent an element in a building model. Further, you learn how to create grids in a building model. Next, you learn how to create levels to define floors of a building model and a keynote that describes an element in a building model. You also learn how to add tags, symbols, and an insulation in a building model. In addition, you learn how to work with labels; that is, you learn how to create and apply labels to a tag in a building model. In the end, you learn how to work with detailing.

Let's start by learning how to create text notes for labeling elements of a building model.

7.1 CREATING TEXT NOTES

A text note is an annotation that consists of a text (message) and a leader line with an arrow. The text of a text note is connected to an element through the leader line. This text note is used to represent an element of a building model. The unit for measuring a text note is paper space. For example, 1.2" paper space of a text note appears as ½" height on a sheet.

Figure 7.1 shows a text note with a leader line followed by an arrow. In Figure 7.1, you can see that the text note represents the curtain system element of the building model.

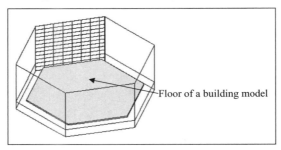

Floor of a building model

FIGURE 7.1

Perform the following steps to create a text note in Autodesk Revit Architecture:

1. *Click* **Start > All Programs > Autodesk > Autodesk Revit Architecture 2010 > Autodesk Revit Architecture 2010** to open the **Autodesk Revit Architecture 2010** window.

2. *Open* the file in which you want to add a text note. In our case, we *open* the **home.rvt** file.

3. *Double-click* the **{3D}** view from the Project Browser to open the 3D view, as shown in **Figure 7.2**.

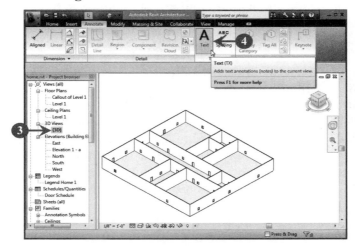

FIGURE 7.2

4. *Click* the **Text** button from the **Text** panel under the **Annotate** tab (Figure 7.2).

5. *Click* the **Change Element Type** (also called **Type Selector**) drop-down button from the **Element** panel under the **Place Text** tab and *select* an option to change the font size from the drop-down list. In our case, we *select* the **1/4" Arial** option, as shown in **Figure 7.3**.

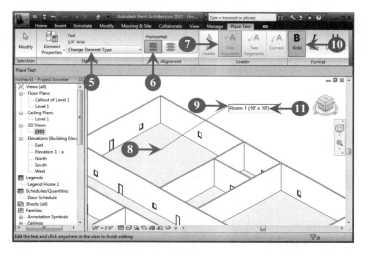

FIGURE 7.3

6. *Click* the **Left** alignment (▤) button from the **Alignment** panel under the **Place Text** tab (Figure 7.3).

7. *Click* the **One Segment** button from the **Leader** panel under the **Place Text** tab (Figure 7.3).

8. *Click* the mouse button in the drawing area (Figure 7.3).

9. *Drag* the mouse button to create a text note (Figure 7.3).

10. *Click* the **Bold** button from the **Format** panel under the **Place Text** tab (Figure 7.3).

11. *Enter* a name of the room element in the note text box. In our case, we *enter* **Room 1 (10' × 10')**, as shown in Figure 7.3.

12. *Press* the **ESC** key to exit the Text tool. The Room 1 (10' × 10') text note is created, as shown in **Figure 7.4**.

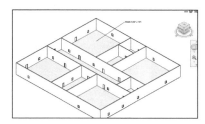

FIGURE 7.4

Now let's learn how to create grids in a building model.

7.2 CREATING GRIDS

Grids are series of lines or arcs that are used to draw or add elements, such as walls, furniture, doors, and windows, in a building model. They help you create a building model and add elements at the specific locations of the building model easily. When you draw grids in the drawing area, Autodesk Revit Architecture automatically inserts numbers at the ending point of each grid. You can also add alphabets at the ending point of each grid.

Perform the following steps to create grids in the drawing area:

1. *Open* the **Autodesk Revit Architecture 2010** window.
2. *Open* the file in which you want to create grids—in our case, the **home.rvt** file.
3. *Double-click* the **Level 1** ceiling plans view from the Project Browser to open it, as shown in **Figure 7.5**.

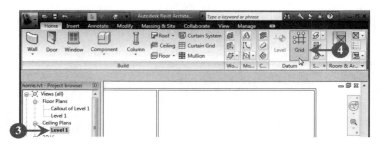

FIGURE 7.5

4. *Click* the **Grid** button from the **Datum** panel under the **Home** tab (Figure 7.5). The **Place Grid** contextual tab appears on the ribbon, as shown in **Figure 7.6**. A contextual tab is similar to a tab that contains a set of tools, drop-down buttons, split buttons, and panels. For example, when you click the **Grid** button on the ribbon (Figure 7.5), the **Place Grid** contextual tab appears on the ribbon, which contains the **Modify** tool, **Element Properties** drop-down button, and **Selection** and **Draw** panels.

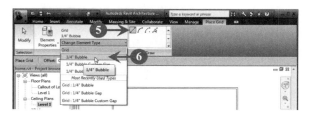

FIGURE 7.6

5. *Click* the **Line** (⬚) button from the **Draw** panel under the **Place Grid** tab (Figure 7.6).

6. *Click* the **Change Element Type** drop-down button from the **Element** panel under the **Place Grid** tab and *select* an option to change the size of grids from the drop-down list. In our case, we *select* the **1/4" Bubble** option (Figure 7.6).

7. *Click* the mouse button in the drawing area to specify the starting point of the grid, as shown in **Figure 7.7**.

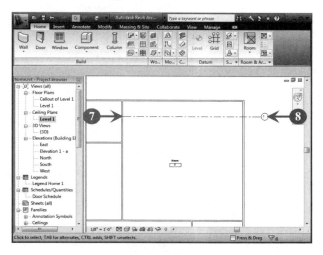

FIGURE 7.7

8. *Click* the mouse button in the drawing area to specify the ending point of the grid (Figure 7.7).

9. *Press* the **ESC** key twice to exit the Grid tool.

Figure 7.7 shows that a grid is created in the drawing area and the number 1 is assigned as the endpoint of the grid. Similarly, you can create more grids, as shown in **Figure 7.8**.

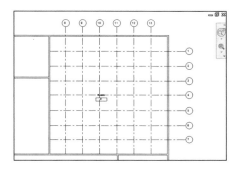

FIGURE 7.8

Let's learn how to create levels in Autodesk Revit Architecture.

7.3 CREATING LEVELS

In Autodesk Revit Architecture, levels are finite horizontal planes of a building model that are divided into different floor levels, such as the first floor and the second floor. Levels are created and visible only in the section or elevation view. Autodesk Revit Architecture provides the Level tool to define the vertical heights, such as first floor, top of wall, or bottom of foundation, in a building model.

> **Note:** You need to create a section or elevation view before creating levels in a building model. Refer to the "Working with Project Views" section of Chapter 3 to learn how to create section views.

Perform the following steps to create levels in a building model:

1. *Open* the **Autodesk Revit Architecture 2010** window.
2. *Open* the file in which you want to create levels—in our case, **home.rvt**.
3. *Double-click* the **Section 1** section view from the Project Browser to open it, as shown in **Figure 7.9**.

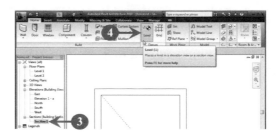

FIGURE 7.9

4. *Click* the **Level** button from the **Datum** panel under the **Home** tab (Figure 7.9). The **Place Level** contextual tab appears on the ribbon, as shown in **Figure 7.10**.

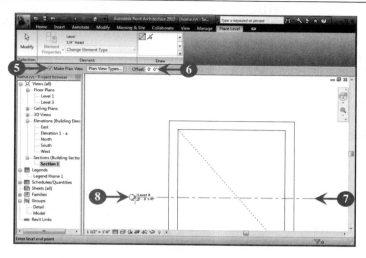

FIGURE 7.10

5. *Select* the **Make Plan View** check box from the options bar (Figure 7.10).
6. *Enter* a distance (in length) of the levels in the **Offset** text box of the options bar. In our case, we *enter* **0' 0"** (Figure 7.10).
7. *Click* the mouse button in the drawing area (Figure 7.10).
8. *Draw* the level lines by moving the cursor horizontally (Figure 7.10).
9. *Press* the **ESC** key to exit the Level tool.

Figure 7.10 shows that the level is created. Similarly, you can create more levels in a building model, as shown in **Figure 7.11**. In Figure 7.11, four levels named Level 8, Level 9, Level 10, and Level 11 are created in the drawing area.

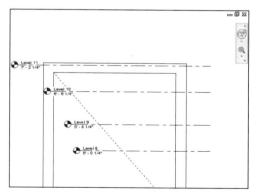

FIGURE 7.11

Let's learn how to create the keynote annotation in Autodesk Revit Architecture.

7.4 CREATING A KEYNOTE

A keynote is a type of annotation that is used to describe an element of a building model. It provides information such as the types of materials used to create an element of a building model. For example, the keynote annotation describes the type and size of bricks used to build the wall element.

Perform the following steps to add keynotes in a building model:

1. *Open* the **Autodesk Revit Architecture 2010** window.
2. *Open* the file in which you want to create a keynote—in our case, **home.rvt**.
3. *Double-click* the **Level 1** plan view from the Project Browser to open it, as shown in **Figure 7.12**.

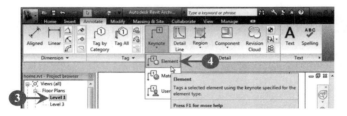

FIGURE 7.12

4. *Click* the **Keynote** drop-down button from the **Tag** panel under the **Annotate** tab and *select* the **Element** option from the drop-down list (Figure 7.12). The **Place Element Keynote** contextual tab appears on the ribbon, as shown in **Figure 7.13**.

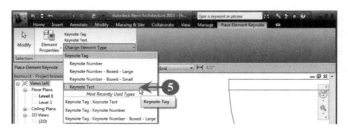

FIGURE 7.13

5. *Click* the **Change Element Type** drop-down button from the **Element** panel under the **Place Element Keynote** tab and *select* an option to specify the type of text of the keynote from the drop-down list. In our case, we *select* the **Keynote Text** option (Figure 7.13).

6. *Select* an option for writing the text of an element from the options bar. In our case, we *select* the **Horizontal** option, as shown in **Figure 7.14**.

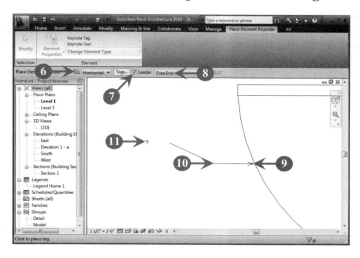

FIGURE 7.14

7. *Select* the **Leader** check box from the options bar (Figure 7.14).

8. *Select* the **Free End** option from the options bar (Figure 7.14).

9. *Click* the mouse button near the door element in the drawing area to create the first leader line of the keynote (Figure 7.14).

10. *Click* the mouse button in the drawing area to create the second leader line of the keynote (Figure 7.14).

11. *Click* the mouse button in the drawing area to specify the ending point of the second leader line of the keynote (Figure 7.14). The **Keynotes** dialog box appears, as shown in **Figure 7.15**.

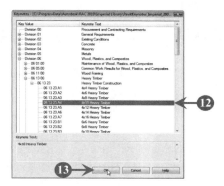

FIGURE 7.15

12. *Expand* **Division 06 > 06 13 00 > 06 13 23** and *select* a key value to define the keynote text. In our case, we *select* the **06 13 23 A4** key value (Figure 7.15).

13. *Click* the **OK** button (Figure 7.15). The keynote of the door element is created with the name **4 × 10 Heavy Timber**, as shown in **Figure 7.16**.

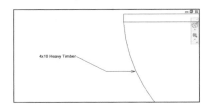

FIGURE 7.16

Let's now learn how to add a tag to identify an element of a building model.

7.5 ADDING A TAG

A tag is another type of annotation that is used to identify elements, such as rooms, doors, walls, and windows, of a building model. It describes information about the element's attributes, such as the room number, room name, computed area, and volume of elements (rooms) used in a building model. Autodesk Revit Architecture provides the Tag tool with which you can add tags in a building model.

Perform the following steps to add a tag of an element in a building model:

1. *Open* the **Autodesk Revit Architecture 2010** window.

2. *Open* the file in which you want to add a tag—in our case, **home.rvt**.

3. *Double-click* the **Level 1** plan view from the Project Browser to open it, as shown in **Figure 7.17**.

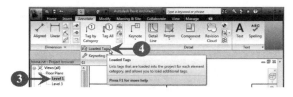

FIGURE 7.17

4. *Click* the drop-down arrow at the bottom of the **Tag** panel under the **Annotate** tab and *select* the **Loaded Tags** option from drop-down list (Figure 7.17). The **Tags** dialog box appears, as shown in **Figure 7.18**.

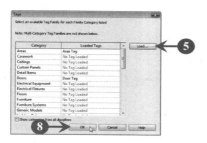

FIGURE 7.18

5. *Click* the **Load** button to load the tag annotation (Figure 7.18). The **Load Family** dialog box appears, as shown in **Figure 7.19**.

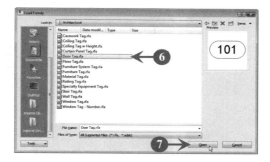

FIGURE 7.19

6. *Select* a file in which you want to create a tag. In our case, we *select* the **Door Tag.rfa** file from the **Architectural** folder by navigating to **Imperial Library>Annotations** (Figure 7.19).

7. *Click* the **Open** button to open the **Door Tag.rfa** file (Figure 7.19). The **Open** dialog box closes.

8. *Click* the **OK** button to close the **Tags** dialog box (Figure 7.18).

9. *Click* the **Tag by Category** button from the **Tag** panel under the **Annotate** tab, as shown in **Figure 7.20**.

FIGURE 7.20

10. *Select* the **Horizontal** option from the options bar, as shown in **Figure 7.21**.

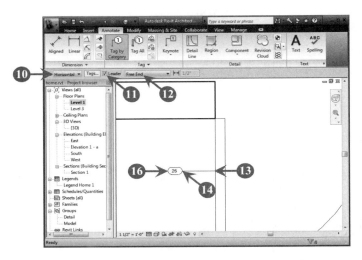

FIGURE 7.21

11. *Select* the **Leader** check box from the options bar (Figure 7.21).

12. *Select* an option to draw a tag in the drawing area from the options bar. In our case, we *select* the **Free End** option (Figure 7.21).

13. *Select* an element of a building model in which you want to add a tag. In our case, we *select* the door element (Figure 7.21).

Note: When you select an element in the drawing area, Autodesk Revit Architecture automatically specifies the starting point of the leader line of the tag.

14. *Click* the mouse button in the drawing area to specify an ending point for the leader line of the door tag (Figure 7.21).

15. *Press* the **ESC** key to exit the Tag tool.

Note: When you add a tag to an element in the drawing area, by default Autodesk Revit Architecture assigns a number (in our case, 26) at the end of the tag annotation. You can modify this number as per your requirement.

16. *Double-click* the **26** number in the door text box, as shown in **Figure 7.22**.

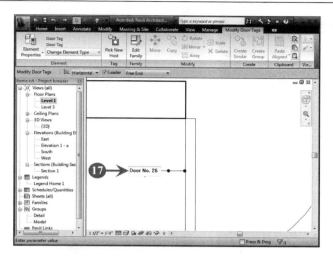

FIGURE 7.22

17. *Enter* a name for the door tag in the tag text box. In our case, we *enter* **Door No. 26** (Figure 7.22).

18. *Press* the **ENTER** key to apply the modified text on the door tag, as shown in **Figure 7.23**. In Figure 7.23, you can see that the door tag shows the door number of a building model.

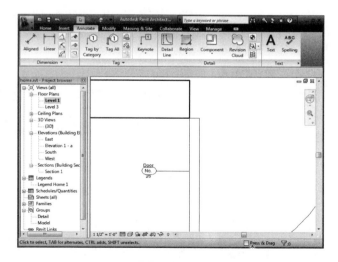

FIGURE 7.23

Let's now learn how to add a symbol that represents an element in a building model.

7.6 ADDING A SYMBOL

A symbol is a graphical representation of an annotation element, such as a keynote, tag, or label. It is used to identify an element of a building model. Symbols are view-specific annotations. Thus, when you add a symbol in a view, the symbol is available only in the view in which it is added.

Perform the following steps to add a symbol in a building model:

1. *Open* the **Autodesk Revit Architecture 2010** window.
2. *Open* the file in which you want to add a symbol—in our case, **home.rvt**.
3. *Double-click* the **Level 1** plan view from the Project Browser to open it, as shown in **Figure 7.24**.

FIGURE 7.24

4. *Click* the **Symbol** button from the **Detail** panel under the **Annotate** tab (Figure 7.24). The **Place Symbol** contextual tab appears on the ribbon, as shown in **Figure 7.25**.

FIGURE 7.25

5. *Enter* a value to specify the number of leaders (lines) added with a symbol in the **Number of Leaders** text box on the options bar. In our case, we *enter* **0** (Figure 7.25).
6. *Click* the **Load Family** button from the **Detail** panel under the **Place Symbol** tab (Figure 7.25). The **Load Family** dialog box appears, as shown in **Figure 7.26**.

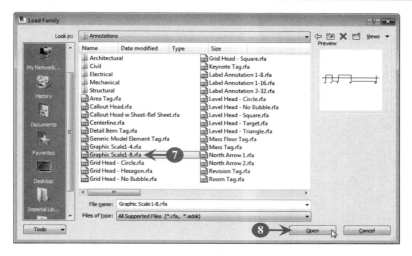

FIGURE 7.26

7. *Select* a file in which you want to load a symbol. In our case, we *select* the **Graphic Scale1-8.rfa** file from the **Annotations** folder (Figure 7.26).

8. *Click* the **Open** button (Figure 7.26).

9. *Click* the **Change Element Type** drop-down button of the **Element** panel under the **Place Symbol** tab and *select* an option from the drop-down list. In our case, we *select* the **Graphic Scale1-8** option, as shown in **Figure 7.27**.

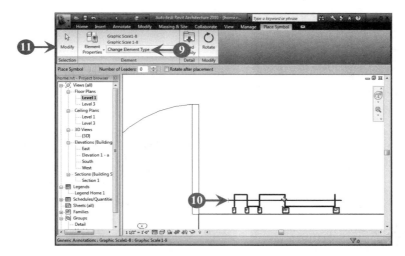

FIGURE 7.27

10. *Click* the mouse button to add the **Graphic Scale1-8** symbol in the drawing area (Figure 7.27).

11. *Click* the **Modify** button from the **Selection** panel under the **Place Symbol** tab (Figure 7.27).
12. *Press* the **ESC** key to exit the Symbol tool. The Graphic Scale 1-8 symbol is added in the building model, as shown in **Figure 7.28**.

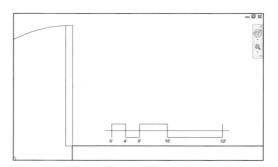

FIGURE 7.28

Next, let's learn how to add an insulating element in a building model.

7.7 ADDING AN INSULATION

Insulation is an element that is used in a building model to retain heat in winter and prevent heat entry in summer. Autodesk Revit Architecture provides the Insulation tool with which you can draw an insulation element in your building model. You can use an insulation element in conjunction with roof and wall elements of a building model.

Perform the following steps to add insulation in your building model:

1. *Open* the **Autodesk Revit Architecture 2010** window.
2. *Open* the file in which you want to add an insulation—in our case, **home.rvt**.
3. *Double-click* the **Level 1** plan view from the Project Browser to open it, as shown in **Figure 7.29**.

FIGURE 7.29

4. *Click* the **Insulation** button from the **Detail** pane under the **Annotate** tab (Figure 7.29). The **Place Insulation** contextual tab appears on the ribbon, as shown in **Figure 7.30**.

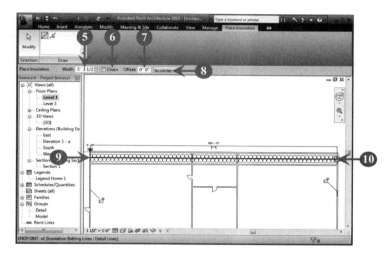

FIGURE 7.30

5. *Enter* the width of the insulation element in the **Width** text box of the options bar. In our case, we *enter* **5' 3** (Figure 7.30).

6. *Clear* the **Chain** check box from the options bar (Figure 7.30).

7. *Enter* the distance between two insulation elements in the **Offset** text box of the options bar. In our case, we *enter* **0' 0"** (Figure 7.30).

8. *Select* the **to center** option from the options bar (Figure 7.30).

9. *Click* the mouse button in the drawing area to specify the starting point of the insulation (Figure 7.30).

10. *Click* the mouse button in the drawing area to specify the ending point of the insulation (Figure 7.30).

11. *Press* the **ESC** key to exit the Insulation tool. The insulation element is added in a building model, as shown in **Figure 7.31**.

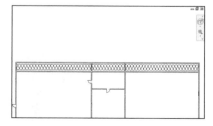

FIGURE 7.31

Let's now learn how a label is used to add a description of an element of a building model.

7.8 WORKING WITH LABELS

A label is text that is used to add information, such as a project name, project date, project number, and name of the architect who creates a project, in Autodesk Revit Architecture. It gives a detailed description of each element, such as walls, doors, windows, and floors, of a building model. In this section you learn how to create a label and apply the newly created label to a tag.

Let's first learn to create a label in Autodesk Revit Architecture.

Creating a Label

A label gives detailed information, such as the height, width, model, and cost, related to the elements used in a building model. Autodesk Revit Architecture provides several files, such as **Callout Head.rft, Door Tag.rft, Room Tag.rft, View Title.rft,** and **Level Head.rft,** with which you can create labels in a project.

Perform the following steps to create labels in Autodesk Revit Architecture:

1. *Open* the **Autodesk Revit Architecture 2010** window.
2. *Click* the **Application (■)** button, as shown in **Figure 7.32**. The application menu appears. The **New Annotation Symbol—Select Template File** dialog box appears, as shown in **Figure 7.33**.

FIGURE 7.32

3. *Select* **New > Annotation Symbol** from the application menu (Figure 7.32).

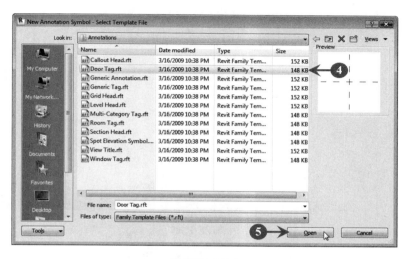

FIGURE 7.33

4. *Select* the file in which you want to load the annotation to add a label. In our case, we *select* the **Door Tag.rft** file from the **Annotations** folder (Figure 7.33).

5. *Click* the **Open** button (Figure 7.33).

6. *Click* the **Label** button from the **Annotate** panel under the **Create** tab, as shown in **Figure 7.34**.

FIGURE 7.34

The **Place Label** contextual tab appears on the ribbon, as shown in **Figure 7.35**.

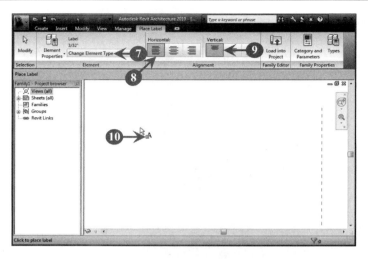

FIGURE 7.35

7. *Click* the **Change Element Type** drop-down button of the **Element** panel under the **Place Label** tab and *select* an option to specify the size of the label from the drop-down list. In our case, we *select* the **3/32** option (Figure 7.35).

8. *Click* the **Left** button from **Alignment** panel under the **Place Label** tab (Figure 7.35).

9. *Click* the **Top** button from **Alignment** panel under the **Place Label** tab (Figure 7.35).

10. *Click* the mouse button in the drawing area (Figure 7.35). The **Edit Label** dialog box appears, as shown in **Figure 7.36**.

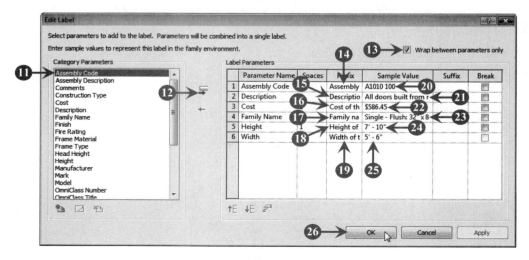

FIGURE 7.36

11. *Select* an option to define the description (attribute) of the door element from the **Category Parameters** list box. In our case, we *select* the **Assembly Code** option (Figure 7.36).

12. *Click* the **Add parameter(s) to label** button (Figure 7.36).

Similarly, repeat steps 11 and 12 to select the **Description, Cost, Family Name, Height**, and **Width** options from the **Category Parameters** list box to define the label of the door element.

13. *Select* the **Wrap between parameters only** check box (Figure 7.36).

14. *Enter* a name for the attribute (assembly code) of the door element in the text box corresponding to the first row of the **Prefix** column. In our case, we *enter* **Assembly code of the doors element:** (Figure 7.36).

15. *Enter* a name for the attribute (description) of the door element in the text box corresponding to the second row of the **Prefix** column. In our case, we *enter* **Description of the doors element:** (Figure 7.36).

16. *Enter* a name for the attribute (cost) of the door element in the text box corresponding to the third row of the **Prefix** column. In our case, we *enter* **Cost of the doors element:** (Figure 7.36).

17. *Enter* a name for the attribute (family name) of the door element in the text box corresponding to the fourth row of the **Prefix** column. In our case, we *enter* **Family name of the doors element:** (Figure 7.36).

18. *Enter* a name for the attribute (height) of the door element in the text box corresponding to the fifth row of the **Prefix** column. In our case, we *enter* **Height of the doors element:** (Figure 7.36).

19. *Enter* a name for the attribute (width) of the door element in the text box corresponding to the sixth row of the **Prefix** column. In our case, we *enter* **Width of the doors element:** (Figure 7.36).

20. *Enter* a value for the attribute (assembly code) of the door element in the text box corresponding to the first row of the **Sample Value** column. In our case, we *enter* **A1010 100** (Figure 7.36).

21. *Enter* a value for the attribute (description) of the door element in the text box corresponding to the second row of the **Sample Value** column. In our case, we *enter* **All doors built from rosewood** (Figure 7.36).

22. *Enter* a value for the attribute (cost) of the door element in the text box corresponding to the third row of the **Sample Value** column. In our case, we *enter* **$586.45** (Figure 7.36).

23. *Enter* a value for the attribute (family name) of the door element in the text box corresponding to the fourth row of the **Sample Value** column. In our case, we *enter* **Single–Flush: 32" × 84"** (Figure 7.36).

24. *Enter* a value for the attribute (height) of the door element in the text box corresponding to the fifth row of the **Sample Value** column. In our case, we *enter* **7'–10"** (Figure 7.36).

25. *Enter* a value for the attribute (width) of the door element in the text box corresponding to the sixth row of the **Sample Value** column. In our case, we *enter* **5'–6"** (Figure 7.36).

26. *Click* the **OK** button (Figure 7.36).

27. *Click* the **Modify** button from the **Selection** panel under the **Place Label** tab, as shown in **Figure 7.37**.

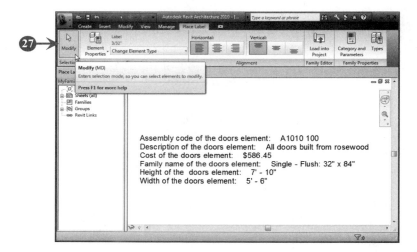

FIGURE 7.37

28. *Save* this label to load the created label in other projects. In our case, we *save* the label with the name **MyFamily.rfa**.

The labels of the doors element are created, as shown in **Figure 7.38**. In Figure 7.38, you can see that the label of the door element, containing its cost, height, width, and family, is stored in the **MyFamily.rfa** file.

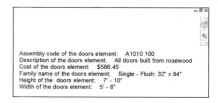

FIGURE 7.38

Applying a Label to a Tag

After creating a label, you can apply it to a tag. Perform the following steps to apply the created label to a door tag:

1. *Open* the **Autodesk Revit Architecture 2010** window.
2. *Open* the file in which you want to apply a label to a tag—in our case, **home.rvt**.
3. *Click* the **Load Family** button from the **Load from Library** panel under the **Insert** tab, as shown in **Figure 7.39**.

FIGURE 7.39

The **Load Family** dialog box appears, as shown in **Figure 7.40**.

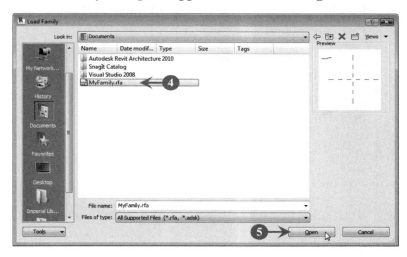

FIGURE 7.40

4. *Select* the file in which you have stored the created label. In our case, we *select* the **MyFamily.rfa** file from the **Documents** folder (Figure 7.40).
5. *Click* the **Open** button (Figure 7.40).
6. *Click* the **Tag by Category** button from the **Tag** panel under the **Annotate** tab, as shown in **Figure 7.41**.

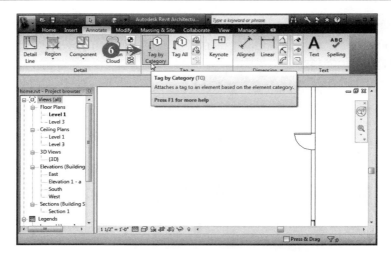

FIGURE 7.41

7. *Select* an element to which you want to apply the created label. In our case, we *select* the door element, as shown in **Figure 7.42**.

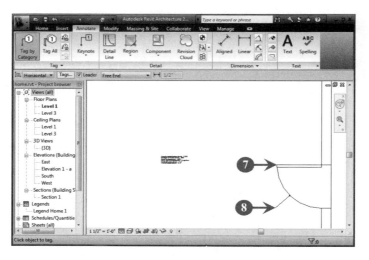

FIGURE 7.42

8. *Double-click* the mouse button in the drawing area to apply the created label to the door element (Figure 7.42). The label created in the **MyFamily.rfa** file is applied to the door element.

9. *Press* the **ESC** key to exit the Tag by Category tool.

10. *Double-click* the label of the door element, as shown in **Figure 7.43**.

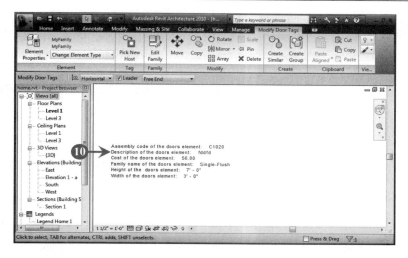

FIGURE 7.43

The **Change Parameter Values** dialog box appears, as shown in **Figure 7.44**.

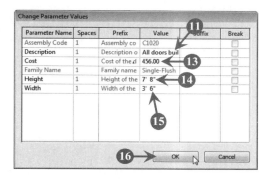

FIGURE 7.44

11. *Enter* a description of the attribute (description) of the door element in the text box corresponding to the **Description** row of the **Value** column. In our case, we *enter* **All doors built from rosewood** (Figure 7.44).

The **Revit** message box appears, as shown in **Figure 7.45**.

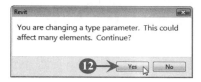

FIGURE 7.45

12. *Click* the **Yes** button (Figure 7.45).

13. *Enter* a value for the attribute (cost) of the door element in the text box corresponding to the **Cost** row of the **Value** column. In our case, we *enter* **456.00** (Figure 7.44).

14. *Enter* a value for the attribute (height) of the door element in the text box corresponding to the **Height** row of the **Value** column. In our case, we *enter* **7' 8"** (Figure 7.44).

15. *Enter* a value for the attribute (width) of the door element in the text box corresponding to the **Width** row of the **Value** column. In our case, we *enter* **3' 6"** (Figure 7.44).

16. *Click* the **OK** button (Figure 7.44). The label of the door element is modified, as shown in **Figure 7.46**.

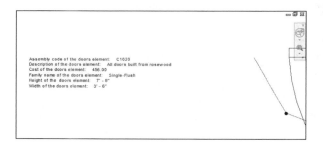

FIGURE 7.46

Let's now learn how detailing helps to construct a building model.

7.9 WORKING WITH DETAILING

In Autodesk Revit Architecture, when an architect designs a building model, it is represented in a digital format. The digital format of a building model is then sent to the constructor to develop the building model. At this point the constructor may need to resolve a series of problems, such as how the elements of a building model are interconnected and how the building model should be built. Detailing provides the necessary information, such as how to interconnect elements of a building model and which type of materials to use to construct the building, to the constructor, thereby solving these problems.

You can create two types of view for detailing:

- Detail view
- Drafting view

Let's first learn how to create a detail view in Autodesk Revit Architecture.

Creating a Detail View

A detail view is a view of a building model that displays a callout or section of a view. It is used to add information, such as the types of materials to be used to construct a part of a building model. Perform the following steps to create a detail view in Autodesk Revit Architecture:

1. *Open* the **Autodesk Revit Architecture 2010** window.
2. *Open* the file in which you want to create a detail view—in our case, **home.rvt**.
3. *Double-click* the **Level 1** plan view from the Project Browser to open it, as shown in **Figure 7.47**.

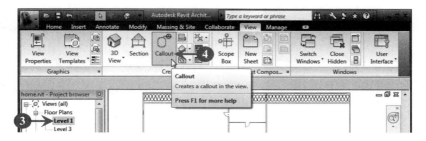

FIGURE 7.47

4. *Click* the **Callout** button from the **Create** panel under the **View** tab (Figure 7.47). The **Callout** contextual tab appears on the ribbon, as shown in **Figure 7.48**.

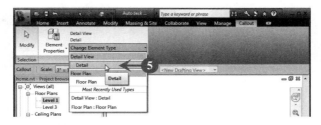

FIGURE 7.48

5. *Click* the **Change Element Type** drop-down button of the **Element** panel under the **Callout** tab and *select* the **Detail** option from the drop-down list (Figure 7.48).
6. *Click* the **Scale** drop-down button of the options bar and *select* an option to set the measurement unit of the detail view from the drop-down list. In our case, we *select* the **1/4" = 1'-0"** option, as shown in **Figure 7.49**.

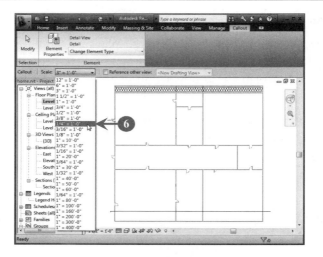

FIGURE 7.49

7. *Click* the mouse button in the drawing area to specify the starting point of the detail view, as shown in **Figure 7.50**.

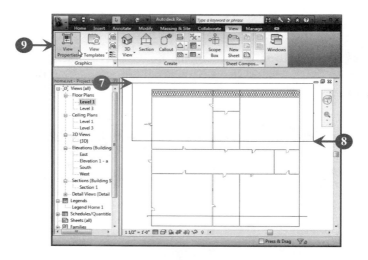

FIGURE 7.50

8. *Click* the mouse button in the drawing area to specify the ending point of the detail view (Figure 7.50).

9. *Click* the **View Properties** button from the **Graphics** panel under the **View** tab (Figure 7.50). The **Instance Properties** dialog box appears, as shown in **Figure 7.51**.

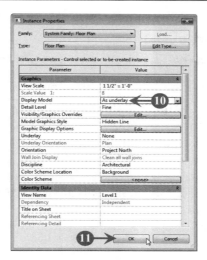

FIGURE 7.51

10. *Select* the **As underlay** option from the **Display Model** drop-down list (Figure 7.51).

11. *Click* the **OK** button (Figure 7.51).

12. *Expand* the **Detail Views (Detail)** folder from the Project Browser, as shown in **Figure 7.52**.

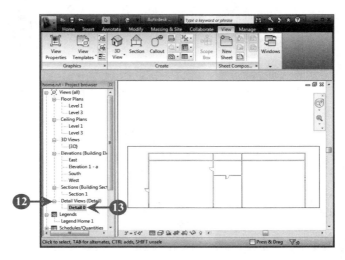

FIGURE 7.52

13. *Double-click* the **Detail 0** detail view (Figure 7.52). The Detail 0 detail view shows the portion of a building model.

Creating a Drafting View

A drafting view is created in an Autodesk Revit Architecture project and is not associated with the project views, such as the 3D, plan, and elevation view. When any changes are made in the drafting view, they are not reflected in other views. A drafting view is just like a 2D view, where you can use 2D detailing tools such as detail lines, detail regions, detail components, insulation, reference planes, dimensions, symbols, and text to design a part of a building model. These detailing tools are available under the Annotation tab of Autodesk Revit Architecture.

Perform the following steps to create a drafting view in Autodesk Revit Architecture:

1. *Open* the **Autodesk Revit Architecture 2010** window.
2. *Open* the file in which you want to create a drafting view—in our case, **home.rvt**.
3. *Click* the **Drafting View** button from the **Create** panel under the **View** tab, as shown in **Figure 7.53**.

FIGURE 7.53

The **New Drafting View** dialog box appears, as shown in **Figure 7.54**.

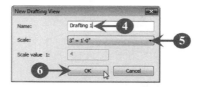

FIGURE 7.54

4. *Enter* a name for the drafting view in the **Name** text box. In our case, we *enter* **Drafting 1** (Figure 7.54).
5. *Select* an option to set the measurement unit of the drafting view from the **Scale** drop-down list. In our case, we *select* the **3" = 1'-0"** option (Figure 7.54).

6. *Click* the **OK** button (Figure 7.54).

7. *Expand* the **Drafting View (Detail)** folder from the Project Browser, as shown in **Figure 7.55**.

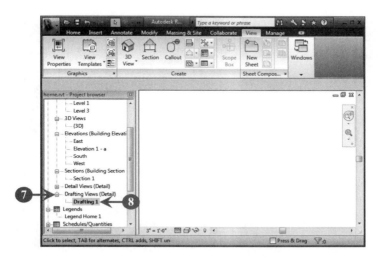

FIGURE 7.55

8. *Double-click* the **Drafting 1** drafting view (Figure 7.55).

9. *Click* the **Detail Line** button from the **Detail** panel under the **Annotate** tab, as shown as **Figure 7.56**.

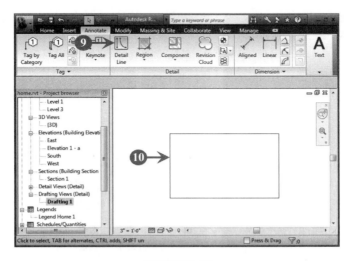

FIGURE 7.56

10. *Sketch* the boundary of the building model in the drawing area (Figure 7.56).

Similarly, you can create cloud, symbol, and insulation elements in the Drafting 1 drafting view, as shown in **Figure 7.57**.

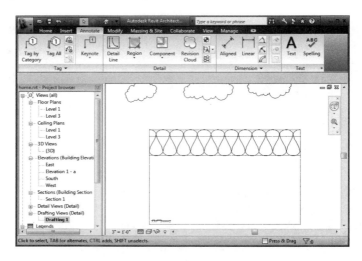

FIGURE 7.57

Chapter 8

WORKING WITH CONSTRUCTION DOCUMENTS

In This Chapter
◊ Using Sheets
◊ Creating a Title Block
◊ Using Viewports
◊ Adding a Schedule to a Sheet
◊ Using Drawing Lists
◊ Using Revisions
◊ Printing a Construction Document

After modeling a building design, you need to create construction documents, which are the records that you share with clients, engineers, and construction professionals to discuss the design. Clients see the floor plans, elevations, and 3D design to approve the building model. Engineers need the construction document to understand the design of the building model in detail. Construction professionals need all of these construction documents to create the design of the building model.

Before creating a construction document, you need to create a sheet and then add drawings and schedules to the sheets. You can then print the sheet; publish it in another format, such as Design Web Format (DWF); or send it to the field, where clients or reviewers can revise the design.

In this chapter, you learn how to use sheets; create a title block; add a schedule to a sheet; use viewports, drawing lists, and revisions; and print a construction document in Autodesk Revit Architecture. We begin by using sheets, as discussed in the next section.

8.1 USING SHEETS

Autodesk Revit Architecture includes sheets as individual pages of a construction document set. A sheet is also referred as a drawing sheet. A sheet is very much similar to a view that is defined by a border and a title block. Autodesk Revit Architecture requires you to create a sheet view for each sheet in a construction document. After creating a sheet view, you can place multiple drawings and schedules on the sheet view. A sheet comprises different parts, such as the project view, schedule, and title block. The project view displays the building model in any of the selected views. The schedule displays information about the project elements in a tabular format. The title block displays project information such as the client's name, project name, project number, and the drawing sheet.

In this section, you learn how to create a sheet, add views to a sheet, and add an image to a sheet. Let's first learn how to create a sheet in Autodesk Revit Architecture.

Creating a Sheet

As stated earlier, before creating a sheet, you need to add a sheet view to a project. When you add sheets to the project, they are listed under the heading "Sheet(s) all" in the Project Browser. After creating a sheet, you can open it later from the Project Browser and use the sheet properties to control the appearance and behavior of that sheet. For example, you can specify a sheet number and name for each sheet in the project and choose whether the sheet will be displayed in the drawing list.

Perform the following steps to create a sheet in Autodesk Revit Architecture:

1. *Open* the **Autodesk Revit Architecture 2010** window.
2. *Open* the project file in which you want to create a sheet. In this case, we open the **Walls** file.
3. *Select* the **View** tab on the ribbon, as shown in **Figure 8.1**.

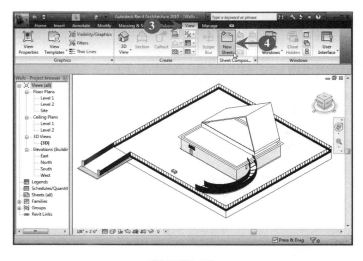

FIGURE 8.1

4. *Click* the **New Sheet** button under the **Sheet Composition** panel (Figure 8.1). The **Select a Titleblock** dialog box appears, as shown in **Figure 8.2**.

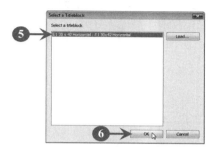

FIGURE 8.2

5. *Select* a title block from the **Select a titleblock** list box. In this case, we *select* **E1 30 × 42 Horizontal : E1 30 × 42 Horizontal** (Figure 8.2).

Note: If you do not find the desired title block in the Select a titleblock list box, click the **Load** button, select the title block from the appropriate location, and then click **Open**.

6. *Click* the **OK** button (Figure 8.2). The title block of the sheet appears in the drawing area, as shown in **Figure 8.3**.

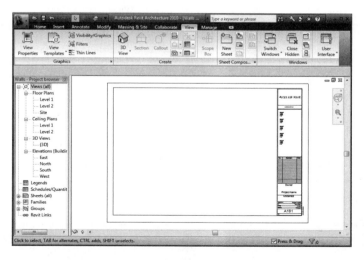

FIGURE 8.3

7. *Zoom in* on the drawing area to see the parameters clearly, as shown in **Figure 8.4**.

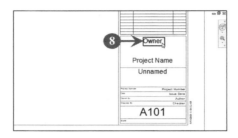

FIGURE 8.4

Note: You can zoom in on the drawing area by using the Zoom tool on the navigation bar. The navigation bar appears at the rightmost side in the drawing area. You can also use the mouse scroll to zoom in or zoom out from the drawing area.

8. *Click* the placeholder text to enter information in the title block. In this case, we *click* the **Owner** placeholder (Figure 8.4). The placeholder appears in editable mode, as shown in **Figure 8.5**.

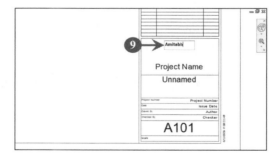

FIGURE 8.5

9. *Enter* the owner name, which you want to provide in the project, in the placeholder. In this case, we *enter* **Amitabh** (Figure 8.5).
10. *Click* outside the placeholder to apply the changes.
11. *Add* views to the sheet.

Note: You can refer to the section "Adding Views to a Sheet," to discover how to add views to a sheet.

12. *Right-click* the sheet name under **Sheet(s) all** in the Project Browser and then *select* the **Rename** option from the context menu to rename the sheet, as shown in **Figure 8.6**.

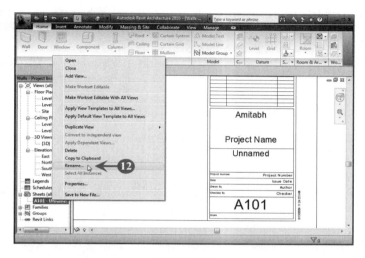

FIGURE 8.6

The **Sheet Title** dialog box appears, as shown in **Figure 8.7**.

FIGURE 8.7

13. *Enter* the sheet number in the **Number** text box. In this case, we *enter* **AM-001** (Figure 8.7).

14. *Enter* the sheet name in the **Name** text box. In this case, we *enter* **Title Block Sheet** (Figure 8.7).

15. *Click* the **OK** button (Figure 8.7). The sheet number and name are changed, as shown in **Figure 8.8**.

FIGURE 8.8

Let's now learn how to add views to a sheet.

Adding Views to a Sheet

Autodesk Revit Architecture includes a number of project views so that you can work with a building model in multiple ways. You can add these views to a sheet, such as floor plans, ceiling plans, elevations, 3D views, and drafting views. Each view can be placed on only one sheet. However, you can add a particular view to multiple sheets by creating a duplicate copy of the view and then placing the duplicate copies on each sheet.

Perform the following steps to add views to a sheet:

1. *Open* the **Autodesk Revit Architecture 2010** window.
2. *Open* the project file that contains the sheet to which you want to add views—in this case, the **Walls** file.
3. *Click* the sheet name to which you want to add views under **Sheet(s) all** in the Project Browser to open the sheet, as shown in **Figure 8.9**.

FIGURE 8.9

4. *Select* the **View** tab on the ribbon (Figure 8.9).
5. *Click* the **Place View** button under the **Sheet Composition** panel (Figure 8.9). The **Views** dialog box appears, as shown in **Figure 8.10**.

FIGURE 8.10

6. *Select* a view that you want to add to a sheet from the list box. In this case, we *select* **3D View: {3D}** (Figure 8.10).

7. *Click* the **Add View to Sheet** button (Figure 8.10). The **Views** dialog box closes and a viewport for the selected view appears in the drawing area, as shown in **Figure 8.11**.

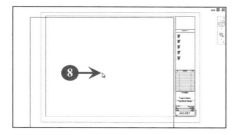

FIGURE 8.11

Note: A viewport is similar to a window through which you can see the actual view of the building model. You can also use the viewport to modify the building model from the sheet.

8. *Move* the mouse pointer to the location where you want to place the viewport (Figure 8.11).

9. *Click* to place the viewport in the drawing area. The viewport appears, as shown in **Figure 8.12**.

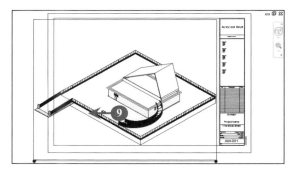

FIGURE 8.12

Note: Repeat steps 5 to 9 to add more views to the sheet.

The view is added to the sheet. After adding a view, you can modify it, such as by changing the view title of the sheet, moving the view to a new location on the sheet, changing the scale of the view, adding dimensions and text notes to the view, and panning the view.

Let's now learn how to add an image to a sheet.

Adding an Image to a Sheet

Apart from the project information, sometimes you need to provide external information, such as text, a spreadsheet, or an image, as part of the sheet. Autodesk Revit Architecture allows you to add text from a file and a spreadsheet to a sheet. In addition, you can add an image to a sheet to provide information as well as improve the appearance of the sheet.

Perform the following steps to add an image to a sheet:

1. *Open* the **Autodesk Revit Architecture 2010** window.
2. *Open* the project file that contains the sheet to which you want to add an image—in this case, **Walls**.
3. *Double-click* the sheet name to which you want to add an image under **Sheet(s) all** in the Project Browser to open the sheet, as shown in **Figure 8.13**.

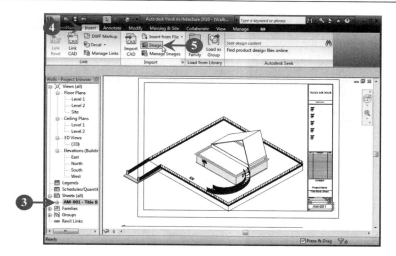

FIGURE 8.13

4. *Select* the **Insert** tab on the ribbon (Figure 8.13).
5. *Click* the **Image** button under the **Import** panel (Figure 8.13). The **Import Image** dialog box appears, as shown in **Figure 8.14**.

FIGURE 8.14

6. *Browse* the location of the image file from the **Look in** drop-down list. In this case, we *browse* the **Sample Pictures** folder (Figure 8.14).
7. *Select* an image file from the list and then *click* the **Open** button (Figure 8.14). In this case, we *select* the file named **Tree**.

8. *Move* the mouse pointer to the appropriate location in the drawing area where you want to place the image, as shown in **Figure 8.15**.

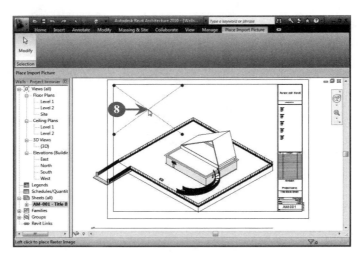

FIGURE 8.15

9. *Click* the mouse button to place the image, as shown in **Figure 8.16**.

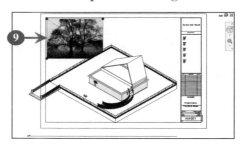

FIGURE 8.16

The image is added to a sheet. After adding the image, you can drag it to another location and resize it by clicking and dragging the dots at the corners of the image.

Let's now move on to the next section to learn how to create a title block.

8.2 CREATING A TITLE BLOCK

A title block provides a template for a sheet, that includes the sheet border and information such as the client name, address, issue date, and revision information about the project, client, and individual sheets. A title block also defines the size and appearance of the drawing sheet. A title block is created using the family editor. You need to specify all pertinent information, such as the sheet size, borders, company logo, company address, and client information, while creating a title block. In simple words, title blocks are external families that include project number, sheet number, or company-specific information, both textual and images.

Perform the following steps to create a title block:

1. *Open* the **Autodesk Revit Architecture 2010** window.
2. *Click* the **Application** button, as shown in **Figure 8.17**. The application menu appears.

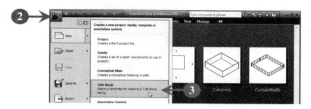

FIGURE 8.17

3. *Select* **New** > **Title Block** from the application menu (Figure 8.17). The **New Title Block** dialog box appears, as shown in **Figure 8.18**.

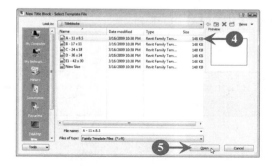

FIGURE 8.18

4. *Select* a predefined template for the title block or *select* **New Size** to create a title block with a new size. In this case, we *select* the default template, **A—11 × 8.5** (Figure 8.18).

5. *Click* the **Open** button (Figure 8.18). The family editor opens, as shown in **Figure 8.19**.

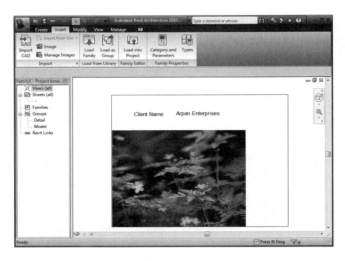

FIGURE 8.19

6. *Add* lines, texts, and labels to the title block using the appropriate tools on the ribbon. In this case, we *add* a label and text (Figure 8.19).

7. *Add* images to the title block using the **Image** tool under the **Insert** tab (Figure 8.19).

Note: You can also add custom fields and revision schedule to the title block. The revision schedule displays information about all the revisions in the project.

8. *Click* the **Application** button and *select* **Save** from the application menu to save the title block, as shown in **Figure 8.20**.

FIGURE 8.20

The **Save As** dialog box appears, as shown in **Figure 8.21**.

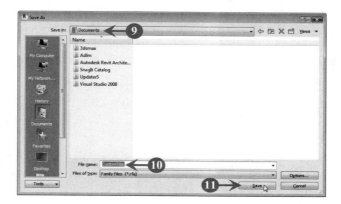

FIGURE 8.21

9. *Browse* the location from the **Save in** drop-down list where you want to save the title block. In this case, we *browse* to the **Documents** folder (Figure 8.21).

10. *Enter* the file name for the title block in the **File name** text box. In this case, we *enter* the name **CustomTitle** (Figure 8.21).

11. *Click* the **Save** button (Figure 8.21). The title block is saved with the specified name.

The title block is created and saved with the name **CustomTitle**. Now you can load it into a project, just as you would load the predefined templates of the title block.

Let's move on to the next section to learn how to use viewports in Autodesk Revit Architecture.

8.3 USING VIEWPORTS

A viewport represents a drawing, schedule, or view when it is placed on a sheet. The viewport is analogous to a window that can be used to see the actual view of the building model. After placing a viewport on the sheet, you can activate and modify the view from the sheet. You can create viewports only for views, such as floor plans, elevations, sections, and 3D view; viewports cannot be created for schedules.

In this section, you learn how to create a viewport type, apply a viewport type to a view, and alter a view title. Let's first create a viewport type.

Creating a Viewport Type

Viewport types (also referred to as title marks) are used to specify settings such as the view title, line weight, and line pattern for the viewport. Autodesk Revit Architecture uses these settings to control which attributes of the view title are displayed on the sheet. For example, you can specify whether the view title and its horizontal line should appear on a sheet. A viewport type can be applied to multiple views on a sheet.

Perform the following steps to create a viewport type:

1. *Open* the **Autodesk Revit Architecture 2010** window.
2. *Open* the project file that contains the views placed on the sheet—in this case, **Walls**.
3. *Double-click* the sheet name under **Sheets (all)** in the Project Browser to open the sheet for which you want to create a viewport. In this case, we *open* the **AM-001—Title Block Sheet**, as shown in **Figure 8.22**.

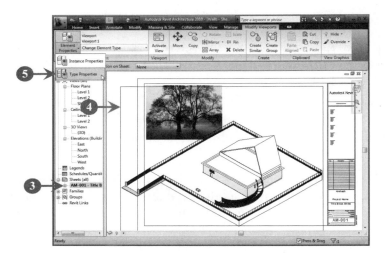

FIGURE 8.22

4. *Select* a viewport for a view on the sheet. In this case, we *select* **Viewport 1** (Figure 8.22). The **Modify Viewports** tab appears on the ribbon in the selected mode.

Note: When you select a viewport, the Type Selector drop-down list under the Element panel of the Modify Viewports tab displays all available viewport types.

5. *Click* the lower part of the **Element Properties** split button and then *select* the **Type Properties** option from the drop-down list (Figure 8.22). The **Type Properties** dialog box appears, as shown in **Figure 8.23**.

FIGURE 8.23

6. *Click* the **Duplicate** button (Figure 8.23). The **Name** dialog box appears, as shown in **Figure 8.24**.

FIGURE 8.24

7. *Enter* the viewport name in the **Name** text box. In this case, we *enter* **AddViewport 2** (Figure 8.24).

8. *Click* the **OK** button (Figure 8.24). The **Name** dialog box closes and the **AddViewport 2** viewport appears in the **Type** drop-down list, as shown in **Figure 8.25**.

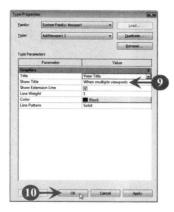

FIGURE 8.25

9. *Set* the parameter values, as required, under the **Type Parameters** section (Figure 8.25). In this case, we *set* the **When multiple viewports** value for the **Show Title** parameter.

10. *Click* the **OK** button (Figure 8.25). The new viewport type is created and applied to the selected viewport.

Next, we learn how to apply a viewport type to a view.

Applying a Viewport Type to a View

After creating a viewport type, you can apply it to a view on sheets in an Autodesk Revit Architecture project. Perform the following steps to apply a viewport type to a view:

1. *Open* the **Autodesk Revit Architecture 2010** window.

2. *Open* the project file that contains the views placed on the sheet—in this case, **Walls**.

3. *Double-click* the sheet name under **Sheets (all)** in the Project Browser to open the sheet containing a view on which you want to apply a viewport. In this case, we open the sheet **AM-001—Title Block Sheet**, as shown in **Figure 8.26**.

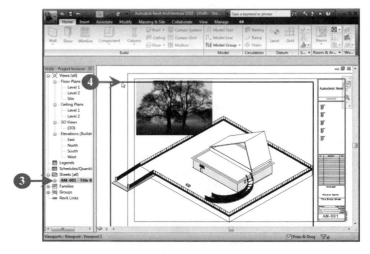

FIGURE 8.26

4. *Select* a viewport in the drawing area (Figure 8.26). The **Modify Viewports** tab appears on the ribbon in the selected mode, as shown in **Figure 8.27**.

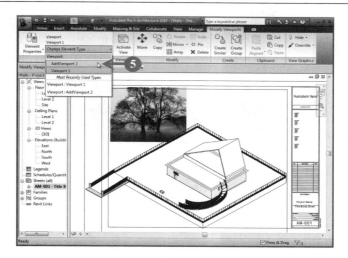

FIGURE 8.27

5. *Select* a viewport type, which you want to apply to a view, from the **Type Selector** drop-down list under the **Element** panel. In this case, we *select* the **AddViewport 2** viewport type (Figure 8.27). The selected viewport is applied to the view.

Let's now learn how to alter a view title.

Altering a View Title

After you place a view on a sheet, the view title automatically appears on the sheet. The view title is displayed only for views, such as floor plans, elevations, sections, and 3D views. You can specify text attributes of the view title in its parameters settings, and you can dictate which information a view title contains in the project. In addition, you can exclude the view titles from sheets as well as define view title types to apply the specified standard settings to view titles.

Perform the following steps to change a view title:

1. *Open* the **Autodesk Revit Architecture 2010** window.
2. *Open* the project file that contains the views placed on the sheet—in this case, **Walls**.

3. Double-click the sheet name under **Sheets (all)** in the Project Browser to open the sheet that contains a view whose title you want to change. In this case, we *open* the sheet **AM-001—Title Block Sheet**, as shown in **Figure 8.28**.

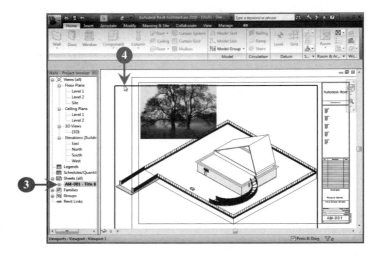

FIGURE 8.28

4. *Select* the viewport for the view whose title you want to change. In this case, we *select* the **Viewport 1** viewport type (Figure 8.28). The **Modify Viewports** tab appears on the ribbon in the selected mode, as shown in **Figure 8.29**.

FIGURE 8.29

5. *Click* the **Element Properties** split button and then *select* the **Instance Properties** option from the drop-down list (Figure 8.29). The **Instance Properties** dialog box appears, as shown in **Figure 8.30**.

FIGURE 8.30

6. *Enter* the value for the sheet title in the **Title on Sheet** parameter under the **Identity Data** section. In this case, we *enter* the value **My Home** (Figure 8.30).

7. *Click* the **OK** button (Figure 8.30). The current view name is retained in the Project Browser, but specifies a different view title to display on the sheet.

Note: You can also rename the view to change the view name in the Project Browser and on the sheet. In addition, you can modify a view title type to change the display attributes for the view title.

Continue with the following steps to change the length of the horizontal line that appears with the view title:

8. *Zoom in* on the view title in the drawing area to display the name of the view title and the drag controls (the points that appear as blue dots) clearly, as shown in **Figure 8.31**.

FIGURE 8.31

9. *Click* and *drag* the **blue drag control** to reduce or extend the length of the horizontal line, as shown in **Figure 8.32**.

FIGURE 8.32

In Figure 8.32, you can see that as we drag the drag control to the right, the length of the horizontal line is reduced. This completes our discussion on altering a view type.

Let's now move on to the next section to learn how to add a schedule to a sheet.

8.4 ADDING A SCHEDULE TO A SHEET

A schedule displays information about a project, which is extracted from the properties of the project elements, in a tabular format. It enumerates items including building elements, such as walls, doors, and windows; calculates material quantities and areas and volumes of the elements, such as rooms and floors; and lists the number of sheets, text notes, and keynotes. In Autodesk Revit Architecture, you can add a single schedule to multiple sheets.

Perform the following steps to add a schedule to a sheet:

1. *Open* the **Autodesk Revit Architecture 2010** window.
2. *Open* the project file that contains the views placed on the sheet—in this case, **Walls**.
3. *Double-click* the sheet name under **Sheets (all)** in the Project Browser to open the sheet to which you want to add a schedule. In this case, we open the **AM-001—Title Block Sheet**, as shown in **Figure 8.33**.

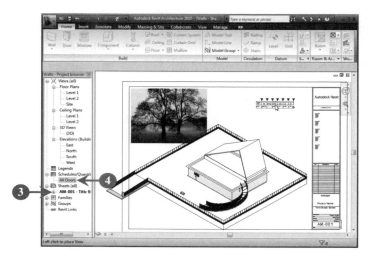

FIGURE 8.33

4. *Click* the schedule that you want to add to the sheet under **Schedules/Quantities** in the Project Browser. In this case, we *click* the **All Doors** schedule (Figure 8.33).

Note: If the project does not have an existing schedule, you can create it and then add it to the sheet. Refer to Chapter 3 for instructions on how to create a schedule.

5. *Drag* the mouse pointer on the sheet in the drawing area and *release* the mouse button once it hovers over the sheet, as shown in **Figure 8.34**.

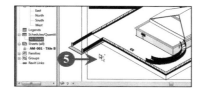

FIGURE 8.34

A preview of the schedule appears with the mouse pointer, as shown in **Figure 8.35**.

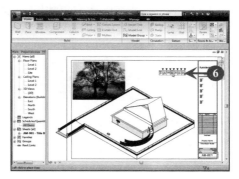

FIGURE 8.35

6. *Move* the mouse pointer to the location in the drawing area where you want to place the schedule (Figure 8.35).
7. *Click* the mouse button to place the schedule, as shown in **Figure 8.36**.

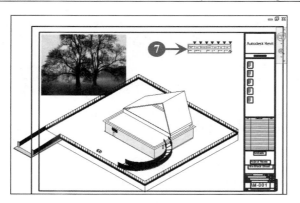

FIGURE 8.36

The schedule is added to a sheet. Let's now move on to the next section to learn how to use drawing lists in Autodesk Revit Architecture.

8.5 USING DRAWING LISTS

A drawing list is also known as a drawing or sheet index. It contains an alphabetically sorted list of the sheets in a project; thus, it acts as a schedule of the lists. A drawing list is generally placed on the title sheet and is treated as a table of contents for a construction document set.

In this section, you learn how to create a drawing list and exclude a sheet from a drawing list. Let's start by creating a drawing list.

Creating a Drawing List

When you create a drawing list, the list identifies all sheets in the project. By default, the sheets are listed alphabetically. While creating a drawing list, you can select the data that you want to display in the schedule. You can also filter out the data that you do not want to display. Autodesk Revit Architecture also provides parameters to control the order in which information is displayed and the graphical aspects of the schedule, such as the font size and type of text for each column and header in the schedule.

Perform the following steps to create a drawing list:

1. *Open* the **Autodesk Revit Architecture 2010** window.
2. *Open* the project file in which you want to create a drawing list—in this case, **Walls**.
3. *Select* the **View** tab on the ribbon, as shown in **Figure 8.37**.

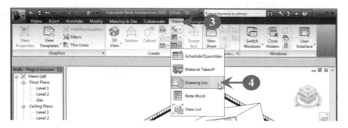

FIGURE 8.37

4. *Click* the **Schedules** drop-down button under the **Create** panel and then *select* the **Drawing List** option from the drop-down list (Figure 8.37). The **Drawing List Properties** dialog box appears, as shown in **Figure 8.38**.

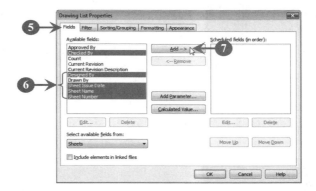

FIGURE 8.38

5. *Select* the **Fields** tab, if not selected (Figure 8.38).
6. *Select* the fields that you want to include in the drawing list from the **Available fields** list. In this case, we *select* the fields named **Checked By, Designed By, Sheet Issue Date, Sheet Name**, and **Sheet Number** (Figure 8.38).
7. *Click* the **Add** button (Figure 8.38). The fields appear under the **Scheduled fields (in order)** list.

Note: You can click the **Add Parameter** button to create custom fields to be included in the drawing list.

---

8. *Select* the **Filter** tab to filter the drawing list, as shown in **Figure 8.39**.

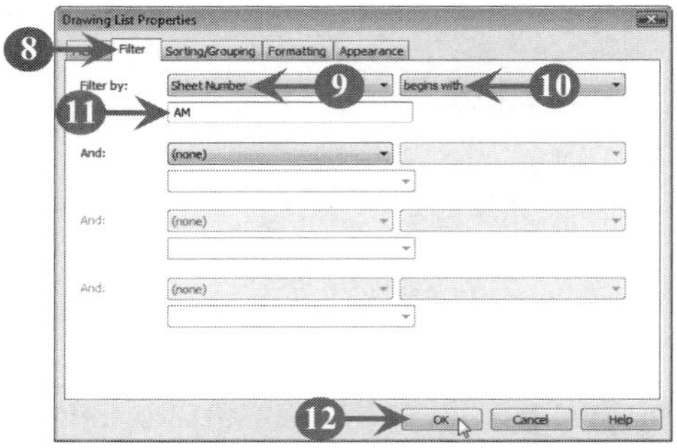

FIGURE 8.39

9. *Select* a parameter that you want to use for filtering the drawing list from the **Filter by** drop-down list. In this case, we *select* **Sheet Number** (Figure 8.39).
10. *Select* an option that you want to use for comparing values from the drop-down list adjacent to the **Filter by** drop-down list. In this case, we *select* **begins with** (Figure 8.39).
11. *Enter* the value that you want to use for comparison purposes in the text box below the **Filter by** drop-down list. In this case, we *enter* the value **AM** (Figure 8.39).

Note: Similar to the options available for filtering, you can specify the sorting/grouping parameters, formatting parameters, and appearance parameters by using the Sorting/Grouping, Formatting, and Appearance tabs, respectively.

12. *Click* the **OK** button (Figure 8.39). The drawing list appears in the drawing area, as shown in **Figure 8.40**.

FIGURE 8.40

The drawing list also appears under Schedules/Quantities in the Project Browser.

Let's now learn how to exclude a sheet from a drawing list.

Excluding a Sheet from a Drawing List

When you create a construction document for a project, you need to create different sheets as per the requirements of the client. Sometimes, you do not want to display particular sheets, such as the cover sheet, in the drawing list. In such a case, Autodesk Revit Architecture allows you to exclude the sheet from the drawing list.

Perform the following steps to exclude a sheet from a drawing list:

1. *Open* the **Autodesk Revit Architecture 2010** window.
2. *Open* the project file containing the drawing list from which you want to exclude a sheet—in this case, **Walls**.
3. *Right-click* the sheet name that you want to exclude from a drawing list in the Project Browser and then *select* the **Properties** option from the context menu, as shown in **Figure 8.41**.

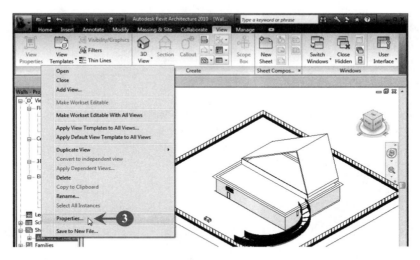

FIGURE 8.41

The **Instance Properties** dialog box appears, as shown in **Figure 8.42**.

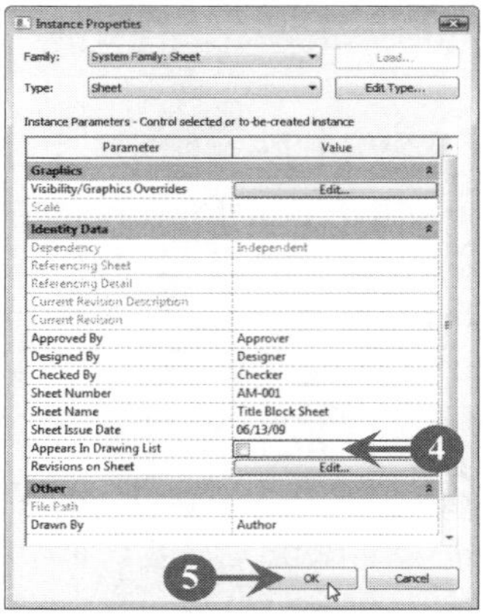

FIGURE 8.42

4. *Clear* the check box adjacent to the **Appears In Drawing List** parameter (Figure 8.42).

Note: The check box adjacent to the Appears In Drawing List parameter is selected for all sheets by default.

5. *Click* the **OK** button (Figure 8.42). The drawing list is updated and the sheet is excluded. Now, when you open the drawing list, the value for the excluded sheet does not appear in the drawing list.

Next, let's learn how to use revisions.

8.6 USING REVISIONS

After you create a building model and the project moves to the construction document phase, you must often make changes in the project to meet the client requirements. These changes need to be tracked for future reference, including such information as when and why these changes were made, and who made them. Revisions allow designers and builders to track changes made to a set of construction documents. Generally, these changes are tracked after a set of documents has been issued. As you already know, construction documents comprise multiple sheets. Revisions allow everyone in the team to view and identify all details of the changes made in the sheets during the construction process.

In this section, you learn about the revision workflow as well as how to insert revision information in a project, use revision clouds, insert revisions in a revision schedule, and issue a revision. Let's first understand the revision workflow.

Describing the Revision Workflow

The revision workflow describes the process of managing revisions in an Autodesk Revit Architecture project, which begins when the revision is created and ends when the revision is issued. When you perform the revision tracking, you need to perform the following steps to process the revision workflow:

1. *Enter* revision information in the **Sheet Issues/Revisions** dialog box and then *update* the project to apply the changes.
2. *Draw* revision clouds in one or more project views to determine the modified areas.
3. *Assign* a revision to each revision cloud.

> **Note:** Revision clouds are discussed later in this chapter.

4. *Assign* a tag to revision clouds to determine the assigned revisions.
5. *Ensure* that the revision schedules on the sheets display the desired information.
6. *Issue* the revisions.

Now that you are familiar with the different processes followed in the revision workflow, let's learn how to insert revision information.

Inserting Revision Information

Revision information is inserted in the project when the building model is revised. Each time you insert revision information, it is placed in a new separate row. These revisions can be assigned to one or more revision clouds in the drawing area.

Perform the following steps to insert the revision information in an Autodesk Revit Architecture project:

1. *Open* the **Autodesk Revit Architecture 2010** window.
2. *Open* the project file in which you want to insert revision information—in this case, **Walls**.

3. *Select* the **View** tab on the ribbon, as shown in **Figure 8.43**.

FIGURE 8.43

4. *Click* the **Sheet Issues/Revisions** dialog box launcher under the **Sheet Composition** panel (Figure 8.43). The **Sheet Issues/Revisions** dialog box appears, as shown in **Figure 8.44**.

FIGURE 8.44

5. *Click* the **Add** button to add a new revision (Figure 8.44). A new row for the revision is added in the revision list, as shown in **Figure 8.45**.

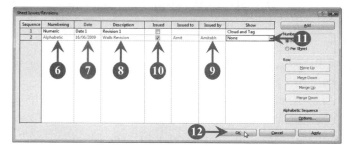

FIGURE 8.45

6. *Select* a numbering scheme for the revision row under **Numbering** to specify how you want to display the sequence of revisions in a project. In this case, we *select* **Alphabetic** (Figure 8.45).

Note: You can select one of three numbering choices—Numeric, Alphabetic, and None—and can track the revisions later using these choices.

7. *Enter* the date for the revision row (i.e., the date on which the revisions are made or sent for review) in the text box provided on row **2** and column **Date**. In this case, we *enter* the date **16/06/2009** (Figure 8.45).

8. *Enter* the description of the revision in the text box provided on row **2** and column **Description** that should be displayed in revision schedules on the sheets. In this case, we *enter* the description **Walls Revision** (Figure 8.45).

9. *Enter* the values in the **Issued to** and **Issued by** text boxes on row **2** if the revision has been issued. In this case, we *enter* the values **Amit** and **Amitabh**, respectively (Figure 8.45).

10. *Select* the check box provided on row **2** and column **Issued** to prevent anyone from modifying the revision information (Figure 8.45).

11. *Select* a value from the list provided on row **2** and column **Show** to specify whether you want to display a revision cloud and tag. In this case, we *select* the value **None** (Figure 8.45).

12. *Click* the **OK** button (Figure 8.45). The revision information is inserted in the project.

Let's now learn how to use revision clouds in Autodesk Revit Architecture.

Using Revision Clouds

Revision clouds indicate the part of the building model that has changed. They can be sketched in all views except 3D view. The revision cloud appears in the view where it is created and on sheets that include the view. For example, if you create a revision cloud in the floor plan view, it appears only in the floor plan view rather than appearing in all project views.

After entering the revision information in the project, you can assign the revision to one or more revision clouds. These assigned revisions can be identified by tagging the revision clouds.

In this section, you learn how to create a revision cloud, assign a revision to a revision cloud, and assign a tag to a revision cloud. Let's first create a revision cloud.

Creating a Revision Cloud

Before creating a revision cloud, you need to open the view in which you have made changes to the building model. When you open this view later, the revision clouds will appear on the sheet automatically. For each sheet, the revision schedule includes revision information represented by the revision clouds that are created on the sheet in the current view.

Perform the following steps to create a revision cloud:

1. *Open* the **Autodesk Revit Architecture 2010** window.
2. *Open* the project file in which you want to display changes—in this case, **Walls**.

3. *Open* the view in which you want to create a revision cloud. In this case, we *open* the floor plan view, as shown in **Figure 8.46**.

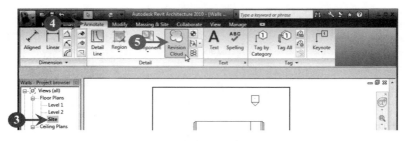

FIGURE 8.46

4. *Select* the **Annotate** tab on the ribbon (Figure 8.46).
5. *Click* the **Revision Cloud** button under the **Detail** panel (Figure 8.46). The **Create Revision Cloud Sketch** tab appears on the ribbon in the selected mode, as shown in **Figure 8.47**.

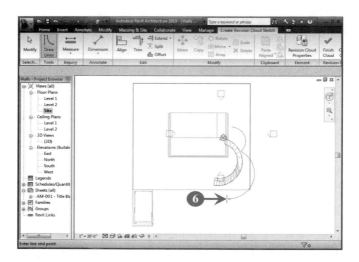

FIGURE 8.47

Note: The revision cloud cannot be created if the revision has been already issued. However, you can create a revision cloud after you create a new revision.

6. *Place* the mouse pointer near the view part that has changed and then *click* and *drag* the mouse pointer in a clockwise direction to sketch a segment of the cloud (Figure 8.47).

7. *Click* the mouse button to finish that segment and start a new segment, as shown in **Figure 8.48**.

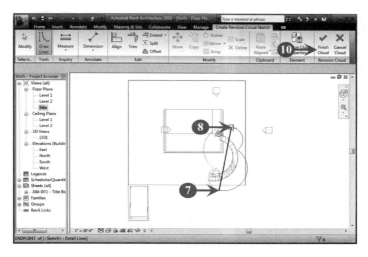

FIGURE 8.48

8. *Click* the endpoint to complete sketching the cloud (Figure 8.48).

9. *Repeat* steps 6 to 8 to create more clouds, if required.

10. *Click* the **Finish Cloud** button under the **Revision Cloud** panel (Figure 8.48). The cloud is created, as shown in **Figure 8.49**.

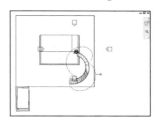

FIGURE 8.49

Next, let's learn how to assign a revision to a revision cloud.

Assigning a Revision to a Revision Cloud

Once the revision cloud is created, by default the most recent revision is assigned to the revision cloud. However, if required, you can assign another revision to the revision cloud. A revision cloud can contain only one revision, but that revision can be the same for multiple revision clouds.

Perform the following steps to assign a revision to a revision cloud:

1. *Open* the **Autodesk Revit Architecture 2010** window.
2. *Open* the project file containing a revision cloud to which you want to assign a revision—in this case, **Walls**.
3. *Open* the view in which you created the revision cloud. In this case, we *open* the floor plan view, as shown in **Figure 8.50**.

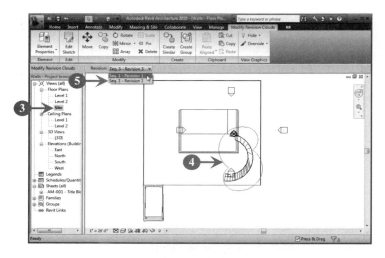

FIGURE 8.50

4. *Select* the revision cloud to which you want to add a revision in the drawing area (Figure 8.50). The **Modify Revision Clouds** tab appears on the ribbon in the selected mode.
5. *Select* the revision that you want to add to the revision cloud from the **Revision** drop-down list on the options bar. In this case, we *select* the revision **Seq. 3—Revision 3** (Figure 8.50).

Note: If you have not yet entered the revision information, refer to the "Inserting Revision Information" section of this chapter.

The selected revision is assigned to the selected revision cloud.

Let's now learn how to assign a tag to a revision cloud.

Assigning a Tag to a Revision Cloud

Similar to other elements in Autodesk Revit Architecture, revision clouds can be tagged. These tags are designed to include the revision number or letter that has been assigned to the cloud. In simple words, a revision tag identifies the revision assigned to each cloud in a view. Before tagging a revision cloud, you need to load the revision tag family in the project. A project created using the default project template includes the Revision Tag or M_Revision Tag family. If a revision tag is not found in the project template, Autodesk Revit Architecture shows the warning that no such tag exists in your project.

Perform the following steps to assign a tag to a revision cloud:

1. *Open* the **Autodesk Revit Architecture 2010** window.
2. *Open* the project file containing a revision cloud to which you want to assign a tag—in this case, **Walls**.
3. *Open* the view in which you created the revision cloud. In this case, we *open* the floor plan view, as shown in **Figure 8.51**.

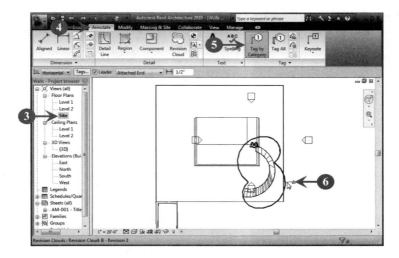

FIGURE 8.51

4. *Select* the **Annotate** tab on the ribbon (Figure 8.51).

5. *Click* the **Tag by Category** button under the **Tag** panel (Figure 8.51).

6. *Click* the revision cloud in the drawing area that you want to tag (Figure 8.51). As you click the revision cloud, a revision tag appears next to it, as shown in **Figure 8.52**.

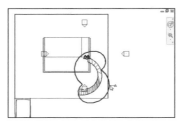

FIGURE 8.52

7. *Press* the **ESC** key to exit the Tag by Category tool.

The numbers within the tag indicate the revisions assigned to the clouds. In addition, you can adjust the positions of the tags and their leader lines.

Next, let's learn how to insert revisions in a revision schedule.

Inserting Revisions in a Revision Schedule

A revision schedule displays information about the revisions contained in a revision cloud. You can use a tile block having a revision schedule to display a revision schedule on a sheet. By default, the revision schedule lists all revisions related to the revision clouds in the views of a sheet. However, you can also insert revisions in a revision schedule that are not related to the revision clouds in the views of that particular sheet.

Perform the following steps to insert revisions in a revision schedule:

1. *Open* the **Autodesk Revit Architecture 2010** window.

2. *Open* the project file containing a revision schedule on a sheet—in this case, **Walls**.

3. *Double-click* the sheet name under **Sheets (all)** in the Project Browser to open the sheet that contains the revision schedule. In this case, we *open* the **AM-001—Title Block Sheet**, as shown in **Figure 8.53**.

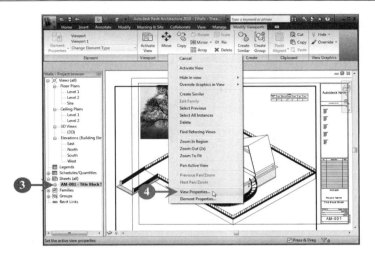

FIGURE 8.53

4. *Right-click* in the drawing area and then *select* the **View Properties** option from the context menu (Figure 8.53). The **Instance Properties** dialog box appears, as shown in **Figure 8.54**.

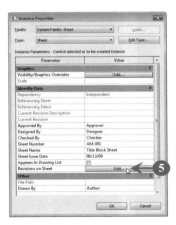

FIGURE 8.54

5. *Click* the **Edit** button adjacent to the **Revisions on Sheet** parameter (Figure 8.54). The **Revisions on Sheet** dialog box appears with a list of all revisions that you have already entered, as shown in **Figure 8.55**.

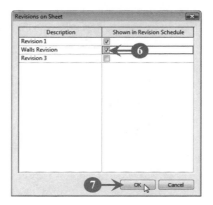

FIGURE 8.55

6. *Select* the check boxes adjacent to the revisions that you want to include in the revision schedule on the current sheet. In this case, we *select* the check boxes adjacent to the revisions named **Revision 1** and **Walls Revision** (Figure 8.55).

7. *Click* the **OK** button (Figure 8.55). The **Instance Properties** dialog box appears with the specified revisions, as shown in **Figure 8.56**.

FIGURE 8.56

8. *Click* the **OK** button (Figure 8.56). The **Instance Properties** dialog box is closed and the selected revisions are included in the revision schedule.

Next, let's learn how to issue a revision.

Issuing a Revision

Issuing a revision is the final process of the revision workflow. After making revisions to a project and adding the revised views to a sheet, you can issue the revision. Once you issue a revision, you cannot make further changes to the revision information, nor can the issued revision be assigned to the newly added revision clouds. If you assign an issued revision to a newly added revision cloud, the revision cloud cannot be edited.

Perform the following steps to issue a revision:

1. *Open* the **Autodesk Revit Architecture 2010** window.
2. *Open* the project file in which you want to issue a revision—in this case, **Walls**.
3. *Select* the **View** tab on the ribbon, as shown in **Figure 8.57**.

FIGURE 8.57

4. *Click* the **Sheet Issues/Revisions** dialog box launcher under the **Sheet Composition** panel (Figure 8.57). The **Sheet Issues/Revisions** dialog box appears, as shown in **Figure 8.58**.

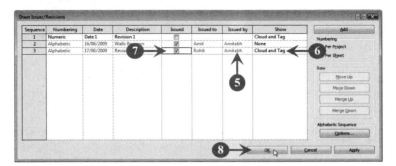

FIGURE 8.58

5.   *Enter* values for the **Issued to** and **Issued by** columns for the revision row that you want to issue. In this case, we *enter* the values **Rohit** and **Amitabh** for row 3 (Figure 8.58).

6.   *Enter* the other values of the revision row 3, such as **Numbering**, **Date**, **Description**, and **Show** (Figure 8.58).

Note: If the revision row already contains values, you can leave it as is or update the values, as required.

7.   *Select* the check box on row **3** and column **Issued** (Figure 8.58).

Note: After selecting the check box, you cannot make further changes to the revision information.

8.   *Click* the **OK** button (Figure 8.58). The revision is issued.

After a revision is issued, you can print or publish the revised sheet. Let's move on to the next section to learn how to print a construction document (sheet).

8.7 PRINTING A CONSTRUCTION DOCUMENT

Printing enables you to create a hard copy of the construction document. Autodesk Revit Architecture allows you to print the current window, a visible portion of the current window, or selected views and sheets. Before making a printout of the construction document, you can also see a draft version of a view or sheet using the print preview feature. The print preview feature is not available if you are printing multiple sheets or views. Using the Print option in the application menu, you can print one or more views and sheets in a project.

Perform the following steps to print a construction document:

1.   *Open* the **Autodesk Revit Architecture 2010** window.

2.   *Open* the project file containing a sheet that you want to print—in this case, **Walls**.

3.   *Open* the sheet that you want to print. In this case, we *open* the **AM-001—Title Block Sheet**, as shown in **Figure 8.59**.

FIGURE 8.59

4. *Click* the **Application** button (Figure 8.59). The application menu appears.

5. *Select* **Print→Print** from the application menu (Figure 8.59). The **Print** dialog box appears, as shown in **Figure 8.60**.

FIGURE 8.60

6. *Select* a radio button under the **Print Range** group to specify whether you want to print the current window, the visible portion of the current window, or selected views and sheets. In this case, we *select* the **Current window** radio button (Figure 8.60).

Note: If you want to print selected views and sheets, select the **Selected views/ sheets** radio button and click the **Select** button. Select the check boxes for the views and sheets in the **View/Sheet Set** dialog box and click the **OK** button.

7. *Enter* the number of copies that you want to print in the **Number of copies** spin box. In this case, we *enter* **2** (Figure 8.60).

Note: Select the **Reverse print order** check box under the **Options** group to print the pages in last-to-first order. Select the **Collate** check box to print all pages of a project of the first copy before printing the first page of the next copy.

8. *Click* the **Setup** button under the **Settings** group to configure the printer settings (Figure 8.60). The **Print Setup** dialog box appears, as shown in **Figure 8.61**.

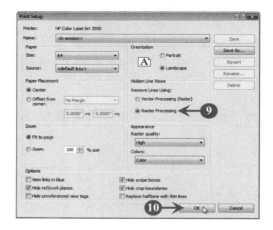

FIGURE 8.61

9. *Configure* the printer settings, as required. In this case, we *select* the **Raster Processing** radio button under the **Hidden Line Views** group (Figure 8.61).

10. *Click* the **OK** button after configuring the printer settings (Figure 8.61). The **Print Setup** dialog box closes and the **Print** dialog box appears, as shown in **Figure 8.62**.

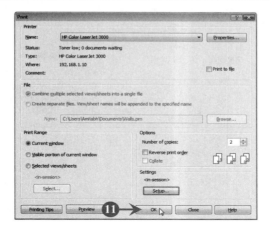

FIGURE 8.62

11. *Click* the **OK** button (Figure 8.62). The sheets and views in the current window are printed.

9

RENDERING BASICS

In This Chapter
◊   Understanding the Rendering Workflow
◊   Using Lights
◊   Adding Plants and an Entourage
◊   Using Decals
◊   Rendering an Image

Rendering is the final process once you have designed a building model. It creates a realistic effect in a 3D view so that you can present the design of the building model to clients or share it with other team members. The rendering process applies various effects to an image before rendering it, such as lighting, plants, decals, people, and cars. After the image is rendered, you can save it to the project itself or export it to a file.

In this chapter, you learn about the workflow of rendering. You then learn how to use lights, add plants and an entourage to a building model, use decals, and render an image in Autodesk Revit Architecture. We start by exploring the rendering workflow.

9.1 UNDERSTANDING THE RENDERING WORKFLOW

The rendering workflow describes the process of rendering a building model in Autodesk Revit Architecture. Once you complete designing the building model, you can perform the following steps to render a 3D view of the building model:

1. *Create* or *open* the 3D view.
2. *Specify* the render appearances for materials and then *apply* these materials to the elements in the building model.
3. *Specify* the lighting settings for the building model.

4. *Add* plants, cars, entourages, and decals to the building model.
5. *Configure* the render settings.
6. *Render* the image.
7. *Save* the rendered image or *export* it to a file.

The order of the first four steps in this rendering process can vary. In step 7, when you export the rendered image to a file, the image is saved with a specified file format, such as .JPEG, .BMP, .GIF, .PNG, or .TIF.

In the next section, we learn how to use lights in Autodesk Revit Architecture.

9.2 USING LIGHTS

Lights play a vital role when you are designing a building model. They affect the appearance of the elements and materials in the building model within the rendered view. After designing a building model, when you render it, you can use natural light (sunlight), artificial light (bulb and lamp), or both to illuminate the building model.

Natural light requires you to specify the direction of the sunlight as well as the location and the date and time of a day to create a realistic appearance of sunlight on the building model. Artificial lights require you to add lighting fixtures to the building model and then specify the light settings to achieve the desired effect.

In this section, you learn how to create a lighting fixture, add a lighting fixture to a building model, set the light source of the lighting fixture, display a light source in a view, and control the position of a spotlight in a building model. Let's first explore how to create a lighting fixture.

Creating a Lighting Fixture

A lighting fixture is an element that provides artificial light or illumination to the building model. It emits light from one or more light sources. In Autodesk Revit Architecture, you will find various types of predefined lighting fixtures, such as wall lights, ceiling lights, table lamps, floor lamps, and exterior lighting. In addition, Autodesk Revit Architecture enables you to create a custom lighting fixture using the family editor.

Perform the following steps to create a lighting fixture:

1. *Open* the **Autodesk Revit Architecture 2010** window.
2. *Click* the **Application** button to open the application menu, as shown in **Figure 9.1**.

FIGURE 9.1

3. *Select* **New > Family** from the application menu (Figure 9.1). The **New Family—Select Template File** dialog box appears, as shown in **Figure 9.2**.

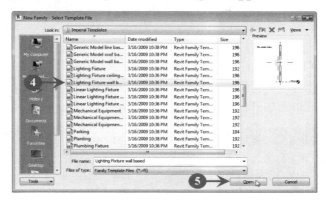

FIGURE 9.2

4. *Select* a lighting fixture template from the list of different lighting fixture templates. In this case, we *select* the **Lighting Fixture wall based** template (Figure 9.2).

Note: The templates for lighting fixtures begin with the words "Lighting Fixture" in the list. You need to select an appropriate template for the lighting fixture that you want to create. For example, you can select the Lighting Fixture ceiling based template to create ceiling-based fixtures and the Lighting Fixture wall based template to create wall-based fixtures.

5. *Click* the **Open** button (Figure 9.2). The family editor opens, as shown in **Figure 9.3**.

FIGURE 9.3

> **Note:** The selected template defines the reference planes and a light source. It also includes a ceiling or wall to host the lighting fixture, depending on the template you select.

Continue with the following steps to define the geometry of the light source for the lighting fixture.

6.   *Select* the light source in the drawing area. The **Modify Light Source** tab appears on the ribbon in the selected mode, as shown in **Figure 9.4**.

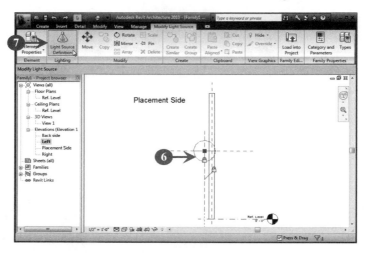

FIGURE 9.4

> **Note:** Typically, the light source appears in the drawing area with a yellow outline.

7.   *Click* the **Light Source Definition** button under the **Lighting** panel (Figure 9.4). The **Light Source Definition** dialog box appears, as shown in **Figure 9.5**.

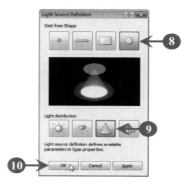

FIGURE 9.5

8. *Select* the shape of the light that emits from the light source, from the **Emit from Shape** section. In this case, we *select* the **Circle** shape (Figure 9.5).

Note: The other shapes of the light are Point, Line, and Rectangle.

9. *Select* the pattern of light distribution for the light source from the **Light Distribution** section. In this case, we *select* the **Spot** pattern (Figure 9.5).

Note: The other patterns of light distribution are Spherical, Hemispherical, and Photometric Web.

10. *Click* the **OK** button (Figure 9.5). The outline shape of the light source is changed in the drawing area, as shown in **Figure 9.6**.

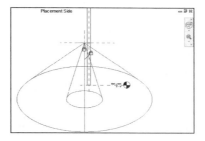

FIGURE 9.6

This defines the geometry of the light source. Now, *save* the file with an appropriate name. In this case, we *save* the file with the name **Lighting**.

Continue with the following steps to create the solid geometry for the lighting fixtures.

11. *Select* the **Create** tab on the ribbon, as shown in **Figure 9.7**.

FIGURE 9.7

12. *Click* the **Solid** drop-down button under the **Forms** panel and then *select* a solid geometry from the drop-down list. In this case, we *select* the **Blend**

geometry (Figure 9.7). The **Create Blend Base Boundary** tab appears on the ribbon in the selected mode, as shown in **Figure 9.8**.

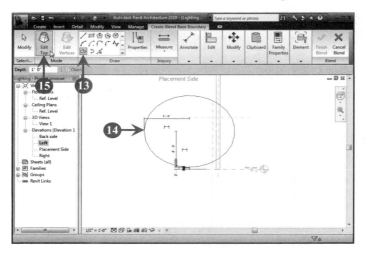

FIGURE 9.8

13. *Select* a sketching tool under the **Draw** panel to draw the base boundary of the blend. In this case, we *select* the **Ellipse** tool (Figure 9.8).

14. *Draw* an ellipse in the drawing area (Figure 9.8).

15. *Click* the **Edit Top** button under the **Mode** panel (Figure 9.8). The **Create Blend Top Boundary** tab appears on the ribbon in the selected mode, as shown in **Figure 9.9**.

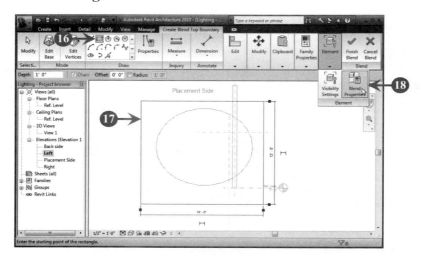

FIGURE 9.9

16. *Select* a sketching tool under the **Draw** panel to draw the top of the blend. In this case, we *select* the **Rectangle** tool (Figure 9.9).

17. *Draw* a rectangle or a square for the top of the blend in the drawing area (Figure 9.9).
18. *Click* the **Element** drop-down button and then *click* the **Blend Properties** button under the **Element** panel to specify the blend properties (Figure 9.9). The **Instance Properties** dialog box appears, as shown in **Figure 9.10**.

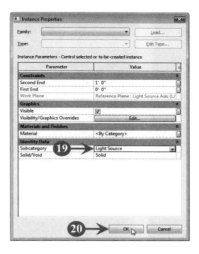

FIGURE 9.10

19. *Set* the blend properties as required. In this case, we *set* the **Light Source** subcategory to the **Subcategory** parameter to assign a solid blend to a subcategory (Figure 9.10).
20. *Click* the **OK** button (Figure 9.10). The **Instance Properties** dialog box closes.
21. *Click* the **Finish Blend** button under the **Blend** panel, as shown in **Figure 9.11**.

FIGURE 9.11

A solid geometry for the lighting fixture is created and the **Modify Light Source** tab appears on the ribbon in the selected mode, as shown in **Figure 9.12**.

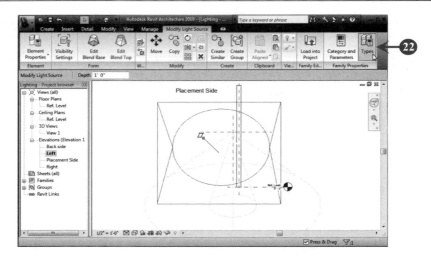

FIGURE 9.12

22. *Click* the **Types** button under the **Family Properties** panel (Figure 9.12). The **Family Types** dialog box appears, as shown in **Figure 9.13**.

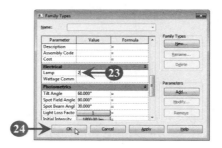

FIGURE 9.13

23. *Specify* appropriate values for the different parameters. In this case, we *specify* the value **2** for the **Lamp** parameter (Figure 9.13).

24. *Click* the **OK** button (Figure 9.13). The **Family Types** dialog box closes.

The lighting fixture is created. You can *click* the **Load into Project** button under the **Family Editor** panel to load the lighting fixture into the current project. You can also *save* the lighting fixture and *exit* the family editor.

Let's learn how to add a lighting fixture to a building model.

Adding a Lighting Fixture to a Building Model

Once you have created a lighting fixture, you can add it to a building model. You can also add predefined lighting fixtures to the building model. Before adding a lighting fixture to a building model, you are required to load the lighting fixtures family that contains the lighting fixture you want to add.

Perform the following steps to add a lighting fixture to a building model:

1. *Open* the **Autodesk Revit Architecture 2010** window.
2. *Open* the file containing a building model to which you want to add a lighting fixture—in this case, **Walls**.
3. *Select* the **Insert** tab on the ribbon, as shown in **Figure 9.14**.

FIGURE 9.14

4. *Click* the **Load Family** button under the **Load from Library** panel (Figure 9.14). The **Load Family** dialog box appears, as shown in **Figure 9.15**.

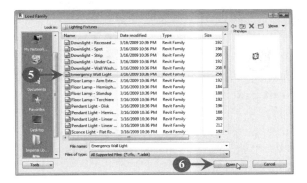

FIGURE 9.15

5. *Open* the **Lighting Fixtures** folder and then *select* one or more lighting fixture families from the list to use in the building model. In this case, we *select* the **Emergency Wall Light** family (Figure 9.15).
6. *Click* the **Open** button (Figure 9.15). The selected family is loaded to the project.
7. *Open* a view in which you can place the lighting fixture on the building. In this case, we *open* the **3D** view.

Note: Some lighting fixtures can be placed only in specific views; therefore, you need to open an appropriate view while placing such a fixture. For example, you can open a ceiling plan view to place a ceiling-based lighting fixture, a section or an elevation view to place a wall-based lighting fixture, and a floor plan or section view to place a table lamp or floor lamp.

8. *Select* the **Home** tab, as shown in **Figure 9.16**.

FIGURE 9.16

9. *Click* the lower part of the **Component** split button under the **Build** panel and then *select* the **Place a Component** option from the drop-down list (Figure 9.16). The **Place Component** tab appears on the ribbon in the selected mode, as shown in **Figure 9.17**.

FIGURE 9.17

10. *Select* a lighting fixture from the **Type Selector** drop-down list under the **Element** panel. In this case, we *select* the **277V** emergency wall light (Figure 9.17).

11. *Click* at an appropriate location in the drawing area to place the lighting fixture. In this case, we *click* at the wall to place the lighting fixture, as shown in **Figure 9.18**.

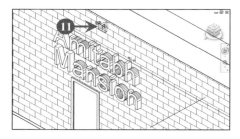

FIGURE 9.18

Note: If required, you can zoom in on the building model to place the lighting fixture at an appropriate location.

The lighting fixture is placed on the wall, as shown in **Figure 9.19**.

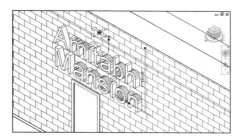

FIGURE 9.19

12. *Press* the **ESC** key twice to exit the Emergency Wall Light tool.

This completes our discussion about adding a lighting fixture to a building model. Now, let's learn how to set the light source.

Setting the Light Source

The light source is the part of the lighting fixture used to emit light, such as a bulb and lamp. Generally, each lighting fixture contains one light source. However, you can create a nested family when a lighting fixture uses multiple light sources. When you set a light source to a lighting fixture, you need to specify the shape of the light element, such as a point, line, rectangle, or circle, as well as the way to distribute the light, such as spherical, hemispherical, spot, or photometric web.

Perform the following steps to set the light source:

1. *Open* the **Autodesk Revit Architecture 2010** window.
2. *Open* the file containing a lighting fixture family. In this case, we open the **Lighting** file.

Note: To set a light source, the lighting fixture family should be open for editing.

3. *Select* the **Create** tab, if not selected, as shown in **Figure 9.20**.

FIGURE 9.20

4. *Click* the **Category and Parameters** button under the **Family Properties** panel (Figure 9.20). The **Family Category and Parameters** dialog box appears, as shown in **Figure 9.21**.

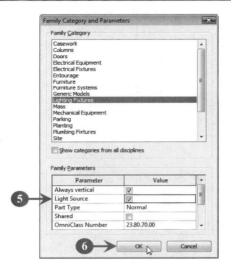

FIGURE 9.21

5. *Select* the **Light Source** check box under the **Family Parameters** group (Figure 9.21).

6. *Click* the **OK** button (Figure 9.21).

7. *Define* the geometry of the light source by repeating *steps* 6 to 10 of the "Creating a Lighting Fixture" section.

8. *Specify* the parameters for the light source by repeating steps 22 to 24 of the "Creating a Lighting Fixture" section.

This completes our discussion about setting a light source. Let's now discuss how to display a light source in a view.

Displaying a Light Source in a View

After adding a lighting fixture to a building model and setting the light source, you can display the light source in a view. Once the light source is visible in a view, you can place it more easily to achieve maximum effect.

Perform the following steps to display a light source in a view:

1. *Open* the **Autodesk Revit Architecture 2010** window.

2. *Open* the file containing a building model to which you have added a lighting fixture. In this case, we open the **Walls** file.

3. *Open* the view in which you want to place the lighting fixture on the building. In this case, we *open* the **3D** view.

4. *Select* the **View** tab on the ribbon, as shown in **Figure 9.22**.

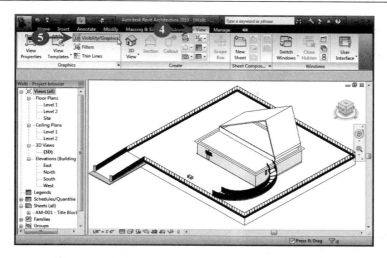

FIGURE 9.22

5. *Click* the **Visibility/Graphics** button under the **Graphics** panel (Figure 9.22). The **Visibility/Graphic Overrides for 3D view: {3D}** dialog box appears, as shown in **Figure 9.23**.

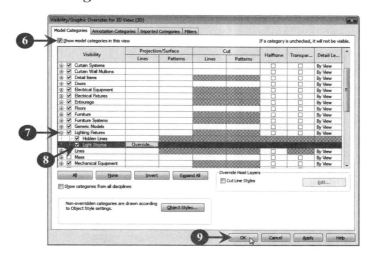

FIGURE 9.23

6. *Select* the **Model Categories** tab (Figure 9.23).
7. *Expand* **Lighting Fixtures** in the **Visibility** column (Figure 9.23).
8. *Select* the **Light Source** check box (Figure 9.23).
9. *Click* the **OK** button (Figure 9.23). The light source in **Figure 9.24** will appear with a yellow outline in the drawing area on your computer screen.

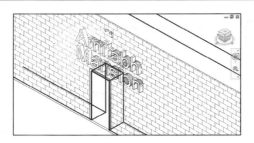

FIGURE 9.24

In addition, you can *click* the **Model Graphics Style** button on the view control bar and then *select* the **Shading or Shading with Edges** option from the context menu to see the difference between the beam angle and field angle for spotlights.

Let's learn how to control the position of a spotlight in a building model.

Controlling the Position of a Spotlight in a Building Model

When you create a spotlight, you need to define its beam angle, field angle, and tilt angle. The beam angle is the angle at which light intensity reaches 50% of the peak intensity, the field angle is the angle at which light intensity reaches 10% of the peak intensity, and the tilt angle is the angle at which the spotlight is bent from its origin. After specifying all three of these angles, you can control the position of the spotlight to achieve the desired lighting effect.

Perform the following steps to control the position of a spotlight in a building model:

1. *Open* the **Autodesk Revit Architecture 2010** window.
2. *Open* the file containing a building model in which you want to control the position of a spotlight—in this case, **Walls**.
3. *Load* the **Spot Light—Exterior** family in the project.
4. *Select* the **Home** tab on the ribbon, as shown in **Figure 9.25**.

FIGURE 9.25

5. *Click* the lower part of the **Component** split button under the **Build** panel and then *select* the **Place a Component** option from the drop-down list (Figure 9.25). The **Place Component** tab appears on the ribbon in the selected mode, as shown in **Figure 9.26**.

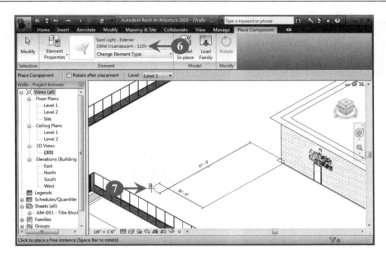

FIGURE 9.26

6. *Select* a spotlight type from the **Type Selector** drop-down list under the **Element** panel. In this case, we *select* the type **300W Incandescent–120V** (Figure 9.26).

7. *Click* at the location in the drawing area where you want to place the spotlight (Figure 9.26).

8. *Press* the **ESC** key twice to exit the Spot Light—Exterior tool.

Continue with the following steps to set up the views in the project.

9. *Leave* the view in which the lighting fixture is added open and *zoom in* on the lighting fixture, as shown in **Figure 9.27**.

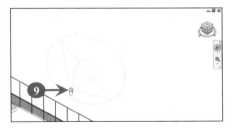

FIGURE 9.27

Note: The view where you have added the lighting fixture is referred to as the placement view. If other views are also open in the project, *select* the **View** tab on the ribbon and then *click* the **Close Hidden** button under the **Windows** panel.

---

10. *Open* another view where you can see the light cast on surfaces, such as an elevation view, section view, or 3D view. In this case, we *open* a duplicate copy of the **3D** view.

> **Note:** This view is referred to as the lighting view. To see both views simultaneously, *select* the **View** tab and then *click* the **Tile Windows** button under the **Windows** panel.

11. *Click* the **Model Graphics Style** button on the view control bar and then *select* the **Shading** or **Shading with Edges** option from the pop-up menu. In this case, we *select* the **Shading with Edges** option, as shown in **Figure 9.28**.

FIGURE 9.28

The spotlight appears, as shown in **Figure 9.29**.

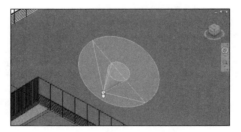

FIGURE 9.29

> **Note:** Turn on the display of light source in a view by performing the steps given in the "Displaying a Light Source in a View" section.

This sets up the views to see the light source in the project. Continue with the following steps to incline or bend a spotlight and to control the size of its beam.

12. *Select* the spotlight in any one of the views, as shown in **Figure 9.30**.

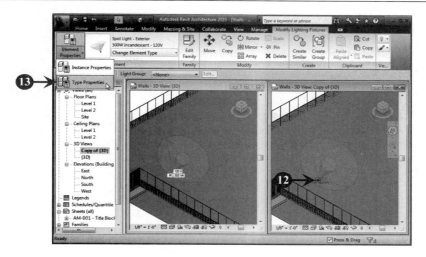

FIGURE 9.30

13. *Click* the lower part of the **Element Properties** split button and then *select* the **Type Properties** option from the drop-down list (Figure 9.30). The **Type Properties** dialog box appears, as shown in **Figure 9.31**.

FIGURE 9.31

14. *Click* the **Duplicate** button to create a new type (Figure 9.31). The **Name** dialog box appears, as shown in **Figure 9.32**.

FIGURE 9.32

15. *Enter* the name of the type in the **Name** text box. In this case, we *enter* the name **Spotlight2** (Figure 9.32).

16. *Click* the **OK** button (Figure 9.32).

17. *Enter* an appropriate value for the **Tilt Angle** parameter under the **Photometrics** section. In this case, we *enter* the value **30.000°**, as shown in **Figure 9.33**.

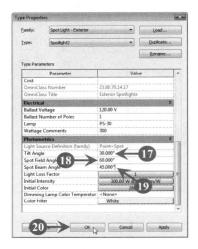

FIGURE 9.33

18. *Enter* an appropriate value for the **Spot Field Angle** parameter under the **Photometrics** section. In this case, we *enter* the value **60.000°** (Figure 9.33).

19. *Enter* an appropriate value for the **Spot Beam Angle** parameter under the **Photometrics** section. In this case, we *enter* the value **45.000°** (Figure 9.33).

20. *Click* the **OK** button (Figure 9.33). The spotlight is tilted, as shown in **Figure 9.34**.

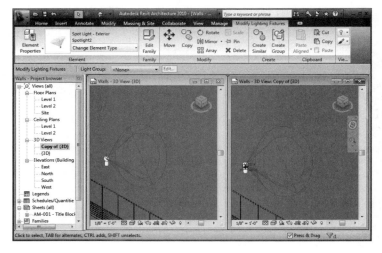

FIGURE 9.34

You can make other adjustments to achieve the desired result by adding or removing spotlights, adjusting their positions, and changing their rotation angles and beam angles to create the desired lighting effect.

This completes our discussion about controlling the position of a spotlight in a building model. Let's move on to the next section, where you learn how to add plants and an entourage to a project.

9.3 ADDING PLANTS AND AN ENTOURAGE

Autodesk Revit Architecture includes the planting and entourage families, which enable you to add plants and entourages to an Autodesk Revit Architecture project. *Plants* imply the families that include different types of shrubs and trees that you can add in the project view. An *entourage* includes landscaping and environmental features such as people, computers, picture frames, cars, and trucks. When you add a tree or an entourage object in the drawing area, it is represented using simple line drawings as placeholders. Once you render the view, photorealistic versions of the entourage objects appear in the rendered image.

Perform the following steps to add plants and an entourage to an Autodesk Revit Architecture project:

1. *Open* the **Autodesk Revit Architecture 2010** window.

2. *Open* the file in which you want to add plants and entourage—in this case, **Walls**.

3. *Open* a floor plan view or a 3D view. In this case, we *open* the **3D** view.

4. *Load* the entourage and planting families in the project. In this case, we *load* the **RPC Female, RPC Male, RPC Tree–Deciduous**, and **RPC Tree–Tropical** families.

5. *Select* the **Home** tab on the ribbon, as shown in **Figure 9.35**.

FIGURE 9.35

6. *Click* the lower part of the **Component** split button under the **Build** panel and then *select* the **Place a Component** option from the drop-down list (Figure 9.35). The **Place Component** tab appears on the ribbon in the selected mode, as shown in **Figure 9.36**.

FIGURE 9.36

7. *Select* the desired family from the **Type Selector** drop-down list under the **Element** panel. In this case, we *select* **Alex** in the **RPC Male** section (Figure 9.36).

8. *Click* at a location in the drawing area to place the entourage object **(Alex)** in the view, as shown in **Figure 9.37**.

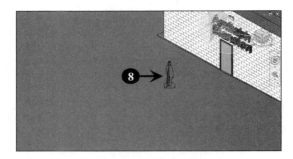

FIGURE 9.37

9. *Press* the **ESC** key twice to exit the Alex tool.

10. *Select* the other families from the **Type Selector** and then *place* them in the drawing area. In this case, we *place* the objects **Cynthia** from the **RPC Female** family and **Red Maple–30'** from the **RPC Tree–Deciduous**, family, as shown in **Figure 9.38**.

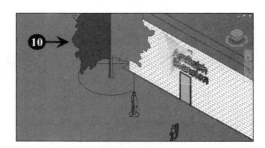

FIGURE 9.38

11. *Press* the **ESC** key twice to exit the Red Maple–30' tool.

Let's move on to the next section to learn how to use decals in Autodesk Revit Architecture.

9.4 USING DECALS

Decals refer to designs such as signs, paintings, and billboards that are fixed to some surface or to a paper bearing the design, which is to be transferred to the surface to display the design. Autodesk Revit Architecture provides you with the Place Decal tool with which you can place images on surfaces of a building model for rendering. Decals can be placed only on flat or cylindrical surfaces. Each decal in the project requires you to specify an image that you want to display as well as its reflectivity, luminance, and texture effects.

A decal is an external graphics file that is linked to the project file. Autodesk Revit Architecture supports decals provided in a variety of file formats, such as .JPEG, .PNG, .TIF, and .BMP. The size of the project file remains constant, as the decal files are only linked—not saved—in the project. You should save the decal files with the project, however, so that the link between the project and the decal file can be maintained.

In this section, you learn how to create a decal type and how to set it in a view. Let's first create a decal type.

Creating a Decal Type

Decal types are used to create decals so as to place images on surfaces of a building model for rendering. You need to create a decal type for each image that you want to use in the building model.

Perform the following steps to create a decal type:

1. *Open* the **Autodesk Revit Architecture 2010** window.
2. *Open* the file in which you want to create a decal type—in this case, **Walls**.
3. *Select* the **Insert** tab on the ribbon, as shown in **Figure 9.39**.

FIGURE 9.39

4. *Click* the **Decal** split button under the **Link** panel and then *select* the **Decal Types** option from the drop-down list (Figure 9.39). The **Decal Types** dialog box appears, as shown in **Figure 9.40**.

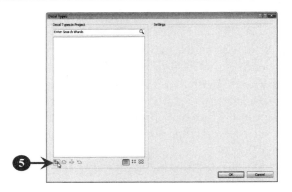

FIGURE 9.40

5. *Click* the **Create new decal** button (Figure 9.40). The **New Decal** dialog box appears, as shown in **Figure 9.41**.

FIGURE 9.41

6. *Enter* the decal name in the **Name** text box. In this case, we *enter* the name **ImgDecal1** (Figure 9.41).
7. *Click* the **OK** button (Figure 9.41). The decal is created, as shown in **Figure 9.42**.

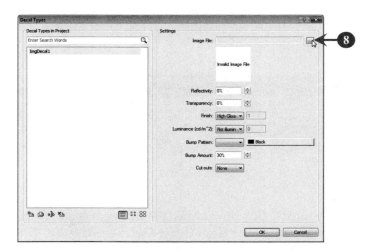

FIGURE 9.42

8. *Click* the ellipsis button next to the **Image File** text box (Figure 9.42). The **Select File** dialog box appears, as shown in **Figure 9.43**.

FIGURE 9.43

9. *Select* the location of the image file from the **Look in** drop-down list. In this case, we *select* the **Sample Pictures** folder (Figure 9.43).

10. *Select* the image file from the list and then *click* the **Open** button (Figure 9.43). The image appears in the **Decal Types** dialog box, as shown in **Figure 9.44**.

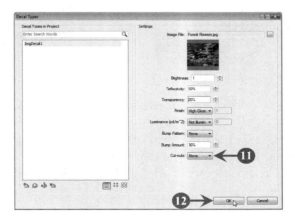

FIGURE 9.44

Note: Autodesk Revit Architecture supports image files of types such as .BMP, .JPG, .JPEG, and .PNG.

11. *Specify* the other parameters of the decal. In this case, we *set* the reflectivity to **50%**, the transparency to **20%**, and the bump pattern to **None** (Figure 9.44).

12. *Click* the **OK** button (Figure 9.44). The decal type is created.

This completes our discussion about creating a decal type. Now, let's learn how to set a decal in a view.

Setting a Decal in a View

After creating a decal type, you can set it in a view to render. As stated earlier, you can place a decal type only on a flat or cylindrical surface. The decal type is placed in a view by using the Place Decal tool.

Perform the following steps to set a decal in a view:

1. *Open* the **Autodesk Revit Architecture 2010** window.
2. *Open* the file in which you want to add a decal—in this case, **Walls**.
3. *Open* the 2D view or 3D orthographic view. In this case, we open the **3D orthographic** view.

> **Note:** The decals cannot be placed in the 3D perspective view because the view must contain a flat or cylindrical surface on which you can place decals.

4. *Select* the **Insert** tab on the ribbon, as shown in **Figure 9.45**.

FIGURE 9.45

5. *Click* the right part of the **Decal** split button and then *select* the **Place Decal** option from the drop-down menu (Figure 9.45). The **Decal** tab appears on the ribbon in the selected mode, as shown in **Figure 9.46**.

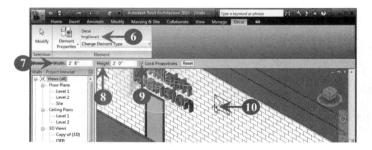

FIGURE 9.46

> **Note:** If the project does not have a decal, the **Decal Types** dialog box appears in which you can create a new decal type. To learn how to create a decal type, refer to the section "Creating a Decal Type."

6. *Select* the decal type from the **Type Selector** drop-down list under the **Element** panel. In this case, we *select* the **ImgDecal1** decal type that we created in the previous section (Figure 9.46).
7. *Enter* the width of the decal in the **Width** text box on the options bar. In this case, we *enter* the width **2' 8"** (Figure 9.46).
8. *Enter* the height of the decal in the **Height** text box on the options bar. In this case, we *enter* the height **2' 0"** (Figure 9.46).
9. *Select* the **Lock Proportions** check box on the options bar to maintain the aspect ratio between the width and the height of the decal (Figure 9.46).
10. *Move* the mouse pointer over a wall or any other flat or cylindrical surface in the drawing area where you want to place the decal and then *click* the mouse button to place the decal. In this case, we *click* on the wall (Figure 9.46).

> **Note:** If required, zoom in on the drawing area to place the decal more accurately. The decal type appears in the drawing area as a placeholder. The detailed decal image becomes visible only when you render the building model. You can also place more decal types in the building model by repeating steps 6 to 10.

11. *Press* the **ESC** key twice to exit the Decal tool.

In the next section, you learn how to configure the render settings.

9.5 RENDERING AN IMAGE

After completing all the tasks of designing a building model, you can render the model to display the rendered image. You can place this rendered image on sheets to present the design to clients. Of course, you require a high-quality rendered image to present a design to clients. However, high-quality rendered images may be generated only slowly; therefore, you may sometimes choose to generate a draft–quality image to test the images. Rendering an image requires you to specify different types of settings, such as quality, output, light, and background.

Perform the following steps to configure the render settings in Autodesk Revit Architecture:

1. *Open* the **Autodesk Revit Architecture 2010** window.
2. *Open* the file for which you want to configure the render settings—in this case, **Walls**.

3. *Click* the **Show Rendering Dialog** button on the view control bar, as shown in **Figure 9.47**.

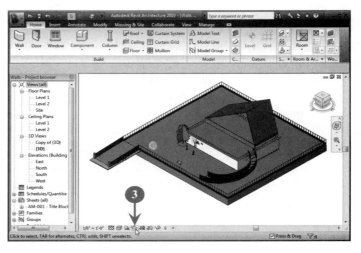

FIGURE 9.47

The **Rendering** dialog box appears, as shown in **Figure 9.48**.

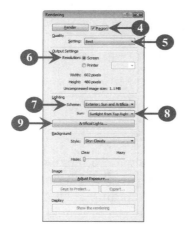

FIGURE 9.48

4. *Select* the **Region** check box to define the view area that you want to render (Figure 9.48).

Note: When you *select* the **Region** check box, the building model is surrounded by a rectangular box. You can *select* the rectangular box and then *drag* the **Adjust Render Region** point to specify the region that you want to render.

5. *Select* an option from the **Setting** drop-down list under the **Quality** group to specify the render quality. In this case, we *select* the **Best** option (Figure 9.48).

6. *Select* a radio button under the **Output Settings** group to specify the resolution of the rendered image. In this case, we *select* the **Screen** radio button, which generates a rendered image for screen display (Figure 9.48).

> **Note:** The other option for resolution setting is the Printer option, which generates a rendered image for printing. When you *select* the **Printer** radio button, you also need to specify the DPI (dots per inch) setting in which to print the image in the drop-down list adjacent to the Printer radio button.

7. *Select* an option from the **Scheme** drop-down list under the **Lighting** group to specify whether you want to use sun, artificial light, or both sun and artificial light. In this case, we *select* the **Exterior: Sun and Artificial** option (Figure 9.48).

> **Note:** If the lighting scheme includes sunlight, the **Sun** drop-down list is activated. If the light scheme includes artificial light, the **Artificial Lights** button is activated. However, if the lighting scheme includes both sunlight and artificial lights, both the **Sun** drop-down list and the **Artificial Lights** button are activated. You can use these items to specify the lighting settings as required.

8. *Select* an option from the **Sun** drop-down list to specify the desired sun position. In this case, we *select* the **Sunlight from Top Right** option (Figure 9.48).

9. *Click* the **Artificial Lights** button (Figure 9.48). The **Artificial Lights–{3D}** dialog box appears, as shown in **Figure 9.49**.

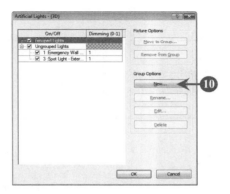

FIGURE 9.49

10. *Click* the **New** button to create a new lighting group (Figure 9.49). The **New Light Group** dialog box appears, as shown in **Figure 9.50**.

FIGURE 9.50

11. *Enter* the name of the light group in the **Name** text box. In this case, we *enter* the name **CustomLights** (Figure 9.50).
12. *Click* the **OK** button (Figure 9.50). The **New Light Group** dialog box closes and the light group is added to the **Artificial Lights–{3D}** dialog box, as shown in **Figure 9.51**.

FIGURE 9.51

> **Note:** If required, *select* the group and *click* the **Edit** button under the **Group Options** group to edit the selected group. The **Rename** button allows you to change the name of the selected group and the **Delete** button allows you to delete the selected group.

13. *Click* the **OK** button (Figure 9.51). The **Artificial Lights–{3D}** dialog box closes.
14. *Select* a background style from the **Style** drop-down list under the **Background** group to specify a background for a rendered image.

In this case, we *select* the **Sky: Cloudy** background style, as shown in **Figure 9.52**.

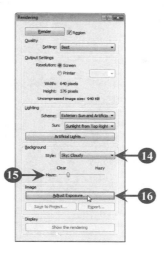

FIGURE 9.52

Note: You can display a solid color or sky and clouds as a background of the rendered image. If you create an interior view that includes natural light, the quality of light in the rendered image can be affected.

15. *Drag* the **Haze** slider between the Clear and Hazy values to change the haziness of the image (Figure 9.52).
16. *Click* the **Adjust Exposure** button to adjust the exposure settings for the image (Figure 9.52). The **Exposure Control** dialog box appears, as shown in **Figure 9.53**.

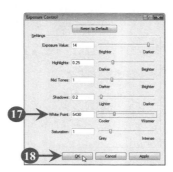

FIGURE 9.53

17. *Drag* the slider for different parameters to specify the settings as required. In this case, we *specify* the **White Point** value of **5430** (Figure 9.53).

18. *Click* the **OK** button (Figure 9.53). The **Exposure Control** dialog box closes and the **Rendering** dialog box appears, as shown in **Figure 9.54**.

FIGURE 9.54

19. *Click* the **Render** button (Figure 9.54). The **Rendering Progress** dialog box appears to show the progress of rendering an image, as shown in **Figure 9.55**.

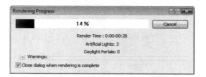

FIGURE 9.55

Once the rendering process is completed, the rendered image appears in the drawing area, as shown in **Figure 9.56**.

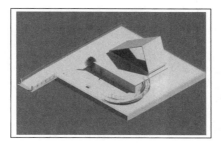

FIGURE 9.56

Note: Once the image is rendered, you can use the **Show the model** button to display the original image of the building model. Once you click this button, it toggles to the **Show the rendering** button, which you can use to display the rendered view of the image. After the image is rendered, you can use the **Save to Project** button under the **Image** group to save the rendering in the current project. You can also export the rendering to a file using the **Export** button under the **Image** group.

INDEX